Britannia & Muscovy

English Silver at the Court of the Tsars

Edited by Olga Dmitrieva and Natalya Abramova

Britannia & Muscovy

English Silver at the Court of the Tsars

Yale Center for British Art, New Haven

The Gilbert Collection, London

Moscow Kremlin Museums

Yale University Press, New Haven and London

This book was produced in connection with the exhibition
Britannia & Muscovy: English Silver at the Court of the Tsars,
held at the Yale Center for British Art, New Haven, CT
(25 May – 10 September 2006) and the Gilbert Collection,
London (14 October 2006 – 28 January 2007).

Major support for this project was provided by grants from the
Samuel H. Kress Foundation and the Lukoil Oil Company

Exhibition conceived by Natalya Abramova, Sergey Orlenko and Irina
Zagorodnaya, and curated by Natalya Abramova and Elena Yablonskaya

Organizing committee for the Moscow Kremlin Museums:
Dr Elena Gagarina
Dr Alexey Levykin
Olga Mironova
Zelfira Tregulova

Receiving curators: Cassandra Albinson (Yale Center for British Art)
and Timothy Stevens (Gilbert Collection). Exhibition coordinated by
Maria Bogoslovskaya and Ainura Yusupova (Moscow Kremlin Museums),
Julia Marciari Alexander and Timothy Goodhue (Yale Center for British Art),
and Sue Thompson (Gilbert Collection)

Catalogue entries:

N.A.   Natalya Abramova
V.F.   Valeria Fedotova
M.M.   Marina Martynova
S.O.   Sergey Orlenko
C.P.   Catherine Phillips
I.V.   Inna Vishnevskaya
E.Y.   Elena Yablonskaya
I.Z.   Irina Zagorodnaya
S.Z.   Svetlana Zyuzeva

Translation and additional research: Catherine Phillips

Photography: S.V. Baranov, M.N. Kravtsov, V.A. Moguchovsky, V.E. Overchenko,
V.N. Seryogin, A.M. Sushenok and A.V. Tarasovsky

Designed by Derek Birdsall
Typeset by Elsa Birdsall / Omnific
Printed in Italy by Conti Tipocolor

Library of Congress Cataloging-in-Publication Data
Britannia & Muscovy : English silver at the court of the tsars / edited by
Olga Dmitrieva and Natalya Abramova.
     p.   cm.
"This book was produced in connection with the exhibition, Britannia &
Muscovy: English Silver at the Court of the Tsars, held at the Yale Center
for British Art, New Haven, CT (25 May/10 September 2006) and the
Gilbert Collection, London (October 2006/January 2007)."
Includes bibliographical references and index.
ISBN 0-300-11678-0 (alk. paper)
1. Silverwork--England--History--Exhibitions. 2. Russia--Foreign
relations--Great Britain--Exhibitions. 3. Great Britain--Foreign relations--
Russia--Exhibitions. 4. Silverwork--Russia (Federation)--Moscow--
Exhibitions. I. Title: Britannia and Muscovy. II. Dmitrieva, Olga. III.
Abramova, Natalya. IV. Yale Center for British Art. V. Gilbert Collection.
NK7143.B68 2006
739.2'309410947--dc22

                          200600535

All measurements are given in both imperial and metric.

Weight for silver and gold is sometimes given as Troy weight:

24 grains	= 1 pennyweight	= 1.5552 grams
20 pennyweight	= 1 Troy ounce	= 31.1035 grams
12 Troy ounces	= 1 Troy pound	= 373.24 grams

Contents

Forewords

The Armoury is one of Russia's longest established institutions, its existence recorded from the very start of the sixteenth century. Part of the Kremlin, official residence of the Princes of Muscovy and then of the Tsars of Russia, it was in effect the royal treasury, where precious goods were kept. Until the eighteenth century it also had workshops where weapons, silverware, court utensils and, later, icons and paintings, were made by the land's finest artists and craftsmen. Over the course of the eighteenth century, when the court itself was based in the new capital, St Petersburg, the collection was gradually put in order and transformed into a storage and display area. This process culminated in 1806 when the Armoury officially became a museum, putting on view to the public many of the state's greatest treasures.

Thus it is that this year, 2006, we are celebrating the 200th anniversary of the foundation of the Armoury, one of the oldest public museums in Russia, and today part of the complex of Moscow Kremlin Museums. It houses an immensely rich collection of applied and decorative arts from the fourth to the twenty-first centuries, works by craftsmen from Russia and other countries worldwide that are not only of artistic value but are also of great historical significance, connected with outstanding individuals and important events in the history of Russia and the world.

But this exhibition celebrates more than 200 years of the Armoury. It celebrates also the rich history of Russo-British relations. Despite the great distance that separates the two lands, the ties between them go back many centuries, even before the arrival in Moscow in 1553 of Richard Chancellor. English sources from as early as the ninth century contain scattered pieces of information about those lands that were later to form part of Ancient Rus.

Dynastic ties between Rus and Britannia were first laid in the late eleventh century, with a marriage between Vladimir Monomakh, Prince of Kiev, and Princess Gytha, daughter of King Harold. At the end of the twelfth century the historian William Fitzstephen wrote a description of the city of London where 'middlemen from every nation under heaven are pleased to bring to the city ships full of merchandize'; he made specific mention of the 'Russ' who brought 'vair and miniver' (squirrel furs and ermine). English maps began to include Kievan Rus from the thirteenth century onwards and English authors provide us with colorful descriptions of the Mongol-Tartar invasion and the pillage of 'Great Russ', events that were to break off Russo-English relations for many long years.

It was only three centuries later that the two lands 'discovered' each other once more and sought to establish both diplomatic and trading ties. From this new era we have not only written sources, but also objects that provide copious evidence of an increasing mutual interest in ever-expanding contacts between Muscovy and England. Among the Armoury's precious works by English craftsmen we find many such objects, some of them gifts to the Tsars of Muscovy from the English Crown, some of them brought to Russia by British trading agents, striking confirmation of the importance attached to the relations between these two countries.

Moreover, the Armoury collection in itself represents a fascinating survival of a whole body of English silver, much of that which remained in England having been melted down or sold during the Civil War. It contains a considerable number of unique pieces and illustrates the great variety of vessel types being produced in a single centre, London, during the sixteenth and seventeenth centuries. Through it, we can trace the evolution of different forms to create a full picture of the national features of English Renaissance and Baroque silver.

Never before has the Armoury's collection of English silver from the sixteenth and seventeenth centuries been so fully represented at exhibitions abroad, here complemented by some of the most outstanding English firearms that also served as gifts during this period. Setting them in context are many commemorative Russian objects, once the property of Russian sovereigns and leading figures in the Ambassadorial Office. Through this exhibition, we hope to convey something of the spirit of the age and to provide visitors with the opportunity to understand, through these magnificent works of art, the history of relations between Muscovy and Britannia in this fascinating period.

Elena Gagarina
General Director, Museums of the Moscow Kremlin

The exhibition *Britannia & Muscovy: English Silver at the Court of the Tsars* and its associated publication are the splendid result of an international collaboration among the Moscow Kremlin Museums, the Yale Center for British Art, and the Gilbert Collection, London, in celebration of the Moscow Kremlin Museums' 200th Anniversary. Focusing on the superb collection of English silver from the Moscow Kremlin Museums (the greatest surviving group of English sixteenth- and seventeenth-century silver in the world), set in context by a group of Russian secular and liturgical material from the same period, the exhibition and publication chart the development of diplomatic, trade, and cultural ties between England and Russia from the time of Queen Elizabeth I and Ivan the Terrible through to the early reigns of Charles II and Alexey Mikhaylovich. They also provide insight into early Anglo-Russian relations and the important series of cultural and commercial exchanges that took place between the two countries during the sixteenth and seventeenth centuries.

In Moscow, we are extremely grateful to all those who have made this exhibition and publication possible, foremost among them: Elena Gagarina, General Director of the Moscow Kremlin Museums, with Olga Mironova, Deputy Director and Curator-in-Chief; Alexey Levykin, Research Director; and Zelfira Tregulova, Deputy Director for Exhibitions. We are indebted to Olga Dmitrieva, Professor of History at Moscow State University, who first conceived the idea of an exhibition to mark the 450th anniversary of the establishment of official Anglo-Russian relations, and to Natalya Abramova and Irina Zagorodnaya of the Moscow Kremlin Museums who turned that idea into reality. Thanks are also due to Natalya Abramova, Irina Zagorodnaya and Elena Yablonskaya, who took on the curatorial organization of *Britannia & Muscovy*, and to Maria Bogoslovskaya and Ainura Yusupova who coordinated all aspects of the exhibition logistics. We are deeply grateful to Olga Dmitrieva, who has continued to serve throughout as an important consultant on the early history of Anglo-Russia relations.

Other institutions in Moscow have also been most generous with material and advice. At the Russian State Archive of Ancient Acts, the Director, Mikhail Ryzhenkov, and the Curator-in-Chief, Ideya Balakayeva, have kindly allowed us to borrow four fragile historic documents for the exhibition at Yale, conserved specially for the event. Staff at the State History Museum have been closely involved in the exhibition from its conception, and we must particularly thank the Director, Alexander Kurko; the Deputy Director, Tamara Igumnova; and Marina Chistyakova, Curator-in-Chief, for their support.

At Yale, we would like to thank Cassandra Albinson, Assistant Curator of Paintings and Sculpture, who expertly curated the exhibition with assistance from Yale undergraduate Laurel Peterson. Barry Shifman, Curator of Decorative Arts at the Indianapolis Museum of Art, was helpful in the early planning stages of the project, and British silver expert Philippa Glanville answered many queries, as did Patricia Kane, Curator of American Decorative Arts at the Yale University Art Gallery. We also wish to acknowledge Cassandra Albinson and the staff of the Department of Exhibitions and Publications, Julia Marciari Alexander, Diane Bowman, Ipek Kaynar, and Anna Magliaro, for collaborating so effectively on the coordination of the publication and exhibition organization. Additional gratitude is expressed to Beth Miller for contract supervision and development efforts on behalf of the exhibition. Elisabeth Fairman and

Maria Rossi provided invaluable expertise with regard to the rare book and manuscript material included in the exhibition, and we thank the Director, Frank Turner, and staff of Yale's Beinecke Rare Book and Manuscript Library for their generous loans. The installation at Yale, designed by Stephen Saitas in collaboration with the Center's installation and design team, led by Richard F. Johnson and Lyn Bell Rose, has allowed the story of the important role that these objects played in the fine art of diplomacy to be told with eloquence and beauty.

At the Gilbert Collection we would like to thank everyone on the exhibition team, including Sue Bond, Amanda Clarke, Sally-Ann Coxon, Jennifer Dinsmore and Sue Thompson, as well as Bridget Heal and Gary Egleton from Ivor Heal Associates, who have been responsible for the exhibition design. As always, Phillipa Glanville has been a source of inspiration. Natalia Makarov and Svetlana Adjoubei from Academia Rossica gave important early encouragement.

Additionally, the exhibition and publication have benefited from the ideas, advice and expertise of Brian Allen, Director of Studies at the Paul Mellon Centre for British Art, London, and Catherine Phillips, who not only compiled and translated the catalogue but also acted as an invaluable curatorial liaison among the three organizing institutions.

Our profound thanks go to those who have contributed in various ways to this publication. Olga Dmitrieva and Natalya Abramova have done a splendid job of editing the volume, which includes substantial essays and contributions by Paul Bushkovitch, Professor of History at Yale University; silver historian Philippa Glanville; Maija Jansson, Director of the Yale Center for Parliamentary History; Edward Kasinec, Curator, and Robert H. Davis, Jr., Assistant Curator, of the Slavic and Baltic Division at The New York Public Library; and from the Moscow Kremlin Museums, Natalya Abramova, Valeria Fedotova, Marina Martynova, Lyubov Kirillova, Sergey Orlenko, Inna Vishnevskaya, Elena Yablonskaya, Irina Zagorodnaya, and Svetlana Zyuzeva. We are greatly indebted to Sally Salvesen at Yale University Press for her unflagging commitment to the publication and to Derek Birdsall and Omnific for designing this beautiful book.

Our gratitude is extended to the Samuel H. Kress Foundation for their support of the exhibition and this accompanying volume. The Gilbert Collection would like to thank most warmly Lukoil for their generous sponsorship of the showing of this exhibition in London. It is excellent that, in this bicentenary year of the Kremlin Armoury Museum, the foundation of this great museum should be commemorated in London by an exhibition that is so central to mutual national histories.

We are pleased to have engaged in this important collaborative project and hope that it will foster further cooperative ventures among our institutions. The collaboration among people, institutions, and nations that produced this exhibition and publication attests to the critical and continued significance of cultural exchange, which is, after all, the subject of this extraordinary project.

Amy Meyers
Director, Yale Center for British Art

Timothy Stevens
Director, The Gilbert Collection

Introduction

'The Golden Chain of Traffic': The First Hundred Years of Anglo-Russian Relations

Olga Dmitrieva

Our men beganne to wonder at the Maiestie of the Emperour ...

—The newe Navigation and discoverie of the kingdoms of Moscovia, by the Northeast, in the yeere 1553

1. 'Ivan IV (the Terrible)', from *Portrety, gerby i pechati Bolshoy gosudarstvennoy knigi 1672 g*, no. 26, Moscow, 1672, reprinted St Petersburg, 1903. Slavic and Baltic Division, The New York Public Library, Astor, Lenox and Tilden Foundations

In 1697 English ambassadors to The Hague presented the diplomats of Peter I of Russia (then travelling through northern Europe, supposedly incognito) with a memorandum. The words recalled that the English, 'above all other peoples that are in Europe' had made trading and friendly ties with Russia that had already continued happily for more than one hundred years, and only time and war had weakened this long-established tie between two peoples.[1] The document returned to the argument that had been commonly employed by the English in the late sixteenth century – their primacy over other nations in the 'discovery' of Russia. This was not, of course, to suggest that the land was totally unknown to other European powers before the English appeared in the state of Muscovy in 1553 (Muscovy maintained contacts with Italy, the Habsburg Empire and other neighbouring lands); rather it referred to the discovery of the northern sea route to Muscovy, opening up radically new opportunities for commercial and political contacts between Muscovy and Western Europe.

At first, however, in setting off 'towards the rising sun' beyond the borders of the explored world – to where, beyond the lands of Tatary and the mythical peoples of Gog and Magog, as was customarily thought, lay Eden – the English had in mind very different destinations than Muscovy. Like most Europeans during this age of exploration, they were seeking new routes to the fantastically rich lands of India and China, and it was this that led to the establishment in London in 1551 of a Society of Merchant-Adventurers, its aim the discovery by sea of new lands, islands, states and territories so far unknown and unvisited. Initiator of the society's foundation was Sebastian Cabot, son of the celebrated traveller John Cabot (who had sought in vain to reach the lands of the Great Chinese Khan, travelling north-west through the ice fields of the Arctic).

In 1553 three ships, the *Bona Speranza*, *Confidentia* and *Edward Bonaventure* (named in honour of King Edward VI) set sail under the command of Sir Hugh Willoughby and the 'pilot' (captain) Richard Chancellor. They were provided with letters of introduction to the rulers of any unknown lands which they might find upon their way, and set off in search of a north-eastern route to the lands of the Far East through the Arctic Ocean. With no suspicion that it would in fact be impossible to make the long trip through the harsh northern latitudes in a single journey, the seafarers passed Scandinavia before their ships were scattered by a storm. Two of the ships managed to reach the Kola Peninsula, but there they became jammed in the ice. Willoughby and many sailors perished, but Chancellor and his men found themselves in the White Sea at the mouth of the northern River Dvina. Stepping onto dry land near the Nikolo-Karelian Monastery, they were met by local coast dwellers. These new arrivals from far-off England were taken to Kholmogory and from there by sledge to Moscow and the court of Ivan IV.[2]

The Englishmen's appearance in the capital of the Russian state occurred at an extremely important stage in the latter's development. During the first half of the sixteenth century Muscovy had gradually been stabilizing its position on the eastern borders of Europe as a new and powerful centralized state with pretensions to a specific religious mission and a role as heir to the Byzantine Empire. Muscovy was the largest Orthodox state since the fall of Constantinople, taken by the Ottomans in 1453, and the grand dukes of Muscovy adopted the title 'Tsar' to recall the title of 'Caesar' of Rome's rulers. The young Ivan IV (soon to be known as 'The Terrible') was crowned Tsar in 1547 (figs. 1, 2). Not long before the arrival of the English merchants he had undertaken a successful mission against the Tatars, annexing the lands of Kazan, and he was maturing plans for further expansion to the east and an attack on the Astrakhan Khanate. Thanks to these new territorial gains, Russia was now an extensive, multi-ethnic state stretching across the broad expanse of two continents, Europe and Asia. Seeking recognition from Europeans of Muscovy's new status, Ivan received Chancellor kindly, the latter having assumed in these unexpected circumstances the role of official representative of the English Crown.

2. Romeyn de Hooghe, 'Coronation of the Russian Tsar', from Balthasar Coyet, *Historisch Verhael, of Beschryving van de Voyagie…*, Amsterdam, 1677. Beinecke Rare Book and Manuscript Library, Yale University

Not only did they have to overcome the complications of the language barrier, during the course of several months the English had to come to terms with many unfamiliar things in Muscovy: although it was a Christian land, the form of Christianity practised there was deeply alien to them, the traditions and habits of the people very different. Chancellor proved to be a perceptive observer. His notes contain a summary but correct assessment of those elements important for the development of further trade and political contacts – natural resources, potential of the local market, system of government, state of the army and cultural aspects of the region. His report reveals his surprise at the very scale of the boundless land so suddenly revealed to him, the mass of its people and goods, the 'exceeding great' wealth and power of its ruler. In Muscovy, Chancellor and his companions noted both the similarities to English life and signs of difference. They did their best to assess what they saw without bias. They found the capital of the Russian state 'as great as the city of London with the suburbs thereof'. Although the city's plan seemed chaotic and the buildings not particularly handsome, the main citadel, the Kremlin, built according to the canons of Italian Renaissance fortification, created a positive impression on the travellers, who described it as 'a very faire Castle, strong, and furnished with artillerie'.[3] The Tsar's palace residences within the Kremlin walls did not impress them, however, being considerably smaller and less richly adorned than English palaces.

Chancellor paid particularly close attention to the nature of the Muscovites' ruling powers and indeed the personality of the Tsar himself – it was, after all, entirely on the latter that all potential mutually beneficial relations depended. To contemporaries, the person of the monarch embodied both the huge state he ruled and the people who were his subjects. His public appearances, particularly his ceremonial reception of representatives of foreign states, were of vast importance in sixteenth-century political culture. The setting for his first ceremonial audience in the Kremlin created a great impression on Chancellor and his companions, who noted the majestic behaviour of the royal dignitaries and the rich attire of the courtiers, 'all apparelled in cloth of golde, downe to their ankles'. The high point and culmination of the whole was, of course, meeting the Tsar himself:

> Being conducted into the chamber of presence, our men beganne to wonder at the Maiestie of the Emperour: his seat was aloft, in a very royall throne, having on his head a Diademe, or Crowne of gold, apparelled with a robe all of Goldsmithes worke, and in his hande he helde a Scepter garnished, and beset with pretious stones: and besides all other notes and apparances of honour, there was a Maiestie in his countenance, proportionable with the excellencie of his estate … This so honourable an assemblie, so great a Maiestie of the Emperour, and of the place, might very wel have amazed our men and have dasht them out of countenance …[4]

Indeed, all English descriptions of official ceremonies at the Russian court were to mention the oriental luxury, the glitter of gold and precious stones.

The next element in the official reception was the ceremonial dinner (fig. 3). Invited to dine in the 'Golden Court' (Gold Chamber), the travellers found the manner in which the food was served very grand, the ritual most solemn: 'They find the Emperour sitting upon a high and stately seate, apparelled with a robe of silver, and with an other Diademe on his head.'[5] On this day Ivan IV changed his precious crown three times, appearing before his guests at the end of the reception in yet another 'diadem'. But the demonstration of his wealth and power was not limited to his official insignia. Precious tableware was set out in the chamber to amaze all those present – which it did. Clement Adams, author of the English edition of Chancellor's report, dedicated a long passage to the royal treasures impressively set forth for general view:

> In the middes of the roome, stoode a mightie Cupboorde upon a square foote, whereuppon stoode also a rounde boorde, in manner of a Diamond, broade beneath, and towardes the toppe narrowe, and every steppe rose uppe more narrowe then another. Upon this Cupboorde was placed the Emperours plate, which was so much, that the very Cupboord it selfe was scant able to sustayne the weight of it: the better part of all the vessels, and goblets, was made of very fine golde: and among the rest, there were foure pots of very large bignesse, which did adorne the rest of the plate, in great measure: for they were so highe, that they thought them at least, five foote long. There were also upon this Cupboorde, certaine silver caskes, not much differing from the quantitie of our Fyrkins, wherein was reserved the Emperours drinke.[6]

The 140 servants attending to the guests were themselves dressed in richly brocaded attire which they too changed three times during the feast. 'This is true,' continued Adams, 'that all the furniture of dishes, and drinking vessels, which were then for the use of a hundred ghests, was all of pure gold, and the tables were so laden with vessels of gold, that there was no roome for some to stand upon them.'[7]

The royal dresser or buffet ('Cupboorde') was to continue to amaze English visitors. Anthony Jenkinson, who visited the Russian court in 1557, noted: 'There was also a Cupbord of plate, most sumptuous, and rich … among the which, was a peece of golde of two yards long, wrought in the toppe with towers, and Dragons heades, also divers barrels of gold and silver, with Castles on the bungs, richly and artificially made.'[8] Half a century later, the author of the report on Sir Thomas Smith's diplomatic mission to Moscow in 1604–5 described enthusiastically the stand with imperial treasures in the Faceted Chamber:

> In the midst of this hall might seeme to stand a great Piller, round about which, a great heigth stood wonderfull great peeces of plate, very curiously wroght with all manner of Beastes, Fishes and fowles, besides some other ordinarye peeces of serviceable plate. Being thus set (some quarter of an houre as it were, feeding our eyes with that fayre Piller of plate) we beheld the Emperors table served by two hund[red] Noblemen, all in coates of cloth of gold.'[9]

Among the precious objects set out in the feasting hall were works by Russian goldsmiths, oriental masters and western European jewellers. The abundance of gold and silver utensils and ceremonial vessels to which great significance was attached at the Russian court was a means of demonstrating the Emperor's power. Foreign guests were always allowed plenty of time to linger and take in the full scale of his wealth. The display was also a valuable prompt to the English, who quickly worked out that elegant items in gold and silver might be welcomed as diplomatic gifts and fruitfully traded in Muscovy.

3. Matthiae Beckeri, 'Foreign Ambassadors Being Received at the Court of Ivan the Terrible in 1578', from Jacob Ulfeldt, *Hodoeporicon Ruthenicum*, plate 3, Frankfurt, 1608. Rare Books Division, The New York Public Library, Astor, Lenox and Tilden Foundations

In 1553 the English were not only permitted to look upon the Tsar in the palace chambers, but also to be present when Ivan IV made his ceremonial departure from the capital. Richard Chancellor found the royal armour 'most notable', while Ivan's own military tents surpassed in richness and beauty anything which could be seen at the courts of England and France: 'The coverings of his tent for the most part, are all of gold, adorned with stones of great price, and with the curious workemanship of plumasiers' (fig. 4).[10]

Chancellor's overall impression was of 'pomp and magnificence'.[11] His vision of the court of Moscow and its rituals was comparable to English perceptions of the courts of European monarchs. Yet in the sixteenth century the image of the Russian Tsar – the architecture and decoration of his residence, the appearance of his court – combined both European and Asian features (fig. 5). Their influence by the rich ceremonial traditions of Byzantium, the Orient and Renaissance Europe endured. As the cultural dialogue between Russia and England developed, magnificent English works in gold and silver came to be added to this complex imperial treasury, just as fine examples of parade armour were added to the arsenal. These gifts formed an essential part of the theatricality that reinforced the Tsars' power. The presents of the English not only contributed to the formation of the new image of the ruler of Muscovy, but reinforced the very western European elements of that image.

4. Romeyn de Hooghe, 'Water wydingth tot Moskow', from Balthasar Coyet, *Historisch Verhael, of Beschryving van de Voyagie…*, Amsterdam, 1677. Beinecke Rare Book and Manuscript Library, Yale University

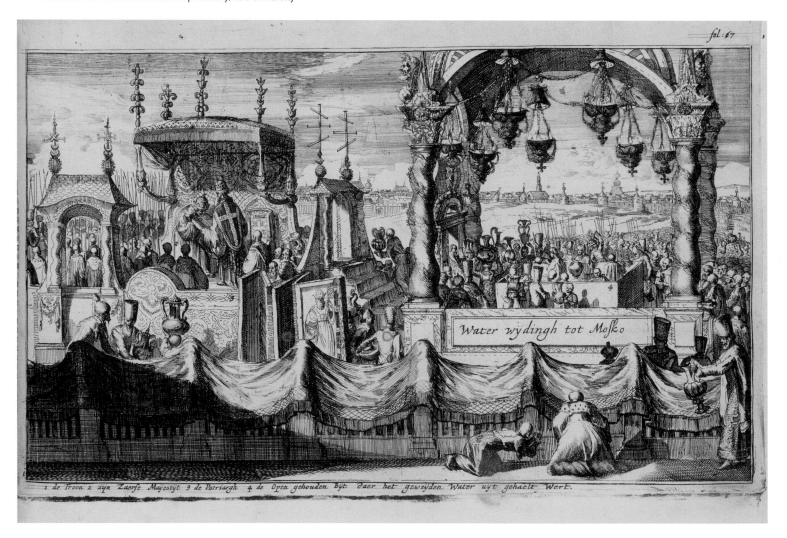

Kremelin.   Porte du Sauveur.   S. Nicolai.

Château Kremelin, dans la Ville de Moscou, avec la célébration de la Fête de Pâques Fleuries.

a Leide. Chez Pierre vander Aa.   34

5. 'Château Kremlin… avec la celebration de la Fête des Pâques Fleuries', from Pieter van der Aa, *La Galerie Agréable du Monde*, plate 34, Leiden, 1729. Yale Center for British Art, Paul Mellon Collection

Trade and diplomacy

Taking advantage of propitious circumstances, Richard Chancellor undertook negotiations with Ivan IV to grant English merchants the right to trade within the realm of Muscovy. Having received Ivan's agreement he departed for London where, in 1555, the Muscovy Company was established, comprising not only merchants but also a number of high-ranking statesmen.[12] In 1556 Chancellor returned to Russia, this time as official ambassador with letters of credence from Philip and Mary, who had by this time replaced Edward VI on the throne. An entry in the 'Patriarch's Chronicle' for 1556 records that the sovereign received the envoys 'with great reward' and permitted the English 'to establish a harbor for ships on the Dvina and trade throughout the whole state'.[13] The Muscovy Company was also presented with a residence on Varvarka Street very close to the Kremlin. In 1557, Ivan IV dispatched the first Russian embassy to England led by Osip Nepeya. Accompanying Chancellor on his return voyage, their ship was wrecked and in a moment of true drama, Chancellor perished saving the Russian ambassador. Nepeya made his way on to London where he was received

6. Romeyn de Hooghe, 'View of Archangel from the sea-side', etching from Balthasar Coyet, *Historisch Verhael, of Beschryving van de Voyagie…,* Amsterdam, 1677. Beinecke Rare Book and Manuscript Library, Yale University

with great honours by the royal couple who reciprocated the kindness of Ivan IV by permitting Russian merchants 'without any duties to trade' in London. At the Tsar's request, the English sent back with Nepeya a number of specialists: physicians, seekers and workers of gold and silver, and other craftsmen.[14]

The basis was thus laid for active trading links and regular diplomatic contacts between Russia and England. The rights granted to the Muscovy Company by Ivan IV were extensive. The English were to have a customs-free monopoly on trade through ports in the White Sea (to which no other European power had the right to send its ships), making England Russia's first privileged trading partner in the sixteenth century.[15] This stimulated the development of the economy in the Russian north and the growth of Kholmogory. It led to the appearance in 1584 of a new port on the River Dvina – Arkhangel'sk, known to the English as Archangel – and towns along the trading routes from the White Sea to Moscow flourished (fig. 6). The English established factories and merchant houses, warehouses and workshops on Rose Island (near Kholmogory) and in Archangel, Vologda, Yaroslavl, Veliky Ustyug, Novgorod Veliky and Pskov. The Muscovy Company brought to Russia mainly prized English cloth, taking back tar, linen, wax, blubber, animal pelts and tall timber for ships' masts. After the establishment of rope production in Kholmogory, on the initiative of the company's agent Richard Grey, the volume of rope exported from Russia grew consistently; it was of strategic importance, for the rope was used for the rigging of the English fleet.

The acquisition of so extensive and promising a market as Russia did not slow the English desire to study the north-eastern sea passage. In 1566 an expedition led by Steven Burrough (Borough) (1525–84) got as far as Novaya Zemlya, but was unable to reach 'the great River Ob' of which the English had heard so much from shore dwellers. Over the course of the sixteenth and seventeenth centuries the English managed nonetheless to get through to Siberia and start trading there.[16]

The position of the English merchants was further reinforced in the 1560s, largely due to the efforts of Anthony Jenkinson (1529–1611). Jenkinson represented the company's interests in Muscovy and repeatedly pressed Ivan IV for permission to seek a passage to China through the wide open spaces of Tatary. He eventually travelled down the Volga to the Caspian Sea and made it to Bukhara (fig. 7). In 1562 he received permission for a new journey, his aim being to reach Persia. An important political result of this expedition was that the English were granted trading rights in Kazan, Astrakhan, Bulgaria and Shemakha and the possibility to move on further to Samarkand and China.[17]

Close and mutually beneficial links were thus established between the two states in the 1550s and 1560s. For England, the White Sea opened up the gates to trade not only with Muscovy but with the Orient. These new markets alleviated some of the problems selling English cloth that had arisen as a result of competition within traditional European markets. For the Muscovite state, the northern passage to England was a window on to

Europe long before Peter the Great created one by founding St Petersburg: the only other means of access to the West, via the ports in the Baltic Sea, involved sharp conflict with Poland, Lithuania and Sweden. It was largely these strategic concerns that determined the particularly warm welcome extended to English merchants by Ivan the Terrible, nicknamed 'The English Tsar' by his enemies, and by Ivan Viskovaty, who was in charge of Muscovy's international policy during the 1550s and 1560s.[18]

In the sixteenth century state diplomacy was in many ways perceived as a personal dialogue between reigning monarchs. The anglophile Ivan IV and Elizabeth I, who succeeded her sister Mary in 1558, justified such a perception for they maintained a regular correspondence of striking intensity. Over the course of her reign the Queen sent Russian monarchs some one hundred documents of various kinds, more than sixty of which qualify as personal letters, half of those being addressed to Ivan IV and half to Fyodor Ivanovich and Boris Godunov.[19] Despite the apparently private nature of much of this correspondence, it was an active political instrument. Its content was in many ways inspired by the interests of merchants of the Muscovy Company. Alongside discussion of policy, Elizabeth's letters to Ivan contained active lobbying for trade interests and petitioning on behalf of specific individuals. This tradition was continued by their royal successors and by the end of the century the letters were ever more elegant, the finesse and richness of their illuminations making them very like those public royal charters that derived from Chancery. During the reign of the early Stuarts official epistolary art flourished.[20] Their decorated letters to the Russian monarchs are of striking beauty, densely covered with heraldic images and symbols of power intended to play an important ceremonial function and reflect the prestige of the royal sender (cats. 56–9).

Despite the numerous privileges and regular private correspondence between Ivan the Terrible and Elizabeth I, whom he described as 'dear sister', the development of Anglo-Russian relations was nonetheless affected by Ivan's unpredictable moods and more deep-rooted political factors. In the 1570s – years of crisis for Ivan's internal policies, with an intensification in the battle for power and the terror of the oprichniki (Ivan's elite forces, selected from among the nobility) – the Tsar took the factories of the English merchants into the oprichnina, the lands and bodies under his personal control, along with the whole economically important region through which lay the path to the White Sea. Moreover, the Muscovy Company was presented with monopoly rights to the importation of precious metals and the stamping of coins from them, as well as rights to pursue the 'interlopers' (in essence smugglers) who had appeared in the northern seas, sharing their takings equally with the imperial treasury. In return, Ivan expected a reciprocal move on England's part in terms of international policy.

Although trade was the main artery of Anglo-Russian relations, political factors came to play an increasingly important role. From the end of the 1560s Russia suffered regular defeats in its wars with Poland and Lithuania for the Livonian lands. Sweden represented no less of a threat in the Baltic region. The battle to hold the country's western borders required up-to-date artillery and firearms and an increase in supplies of gunpowder, saltpetre and other ordnance. The Russian army had need of modernization and experienced military specialists. Facing numerous opponents, Muscovy turned its diplomatic gaze to England in its search for an ally in the northern regions. Ivan suggested a military and political alliance between the two countries which would have brought England into the Livonian war, and – to reinforce that alliance – a dynastic marriage between the Russian Tsar and Queen Elizabeth. In addition, he proposed that the monarchs agree to offer each other refuge in the event that either was forced to flee as a result of internal revolt or intervention from without. Such suggestions were greeted with a complete absence of enthusiasm on the part of the English, who sought to lead the negotiations towards more superficial assertions of friendship and discussion of matters of trade. The obvious attempts by the English – so zealous in their lobbying of commercial interests – to back away from signing any political agreement aroused Ivan's undisguised ire; in spite of all diplomatic protocol, he expressed a notoriously unflattering opinion of the nature of Elizabeth's reign:

> And wee had thought that you had been ruler over your lande and had sought honor to your self and profitt to your countrie, and therefore wee did pretend those weightie affaires betweene you and us; But now wee perceive that there be other men that doe rule, and not men but bowers and merchaunts the which seeke not the wealth and honour of our maiesties, but they seeke there owne profit of marchauntdize: and you flowe in your maydenlie estate like a maide.[21]

Over the next years, English diplomats were to feel all the force of the Tsar's anger and that of his administration.

Against the background of Ivan's displeasure, the different attitudes to diplomatic protocol on the part of the Russians and the English stood out all the more starkly. The original initiative to establish contacts with Russia

7. 'Map of the Volga River', from Adam Olearius, *The Voyages and Travels of the Ambassadors Sent by Frederick Duke of Holstein, to the Great Duke of Muscovy, and the King of Persia*, London, 2nd edition, 1669. Beinecke Rare Book and Manuscript Library, Yale University

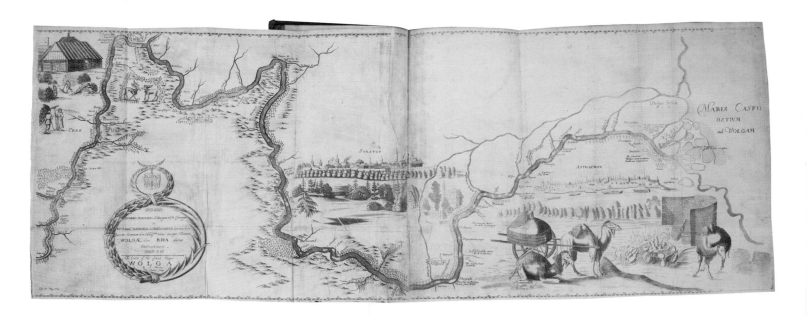

came from English merchants, who continued to play an important role in developing England's official international policy and in organizing the diplomatic missions, selecting the candidates to act as envoys and indeed financing their journeys. Quite often, the trading agents of the Muscovy Company simultaneously performed official tasks on behalf of the Queen. During the most propitious period in their mutual relations, Ivan IV and the administration of the Ambassadorial Office closed their eyes to such liberties on the part of the English, but Muscovy's diplomatic traditions were strict and highly regulated. Russian political culture was marked by its Byzantine traditions: an extreme sensitivity to the social status of ambassadors sent to the Tsar, as well as to those ambassadors' observation of written and unwritten codes of conduct, including the full use of the Tsar's numerous titles. [22] Any departure from those codes was perceived as an insult to the throne. The relatively low status of English diplomatic representatives, frequently without even the rank of knight (or having had that rank thrust upon them only on the eve of their departure to Russia), and the nature of the diplomacy conducted by these 'men of commerce' increased the annoyance of the already irritated Russian side. Moreover, Elizabeth's last two envoys to Ivan the Terrible – Thomas Randolph (1525/6–90) in 1568[23] and Jerome Bowes (d. 1616) in 1583–4[24] – conducted themselves in a manner considered so provocative by the Russians that they placed under threat the whole success of their negotiations.

Meanwhile, the English had their own causes for concern. Continuing to count on trading privileges with Russia, they insisted that the Russians prevent English merchants who were not part of the Muscovy Company from supplying goods to the Baltic area via Narva,[25] as well as keeping the White Sea clear of merchants from other European lands. Their argument was that it was they who had opened up the northern passage and their nation alone should enjoy its fruits. Such demands were in direct conflict with the economic interests of the Russian state, which in the 1570s to 1590s was actively seeking to trade with other European powers, and were forcefully rejected. Ivan IV and the new head of the Ambassadorial Office, Andrey Shchelkalov, immediately demonstrated to the English that they had their own means of putting pressure on intractable partners: in 1571 the Muscovy Company was deprived of its right to customs-free trade and navigation down the Volga, and part of its property was confiscated. Dutch merchants did not hesitate to take advantage of this cooling in Anglo-Russian relations and in 1577 Dutch ships sailed into the mouth of the River Dvina. While the conflict was resolved and English merchants retained their right to trade in the Russian market, they lost forever their former monopoly; they were forced to pay customs and accept the presence of competitors in the Russian north.

The pause in the Anglo-Russian political dialogue was brief. By the start of the 1580s both states had many reasons to be interested in reviving it. The situation on Muscovy's western borders was catastrophic and the successes enjoyed by Polish King Stephen Báthory (1575–86) forced Ivan IV to conclude a peace treaty in 1582 that ceded the Livonian lands to Poland. At the same time the Swedes gained key fortresses on the Baltic, at Narva and

Ivangorod, Yam (modern Kingisepp) and Koporye. Access to the Baltic was now closed, thereby enhancing the strategic significance of the northern sea passage and of friendly relations with England. The latter's situation in northern Europe was in many ways similar. England was experiencing a period of isolation and threat from Catholic states, while unable to find a common language with the Protestant States, Holland, Denmark and Sweden all being the country's trading competitors. Under such conditions, Russia remained England's sole potential ally in the north and for an island such as England, trade was a crucial factor in political survival, particularly as regarded those goods needed to equip its fleet.

Ivan IV and Elizabeth I renewed their contacts through the mediation of the head of the Muscovy Company in Moscow, Jerome Horsey (before 1560–1627). In 1582 another embassy was sent to London with the offer of a military alliance and a marriage between the Russian Tsar and a relative of the Queen, Mary Hastings. Once again, however, it proved impossible to persuade the English that both countries would stand 'as one' against all enemies. In their turn the English were unable to revive their exclusive privileges in Russia, being told in no uncertain terms that 'the Russian people shall not live by English trade alone'.[26] The death of Ivan the Terrible in 1584 finally laid to rest the company's hopes of restoring its former status.

During the reign of Ivan's son, Fyodor Ivanovich (1584–98), the Russian court was dominated by anti-English feeling; even his brother-in-law, that celebrated 'friend of the English' Boris Godunov, did not speak out in favour of closer relations, although he did repeatedly assist the Muscovy Company in settling conflicts with the local administration. Russian interests in the international arena were steadily tending towards an alliance with the Catholic Habsburg Empire, a matter which could not but be of concern to the English. Godunov's arrival on the throne in 1598 aroused great hopes and Elizabeth I expressed her joy that their 'well-wisher' had come to power. The reign of Boris Godunov (1598–1605) was indeed favourable to the English, for he immediately re-established a number of the Muscovy Company's earlier privileges.

Under Godunov's rule the influx of English specialists to Russia increased, among them silversmiths, apothecaries and doctors. The private physicians of both Tsar Fyodor and Boris Godunov – Mark Ridley (d. 1624) and Timothy Willis – were also sent from England. Boris was the first to allow foreigners, including the English, to own their own houses in Moscow (they had previously been forced to live together in the English Yard on the Varvarka). Aware of the importance of European contacts, he was the first Russian ruler to send his own subjects to study at English universities.

By the beginning of the seventeenth century the very tone of Anglo-Russian political dialogue had changed. Now the two powers were united by common anti-Polish interests and the search for an alliance with Denmark. Such a similarity in their political outlook ensured previously unheard of success for the mission to Russia led by Sir Thomas Smith (c.1558–1625) in 1604–5, during the course of which he was granted a reception unprecedented in the history of Anglo-Russian political relations.

Despite the unease that marked Anglo-Russian political contacts at the end of the sixteenth century, trade continued to develop and the number of Englishmen resident in Russia for long periods grew. One contemporary, author of the report on Sir Thomas Smith's journey, noted that trade formed a cement tying the hearts and souls of nations so 'different in shapes, disagreeing in manners, in speech, in religion'. 'Traffike,' he wrote, 'is the golden chain concatenation, that tyes kingdoms together in mutuall Amitie.'[27] The English merchant 'world' that had taken shape in Muscovy took the usual European form, although adapted somewhat to suit local customs. Fyodor Ivanovich wrote to Elizabeth: 'they have in o[u]r kingdome in Muscove and in enie towne at Yeroslowe at Valagdaie and upon the Dvyna many houses, and they lyve all one w[i]th o[u]r people …'[28] Thomas Smith, sent by James I, travelled to Moscow in 1604–5 and conducted an unusual 'inspection' of the conditions in which his compatriots were living in the Russian north. He noted that the house of the Muscovy Company in Kholmogory was the most spacious, well-built and handsome building in the town, with warehouses, barns and workshops. He was also pleased at the English factory in Yaroslavl, the centre of which was 'a very faire and right house'. Only in Vologda did the building seem to him somewhat run down, and although 'it hath a great many of roomes, as chambers, worke-houses and the lyke, but the house it selfe is very old, and stands with an humble body as though it would shortly kisse the earth'.[29]

In the northern regions – unlike Moscow itself – the English were permitted to reside not only on the site of the company's offices, but independently, renting wooden houses and hiring local servants, which facilitated closer and freer contact with the Russian population. The atmosphere recalled a 'little England' filled with European utensils and equipment, and the receptions held by the company's agents were organized in the normal fashion. The few women present (bearing in mind that no women sat at table in Russian society until the very end of the seventeenth century) were dressed in the latest fashions, English sweets were served and presents exchanged at New Year. Nonetheless, the English did not shun those elements of local life which they found pleasant, paying tribute to Russian bread, honey and *kvas* (a slightly bitter drink made from sour bread) and to monastery recipes for cooking fish. It was easier to establish ties of commerce and friendship with Russian merchants in the north. Frequent informal contacts with the local population even led to some concern on the part of the governors of the Muscovy Company, who in 1567 reproached the Yaroslavl and Vologda Englishmen that they:

> have accustomed to give wyne and meate to comers and goers to or houses th[a]t the same maye be left by little and little we knowe the manner of the contrie is not to welcom with wine except we have brought up this coruptio[n] … It is also notorious that our prentesis and stipendaries make sup[er]fluous buildinge at Colmogro [Kholmogory] and Vologda rather for ostentation fancy and pleasure then for necessitie w[hi]ch causeth many comers and goers to our great hinderunnce …[30]

Participation by employees of the company in feasting and traditional Russian and English pastimes such as bear-baiting also attracted 'too many guests' (fig. 8) and the governors threatened to reduce the supply of wine and other provisions from England in order to prevent such wastage.

By no means all the English left Russia at the end of their contract with the Muscovy Company. Some stayed on in the service of the Tsar, particularly sailors, gunners and captains of vessels, all of whom received high wages. They married local women (for instance Thomas Glover, agent of the company, married a member of the noble boyar family, the Basmanovs), although they usually took wives from among captured Livonian women. Merchants, physicians, apothecaries, mining and military specialists endured alongside the Russians the political terror of Ivan the Terrible, the attack in 1571 by the Tatars under Devlet-Girey and the great fire that swept through Moscow during which some thirty English perished. Those who survived joined the locals in rebuilding the city's fortifications.

By the start of the seventeenth century, there was a whole generation of English who had been brought up in Muscovy since childhood and who spoke Russian well.[31] Well versed in local politics and economies as well as Russian customs, they enjoyed the confidence of the court and the *d'yaks* or secretaries of the Ambassadorial and Foreign Offices. They also enjoyed a high reputation among their trading partners. Russian merchants called them respectfully – according to Russian tradition – by both their first name and patronymic: thus John Merrick, agent of the Muscovy Company, became Ivan Ulyanov or Williamovich (his father's name being William), Francis Cherry became Fryanchik Ivanov (his father being John or Ivan), Anthony Marsh was known as Onton Ivanov, and Thomas Lind signed himself in Russia 'Tomas son of Ulyan [William] Lind'.[32] Many of these people might have applied to themselves the words of John Merrick: 'I was born in my native English land, and grew up in Rus; I never ate as many meals in my homeland as I did in the state of Muscovy.'[33] Thus it was the Russian north, and not the Russian capital, that formed the natural environment in which the dialogue of two nations and two cultures took its unhindered course.

The political experience of the company's members and agents did much to smooth the path enjoyed by English diplomatic missions during the early seventeenth century. They took care of arriving ambassadors and envoys, so that no serious breaches of Russian ambassadorial ceremony or local custom arose. Sir Thomas Smith, for instance, carried out his task impeccably.[34] Half a century of contacts with Russians had not passed in vain, and at last the English had introduced the necessary corrections – from the point of view of Russian political culture – to their ambassadors' public behaviour. In the interests of his business, Smith – a governor of the Muscovy Company in London – first demonstratively distanced himself from his compatriot merchants and turned down the invitation to stay in the home of the agent John Merrick, thereby emphasizing his own diplomatic rank and surrounding his person with the necessary aura of mystery. In the words of one participant in his mission, 'it could not be performed according to the respect ambassadors are used with there, nor perhaps would it be well agreeing to their more private fashion, who hold it greatest glory for greatest men rather to be reported of, then seene.'[35] Smith did nothing to damage his own reputation or to lower the esteem accorded to him by carefully observing the 'strange Ceremony of first allighting from their horses'[36] to which the Russians attached great significance. He unerringly recited the full and complex titles of the Russian Tsar, demonstrating also a superb knowledge of local table ceremonies, such as the ability to raise his cup to toast in fitting manner the health of the representatives of the ruling dynasties of both countries.

The report of Smith's mission, published in London in 1605 (cat. 78), records the symptoms of mutual cultural adaptation on the part of both the English and the Russians and their mastery of each other's customs. It also contains accounts of the use of English silver in everyday and official life. The cups and other vessels figured as prestigious New Year's gifts among the English living in Muscovy and served as a means of rewarding the Russians with whom the English worked and came into contact. Just such a gift, for instance, was made to Thomas Smith by John Merrick: 'the honest and kind Agent . . . presented his Lordship with a faire standing gilt cup and cover, worth thirty pound, likewise his Prestave and Enterpreter very bountifully'.[37] On his part, the ambassador gave the Russian noble assigned to him 'two standing cups with covers'.[38] Thus elegant works by English masters not only came into the imperial treasury, but also adorned the buffets of the Russian aristocracy and those serving in the Ambassadorial Office.

8. Romeyn de Hooghe, 'Sledges and skiers on the Volga River,' from Balthasar Coyet, *Historisch Verhael, of Beschryving van de Voyagie*, Amsterdam, 1677. Beinecke Rare Book and Manuscript Library, Yale University

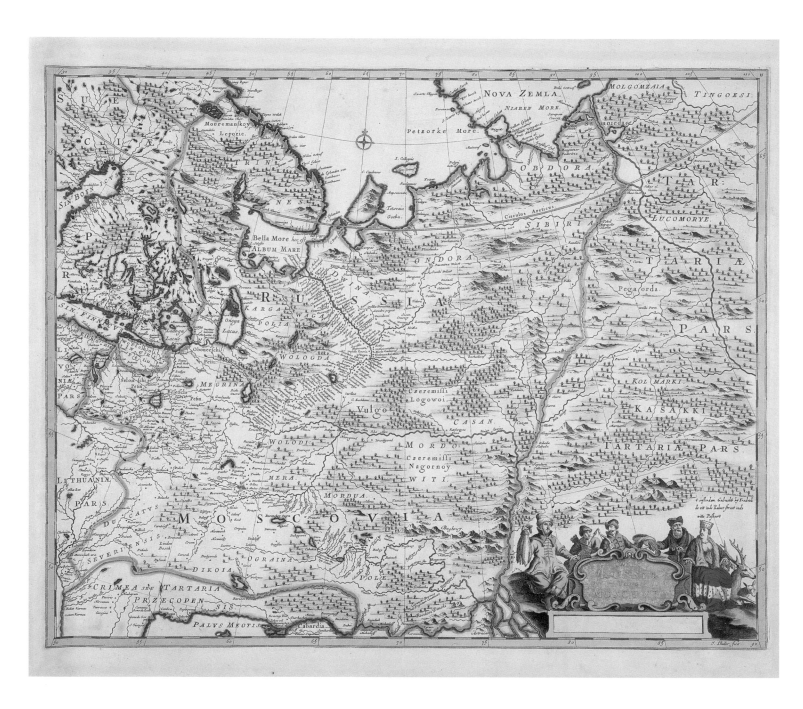

9. 'Tabula Russia Vulgo Moscovia', by F. Shuillier, from
Nicolaes Visscher, *Atlas Minor*, plate 13, Amsterdam, 1745.
Yale Center for British Art, Paul Mellon Collection

Cultural perceptions

Thanks to intensive diplomatic relations and trading links with Muscovy, by the early seventeenth century the English were better informed about the Russian land than any other nation. Like other Europeans they had in the first half of the sixteenth century sought information on Russia mainly in the works of learned Italians or in the authoritative treatise *Rerum Moscoviticarum* (1549) by the Austrian diplomat Sigismund von Herberstein.[39] But from the middle of the century the cosmographia or written sources on Russia came to include more and more information supplied by the English.[40] As a result of the unique talents of the English navigators Steven Burrough and his brother William (1536–99), who were both in the service of the Muscovy Company, maps appeared of the shores of the Kara Sea and the northern sea passage to Siberia and the mouth of the River Ob. One of the most important scholarly results of Anthony Jenkinson's journey was his corrected map of Muscovy and Tatary with a detailed depiction of the route along the Volga to the Caspian Sea (cat. 87). New information received from English travellers and navigators was rapidly disseminated by leading geographers and publishers of atlases – Abraham Ortelius (cat. 87), Joan Blaeu (cats. 88–9), John Seller (cat. 90) and Moses Pitt. In these learned publications, Muscovy gradually took on its true shape, appearing before European eyes with its plethora of geographical features and its variety of ethnic groups (Russians, Lapps, Tatars, Samoyeds and many more).

Many travellers and diplomats (Chancellor, Jenkinson, Randolph, the poet George Turberville, Horsey, Fletcher and Smith) left behind their own memoirs of Russia. Their reports, varying from travel notes and letters in verse to weighty treatises, were gathered together and first published in 1589 by the celebrated amateur historian Richard Hakluyt. *The Principall Navigations, Voiages and Discoveries of the English Nation, made by Sea or over Land* (cat. 76) provides a wide range of information regarding natural and climactic conditions, the appearance of towns and villages, the capital of the Muscovite state, ceremonies at the court of the Russian Tsar, as well as political institutions, the legal system, the state of the army and the religion of the Muscovites. It must be treated with caution. Not every author's observations were original: they frequently reproduced whole passages from the same sources every Englishman used to prepare himself on the eve of his journey to Muscovy. Travel literature was also unreliable as diplomats spent only a short time in Russia and most had no knowledge of the Russian language. The level of the author's objectivity and benevolence depended largely on the reception he was accorded and the success of his mission, as well as the general overall state of Anglo-Russian relations at the time. As a result, the image of Muscovy presented by English diplomats to their readers was at times contradictory.

Without exception the land was described as an attractive market for English goods. The great power concentrated in the Tsar seemed to guarantee the stability necessary for commerce to flourish. In the 1550s Chancellor's report – compiled in a tone well-disposed toward Muscovy – gave the power of the young Russian state its due, but by the end of the century the political literature was dominated by a negative image of Muscovy. It had become to English eyes 'a barbarian state' with a tyrannical form of government headed by an autocratic Tsar, a corrupt bureaucracy and a nobility slavishly dependent on the whim of the sovereign. All layers of society were seen to be rudely subordinated (the bitter reality of the twilight of Ivan IV's reign could not but arouse the hostility of the English, brought up as they were within a very different political culture). Other negative clichés occur in the persistent mention of the Russians' 'superstition', 'idolatry', low morals, drunkenness and debauchery. Still, there was general praise for the Russians' hardiness, their hospitality and sound wooden houses, and of course there was amazement at Muscovy's boundless expanses.[41]

The tendency towards criticism of the state of things in Muscovy and of Russian morals and habits in the late 1560s to 1580s took shape at a time of increasing political friction between the two states, when the status of English merchants on the Russian market was threatened. A major contribution was made by the peevish poetical satires of George Turberville, who formed part of the suite of Thomas Randolph's unsuccessful mission. Negative attitudes were exacerbated by Jerome Bowes, also something of a failure as a diplomat, but one who gained a reputation in English society as an unfailing gentleman disdainful of alien habits and protocol. Critical literature reached its sneering height in a book by Giles Fletcher, *Of the Russe Commonwealth* (fig. 10).[42] Fletcher arrived as envoy to Moscow in 1588, during the reign of the even-tempered Fyodor Ivanovich, but his treatise created a picture of a despotic ruler that was surely more applicable to the reign of Fyodor's father, Ivan the Terrible. The merchants of the Muscovy Company immediately perceived his work as not only prejudiced but dangerous to Anglo-Russian relations. Through their efforts the book was banned.[43] Only a few excerpts managed to get through the censor and were published by Hakluyt.

Such an attitude to Muscovy as a 'barbarian' land, its inhabitants wallowing in sin and superstition, was largely dictated by the religious leanings of some English authors. In the sixteenth century the Reformation had split Europe and harsh polemics regarding the true faith affected not only Catholics and Protestants, but flew between the different branches of Protestantism itself. Alongside nationality, religious faith was one of the most important forms of individual and collective self-identity. Each believed that they followed the one true faith, an approach that encouraged intolerance of other beliefs. English travellers, who included both moderate Anglicans and upholders of more radical Puritan beliefs, perceived the religion of the Muscovites through the prism of their own polemics with Catholicism. While admitting the common origins of different branches of Christianity, they nonetheless saw Orthodoxy, like Catholicism, as misguided, having departed from the 'true way'. The English were cautious of those forms of piety practised by the Russians, describing them as popery – reverence for icons, which they called idol-worship, magnificent ritual, processions of the cross, pilgrimage to monasteries. Everything was grouped together under a single term: superstition (fig. 11).

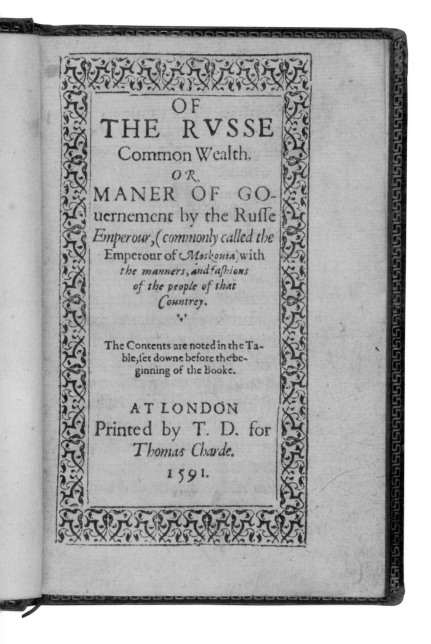

10. Title page of *Of the Russe Common Wealth, or, Maner of Gouernement by the Russe Emperour (commonly called the Emperour of Moskouia): with the Manners, and Fashions of the People of that Countrey*, by Giles Fletcher, London, 1591. Beinecke Rare Book and Manuscript Library, Yale University

OF
THE RVSSE
Common Wealth.
OR
MANER OF GO-
uernement by the Russe
Emperour, (*commonly called the*
Emperour of *Moskouia*) with
the manners, and fashions
of the people of that
Countrey.

The Contents are noted in the Table, set downe before the beginning of the Booke.

AT LONDON
Printed by T. D. for
Thomas Charde.
1591.

Russian church art, continuing the artistic traditions of Byzantium, the frescoes, icons and fine metalwork and the jewels used to adorn them all (see cats. 60–9) served only to disgust Protestant authors. Although many of the English took an interest in the religious practices of the Muscovites (Giles Fletcher was himself a priest and it is he who left the most detailed description), their assessment of them was a foregone conclusion, as was their conviction that the Russians were 'unenlightened' or 'barbarous', sinful and not to be accepted as Christians in the true sense of the word. (To be just, the attitude of the Orthodox Church and Russians to followers of other faiths was much the same: they saw them as heretics, did not recognize the validity of their baptism and called them 'unbaptized Germans', the word 'German' being used to signify all foreigners during this period. Russian fresco depictions of the Last Judgment from the sixteenth and seventeenth centuries frequently depict people in 'foreign' attire burning in the fires of hell.)

English perceptions of remote Russia were based not only on the records of diplomats, of course. There was an extensive oral tradition, based on the reminiscences of those who had spent long years there, and there were those who came into contact with the merchants of the Muscovy Company, in whom there was a kinder, more even attitude towards Russia. It is probably to this circle that we owe the more positive image of Russia that features in literature and plays of the age of Shakespeare.

Muscovy is frequently mentioned in Elizabethan and Jacobean literature, evidence certainly of a genuine interest in Russia. General information was widespread. References to Russian matters and trade can be found in the sonnets of court poets such as Sir Philip Sidney, Edmund Spenser, Fulke Greville and John Donne, whose letter to E. Guilpin – 'To Mr E.G.' – avows:

> Therefore I'll leave it, and in the Country strive
> Pleasure, now fled from London, to retrive.
> Do thou so too; and fill not like a Bee
> The things with hony, but as plenteously
> As Russian Marchants, thy selfes whole vessel load,
> And then at Winter retaile it here abroad.

The achievements of English navigators who opened up the way to Muscovy, suffering great deprivations during their many months sailing through the icy latitudes, became part of a national myth. The ninth song of Michael Drayton's historical poem *Poly-Olbion* (1612) praises the 'brave adventurous Knight, our Sir Hugh Willougby' and remarks

> Two others follow then, eternal fame that wonne,
> Our Chancellor, and with him, compare we Jenkinson:
> For Russia both embarqu'd …

Nor was the Russian theme less common on the English stage, confirming that perceptions of Muscovy were an ingrained element of the English consciousness and included the existence of recognizable and consistent stereotypes. At the same time those stereotypes reveal that to English minds far-off Russia remained an exotic land of extremes. Its unencompassed spaces were dominated by ferociously cold weather and eternal snows, and the only thing comparable to the fury of 'the rugged Russian bear' (*Macbeth* 3.4.100) was the anger of the autocratic Tsar of the Muscovites. Russia and its inhabitants cropped up in the most varied contexts in the works of popular dramatists: Christopher Marlowe, William Shakespeare, Robert Greene, Thomas Heywood, Francis Beaumont and John Fletcher, Thomas Middleton, Thomas Dekker and John Marston. Prose writers too – Thomas Nashe and Thomas Lodge – showed off their knowledge of Russian life and terms.[44]

The distant court of the Russian Emperor haunted the imagination of Elizabethan authors and the mention of Muscovy – even the setting of the action there – became fashionable in English literature as the century waned. Russia allowed dramatists to satisfy the public's taste for the exotic and the fabulous, for unbridled 'barbarian' passions. The heroines of Greene's *Pandosto* (1588) and Shakespeare's *A Winter's Tale* (1610) are daughters of the Russian Emperor. Lodge, who had moved in the circles of merchants of the Muscovy Company since childhood, went even further. His novel, *A Margarite of America* (1596), unfolds in Muscovy. The author creates a fantastical image of the Russian 'Renaissance' court which seems to be the epitome of courtly culture, with a wise sovereign and his advisers citing Plato, the apartments of the ladies of the court adorned with quotations from Greek philosophers, and the Russian 'gentlemen' doing battle at courtly tournaments in honour of the royal daughter.

Lodge mentions that 'Muscovian strangers' and 'Scithian monsters' were popular on the English stage.[45] Shakespeare included the celebrated 'Russian' scene (act 5, scene 2) in *Love's Labour's Lost* (1595) in which a group of the King of Navarre's courtiers dress up as Muscovites to assist the hero in courting his beloved, a French princess. Shakespeare seems to have been inspired by the arrival in London of the Russian embassy led by Fyodor Pisemsky (1582), whose mission included the engagement of Ivan IV and Mary Hastings. We cannot know if the playwright witnessed the reception of this staid and stately imperial ambassador dressed in heavy brocade robes and surrounded by his entourage, but clearly most English people imagined the Russians just as they were described, with some irony, by Shakespeare: 'My frozen Muscovites . . . well-liking wits they have; gross, gross, fat, fat.'[46]

In the case of Thomas Heywood, we know that his interest was aroused by the memorable appearance of the Russian envoys in London. His play *If you know not me, you know no body* (1605), dedicated to the reign of the late Queen Elizabeth and based on true historical events, describes the opening of the Exchange in London, at which the honoured guest of the City merchants and of Thomas Gresham, founder of the Exchange, is the Russian ambassador. The Muscovite greets the London merchants in Latin and raises a toast to the English capital, after which, during the reception, he consults the merchants regarding the official language and order of events for his forthcoming audience with the Queen. This is absolutely in keeping with historical reality, since the Muscovy Company played the most important role in organizing the stay of Russian ambassadors and envoys in London. The image of the Russian diplomat also carried a certain symbolic meaning, since the ambassador represented the Emperor, one who, in the eyes of the

11. 'S. Trinité, ou, Jerusalem, Eglise de Moscou…', unknown artist, from Pieter van der Aa, *La Galerie Agréable du Monde*, plate 33, Leiden, 1729. Yale Center for British Art, Paul Mellon Collection

to Lord Burghley: British Library, MS Lansdowne 10, extract 34, f. 130, The great cawses of offence given to the English Ambassador Thomas Randolf, 1568; extract 36, f. 134, A copy of a letter of Mr Randolph to the Russian Emperor, 12 April 1568; MS Lansdowne 11, extract 35, f. 89, a copy of two letters from Randolph addressed to the Russian 'council' and to the Emperor, May 1569; extract 37, f. 93, a letter from the Russian Company to Thomas Randolph, April 1569.

24 Jerome Bowes' scandalous behavior has been the subject of much attention from historians: see subject bibliography.

25 British Library, MS Cotton Nero, B.VIII, extract 6, f. 7v, The answer of Wm. and Geo. Bond and John Foxall, to a bill of complaint exhibited against them by the governors of the commonalty of the merchant adventurers for the discovery of lands: two articles; extract 7, f. 11, The replication of the governors of the merchant adventurers, to the answers of Wm. and Geo. Bond and John Foxall, and those partners trading to the Narve; with the oath of the freemen of the said company annexed.

26 'Spisok posol'stva Fyodora Pisemkogo da pod'yachego Neudachi Khovralyova kak sya u nikh v Aglinskoy zemle gosudarevo delo delalos" ['Report of the Embassy of Fyodor Pisemky and Pod'yachy Neudacha Khovralyov and How the Sovereign's Affairs Went in the English Lands'] in Sbornik Russkogo Istoricheskogo Obshchestva ['Anthology of the Russian Historical Society'], vol. 38 (St Petersburg, 1883), pp. 37, 49–50.

27 Smith 1605, f. B.

28 British Library, MS Cotton Nero B. XI, extract 98, f. 337, The emperor of Russia (Foedor Iwanowitz) to Q. Elizabeth; by Dr. Giles Fletcher, her ambassador; chiefly conc[e]rning trade. Muscow, 1589.

29 Smith 1605, f. H.

30 British Library, MS Cotton Nero B.XI, extract 93, f. 324r,v, Instructions of the governors of the Levant [Russia] company, W. Garrard and Rowland Hayward, to one of their ambassadors or agents. Lond. April 18, 1567.

31 Evidence includes inscriptions in Russian recording ownership of books belonging to Englishmen, as well as Russian passages in their correspondence (such as British Library, MS Lansdowne 15, extract 76, ff. 162–3, A private letter from William Smith, merchant, from Yaroslav to his brother James with a postscript in Russian) and numerous mentions by the English themselves regarding the level of their knowledge of Russian. Such evidence is gathered in M. P. Alexeev, 'Angliyskiy yazyk v Rossii i russkiy yazyk v Anglii' ['The English Language in Russia and the Russian Language in England'], Uchenye Zapiski LGU: Seriya filologicheskiy nauk ['Scientific Notes of Leningrad State University: Philological Sciences Series'] 9, no. 72 (1944), pp. 77–85; Y. N. Bespyatkh, 'Angliyskiy yazyk Dzheroma Gorseya i russkie realii' ['The English Language of Jerome Horsey and the Realities of Russian Life'], Istoriya SSSR ['History of the USSR'] 2 (1991), pp. 188–92; A. E. Pennington, 'A Sixteenth–Century English Slavist', Modern Language Review 62, no. 4 (1967), pp. 680–6; C. Thomas, 'Two East Slavonic Primers: Lvov, 1574 and Moscow, 1637', British Library Journal 10, no. 11 (1984), pp. 32–47.

32 Vremennik Moskovskogo Obshchestva istorii i drevnostey rossiyskikh ['Annals of the Moscow Society for Russian History and Antiquities'] book 8 (Moscow, 1850), pp. 18, 54.

33 Cited in Sokolov 1992, pp. 84–5.

34 On Smith's mission, see subject bibliography.

35 Smith 1605, ff. C4v–Dr.

36 Smith 1605, f. D.

37 Smith 1605, f. G3v.

38 Smith 1605, f. F2r.

39 Even William Cunningham, author of The Cosmographical Glasse, conteinyng the pleasant Principles of Cosmographie, Geographie, Hydrographie, or Navigation (London, 1559), though aware of Chancellor's journey, preferred to refer to Herberstein (p. 182).

40 'Anglorum navigatio ad Moscovitas' in Rerum Moscoviticarum auctores varii … (Frankfurt, 1600), pp. 142–53.

41 Analysis of the writings of travellers to Russia is found in V. O. Klyuchevsky, Skazaniya Inostrantsev o Moskovskom gosudarstve ['The Tales of Foreigners about the Muscovite State'] (Moscow, 1991); Y. S. Lure, 'Pis'ma Dzheroma Gorseya' ['The Letters of Jerome Horsey'], Uchenye Zapiski LGU: Seriya istoricheskikh nauk ['Scientific Notes of Leningrad State University: Historical Sciences Series'] 8 (1941), pp. 189–201; A. A. Sevastyanova, Sochineniya Dzheroma Gorseya kak istochnik po istorii Rossii XVI – nach. XVII v. ['The Writings of Jerome Horsey as a Source in Russian History of the Sixteenth and early Seventeenth Centuries'], M.Phil. dissertation (Moscow, 1974); A. A. Sevastyanova, 'Dzherom Gorsey i ego sochineniya o Rossii' ['Jerome Horsey and his Writings on Russia'] in Dzherom Gorsey: Zapiski o Rossii XVI–nachala XVII v. ['Jerome Horsey: Notes on Russia of the Sixteenth–early Seventeenth Centuries] (Moscow, 1990); S. M. Seredonin, Sochinenie Dzhil'sa Fletchera 'Of the Russe Commonwealth' kak istorichyeskiy istochnik ['Giles Fletcher's "Of the Russe Commonwealth" as a Historical Source'] (St Petersburg, 1891); Y. V. Tolstoy, 'Skazaniya anglichanina Gorseya o Rossii v iskhode XVI stoletiya' ['Tales of Russia by the Englishman Horsey at the End of the Sixteenth Century'], Otechestvennye zapiski ['Notes of the Fatherland'] 107 (St Petersburg, 1859); R. Croskey, 'The Composition of Sir Jerome Horsey's Travels', Jahrbucher für Geschichte Osteuropas ['Yearbook of East European History'] 26, no. 3 (1978), pp. 362–75; M. Perrie, 'Jerome Horsey's Account of the Events of May 1591', Oxford Slavonic Papers, new series 13 (1980), pp. 28–49; S. Mund, 'La représentation de la Moscovie à la Renaissance: Le regard des voyageurs Anglais face à la tradition "continentale"', Slavica Gandensia 29 (2002), pp. 123–35.

42 For more information on Fletcher and his writings, see subject bibliography.

43 The 1591 petition from the merchants of the Muscovy Company to Lord Burleigh that Giles Fletcher's book be banned is in British Library, MS Lansdowne 112, extract 39, f. 134.

44 Detailed studies of references to Russia in English literature can be found in Alexeev 1982, pp. 29–36; M. P. Alexeev, 'Shekspir i russkoe gosudarstvo ego vremeni' ['Shakespeare and the Russian State of his Time'] in Shekspir i russkaya kul'tura ['Shakespeare and Russian Culture'], (Moscow and Leningrad, 1965), pp. 784–805; L. A. Nikitina, '"Russkie" istochniki i priemy ikh obrabotki v proizvedeniyakh T. Nesha' ['"Russian" Sources and Devices in their Reworking in the Works of T. Nashe'], Arkheograficheskiy ezhegodnik za 1971 g. ['Archaeographical Annual for 1971'] (Moscow, 1972), pp. 148–53; E. H. Sugden, Topographical Dictionary to the Works of Shakespeare and his Fellow Dramatists (Manchester, 1925); J. W. Draper, 'Shakespeare and Muscovy', Slavonic and East European Review 38 (1954), pp. 217–25; A. G. Cross, The Russian Theme in English Literature from the Sixteenth Century to 1980 (Oxford, 1985).

45 T. Lodge, 'A Reply to Stephen Gosson's Schoole of abuse in defence of Poetry musick and stage plays', 1580; published in The Complete Works of Thomas Lodge, 4 vols. (New York, 1963), vol. 1, p. 20.

46 W. Shakespeare, Love's Labours Lost, 5.2.265–8.

47 T. Heywood, If You know not me, you know no body, part two, published in Two Historical Plays on the Life and Reign of Queen Elizabeth by Thomas Heywood (London, 1851), pp. 115–17.

48 The original reports of Russian embassies to England in the sixteenth and seventeenth centuries have been published in Sbornik Russkogo Istoricheskogo Obshchestva ['Anthology of the Russian Historical Society'], vol. 38 (St Petersburg, 1883); Ambassadors' Travels 1954. For Russian sources of information on England, see subject bibliography.

49 'Proekt vzyatiya Moskovskogo gosudarstva pod pokrovitel'stvo Anglii, predlozhennyy angliyskim rezidentom Dzhonom Merikom' ['Plan for Taking the Muscovite State Under English Protection, Put Forward by the English Resident John Merrick'] in Chteniya moskovskogo Obshchestva istorii i drevnostey Rossiyskikh ['Readings of the Moscow Society of Russian History and

Antiquities'] (Moscow, 1874), book 3, pp. 76–81; UK National Archives, PRO, State Papers, Foreign, 91/1, f. 228v; I. I. Lubimenko, 'Project for the Acquisition of Russia by James I', *English Historical Review* 29 (1914), pp. 246–56; C. Dunning, 'James I, the Russia Company and the Plan to Establish a Protectorate Over North Russia', *Albion* 21, no. 2 (1982), pp. 206–26; C. Dunning, 'A Letter to James I Concerning the English Plan for Military Intervention in Russia', *Slavonic and East European Review* 67, no. 1 (1989), pp. 94–108.

50 A full analysis of the international situation on the eve of Zyuzin's embassy appears in the anthology England and the North (1994), which provides considerable additions to the information provided in an earlier publication, *Posol'skaya kniga po svyazyam Rossii s Angliey (1613–14)* ['The Ambassadorial Book on Links Between Russia and England (1613–14)'] (Moscow, 1979).

51 For a political biography of Merrick, see G. M. Phipps, *Sir John Merrick: English Merchant-Diplomat in Seventeenth-Century Russia* (Newtonville, MS, 1983).

52 Dokhutorov's report was published with commentaries in Z. I. Roginsky, *Poezdka gontsa Gerasima Semyonovich Dokhutorova v Angliyu v 1645–6* ['The Journey of Messenger Gerasim Semyonovich Dokhutorov to England in 1645–6'] (Yaroslavl, 1959).

53 *Sobranie gosudarstvennykh gramot i dogovorov* ['Collection of State Letters and Agreements'], part 3 (Moscow, 1822), pp. 162–4.

54 S. I. Arkhangelsky, 'Diplomaticheskie agenty Kromvelya v peregovorakh s Moskvoy' ['Cromwell's Diplomatic Agents in Negotiations with Moscow'], *Istoricheskie zapiski Instituta istorii AN SSSR* ['Historical Notes of the Institute of History of the USSR Academy of Sciences'] 5 (1939), pp. 118–40; I. I. Lubimenko, 'Angliya i Rossiya v XVII veke' ['England and Russia in the Seventeenth Century'] in *Angliyskaya burzhuaznaya revolyutsiya XVII v.* ['The English Bourgeois Revolution of the Seventeenth Century'] (Moscow, 1954), vol. 2, pp. 90–118.

55 *The First Printed Catalogue of the Bodleian Library 1605: A Facsimile / Catalogus librorum bibliothecae publicae quam vir ornatissimus Thomas Bodleius eques auratus in Academia Oxoniensi nuper instituit / [Thomas James]* (Oxford, 1986), p. 349; J. S. G. Simmons and B. O. Unbegaun, 'Slavonic Manuscript Vocabularies in the Bodleian Library', *Oxford Slavonic Papers* 2 (1951), pp. 119–27; W. F. Ryan, 'A Russian Version of the "Secreta Secretorum" in the Bodleian Library', *Oxford Slavonic Papers* 12 (1965), pp. 40–9; J. D. A. Barnicot and J. S. G. Simmons, 'Some Unrecorded Early Printed Slavonic Books in English Libraries', *Oxford Slavonic Papers* 2 (1951), pp. 98–118; P. Dent, 'Early Anglo-Russian Relations', *British Museum Society Bulletin* 10 (1972), pp. 16–17.

56 One can see how Anglican theologians changed their approach to the Russian Orthodox Church, for instance, through Ephraim Paggit, *Christianographie, or the Description of the Multitude and Sundry Sorts of Christians in the World not Subject to the Pope* (London, 1620).

57 *Annals of the Bodleian Library, Oxford, A.D. 1598–1867* (London, 1867), pp. 309–10.

58 *A Dictionarie of the vulgar Russe Tongue, attributed to Mark Ridley*, ed. G. Stone (Cologne, 1996).

59 Bodleian Library, Oxford, MS James 43; B. A. Larin, *Russko-angliyskiy slovar'-dnevnik Richarda Dzhemsa (1618–19)* ['The Russian-English Dictionary-Diary of Richard James (1618–19)'] (Leningrad, 1959).

60 P. Simoni, 'Pesni, zapisannye dlya Richarda Dzheymsa v 1619–1620 gg.' ['Songs Recorded for Richard James in 1619–20'], *Pamyatniki starinnogo russkogo yazyka i slovesnosti XVI–XVII stoletiy* ['Monuments of the Old Russian Language and Philology of the Sixteenth-Seventeenth Centuries'] vol. 2 (St Petersburg, 1907).

61 G. S. Boulger, 'The First Russian Botanist', *Journal of Botany* 82 (1895); J. Hamel, *Tradescant der ältere 1618 in Russland* (St Petersburg and Leipzig, 1847); P. Leith-Ross, *The John Tradescants: Gardeners to the Rose and Lily Queen* (London, 1981).

62 A reference from the *Musaeum Tradescantianum*, cited in P. Leith-Ross, *The John Tradescants*, p. 67.

63 W. F. Ryan, 'John Tradescant's Russian Abacus', *Oxford Slavonic Papers*, new series 5 (1972), pp. 83–8.

64 Milton 1682, p. 1.

65 P. Dukes, 'The Leslie Family in the Swedish Period (1630–5) of the Thirty Years War', *European Studies Review* 12, no. 4 (1982), pp. 401–24.

66 On Gordon's life in Moscow, see Gordon 2002: 'Dnevnik generala Patrika Gordona vedennyy im vo vremya ego prebyvaniya v Rossii 1661–78 gg.' ['The Diary of General Patrick Gordon Kept During his Stay in Russia 1661–78'] in *Moskoviya i Evropa* ['Muscovy and Europe'] (Moscow, 2000); Baroness Sophie Buxhoeveden, *A Cavalier in Muscovy: A Biography of General Patrick Gordon* (London, 1932); P. Gordon, *Passages from the Diary of General Patrick Gordon of Auchleuchries in the Years 1635–99* (Aberdeen, 1859; repr. London, 1968); G. P. Herd, *General Patrick Gordon of Auchleuchries (1635–99): A Scot in Russian Service*, PhD dissertation (University of Aberdeen, 1995).

67 Collins 1671.

68 Information regarding such translations is provided in Alexeev 1982, pp. 46–8.

69 'Book entitled the Cosmographia, That is a Description of the whole earthly land', cited in Alexeev 1946, pp. 75–9.

70 Z. I. Roginsky, *London 1645–6 godov': Novye istochniki o poezdki gontsa G. S. Dokhutorova v Angliyu* ['London in 1645–6: New Sources Regarding the Journey by Messenger G. S. Dokhutorov to England'] (Yaroslavl, 1960), p. 10.

71 On Hebdon's task of seeking actors see I. Shlyapkin, 'K istorii russkogo teatra pri Aleksee Mikhayloviche' ['On the History of the Russian Theater Under Alexey Mikhaylovich'], *Zhurnal Ministerstva Narodnogo Prosveshcheniya* ['Journal of the Ministry of Public Education'] 3 (1903), pp. 210–11; I. Y. Gurlyand, *Ivan Gebdon, kommissarius i resident* ['John Hebdon, Commissary and Resident'] (Yaroslavl, 1903), pp. 26–7.

72 M. S. Anderson, *Britain's Discovery of Russia, 1553–1815* (London, 1958), p. 48.

73 Rude and Barbarous Kingdom 1968, p. xi; Russian State Archive of Ancient Acts, Moscow, fund 35, *opis'* 2, documents, no. 37, 1 February 1626, Letter from Charles I to Tsar Mikhail Fyodorovich.

74 Milton 1682, p. 2.

1

English Silver in Moscow

A preasent to the greate Emperor and greate Duke Borris Pheodorow[ch] of all Russia and to the Empriss Marya Gryoryevna from James the Great, Kinge of all England.

> A charyott,
> Two greate flaggons,
> A christall cuppe,
> A bason and ewre,
> Two haunche ottes,
> One standinge cuppe,
> One peece of scarlett and fowre peeces of other fine cloathe.

—Gifts brought by the embassy of Sir Thomas Smith, 1604–5

English Silver
of the Sixteenth and Seventeenth Centuries
in the Kremlin

Natalya Abramova

12. Interior of the Facet Chamber in the Armoury, Moscow Kremlin.
Nineteenth-century photograph

There are more than 500 pieces of silver by English masters in the Armoury, part of the Moscow Kremlin Museums (fig. 12). Some one hundred of these date from the early period of English silverwork, the late Tudor and early Stuart era between the middle of the sixteenth century and the middle of the seventeenth. It is one of the world's largest collections of English silver from this period.[1]

The Armoury collection is of particular historical and artistic significance because of the way in which it was formed. English silver was not widely traded in Europe in the sixteenth and seventeenth centuries, but arrived on the Continent as single examples, usually as gifts. Indeed, many of the pieces in the Armoury were diplomatic gifts, brought for Russian rulers by English ambassadors, while others were purchased by merchants and agents specially for the Tsar's treasury.

Whereas the composition of English diplomatic gifts in the sixteenth century was extremely varied, by the seventeenth century they had come to be dominated by textiles and all kinds of silver plate.[2] Naturally, those gifts selected for presentation to the rulers of Muscovy included the very best examples of work by English silversmiths. The royal instructions given to Thomas Randolph, an ambassador during the reign of Elizabeth I, were to present to the Tsar in the Queen's name 'a rich standing cup of silver, containing in it a great number of pieces of plate artificially wrought' which was to be prized rather for the 'newness of the device than ... its intrinsic value' and which was 'the first that was ever made in England'.[3] Such an attitude explains the presence of so many truly unique pieces in the Armoury and why this one collection provides us with so many opportunities to study the stylistic features of English Renaissance and Baroque silver.

English Renaissance silver

English Renaissance silver produced from about 1520 to 1620 can be characterized in general by its precise, symmetrical form and a clear division between the functional parts. Decoration is always subordinated to the object's physical structure. The composition and adornment of such works are dominated by a horizontal articulation of form with any ornament generally arranged in bands or around the centre. English Renaissance silversmiths favoured such forms as the font-shaped cup, ewer and basin sets, all kinds of cups, large pillar-shaped salts, livery pots, candlesticks and flagons, all of which are represented in the Armoury by rare pieces, many of which find no analogy in other collections.

Among the earliest pieces is a font-shaped cup of 1557–8 (cat. 1). Such vessels recall the Italian *tazza* or wine-bowl, but differ significantly in having a broad, massive stem. They were widespread in England during the first half of the sixteenth century. The latest examples date from the 1570s. Traditionally such vessels were found in parish churches, where they were used as chalices, and they are still found today in local churches in Kent, Oxford and Leicestershire.[4] More luxurious versions appear in paintings such as *The Last Supper* by Frans Pourbus the Elder (1545–81; Museum voor

Schone Kunsten, Ghent), and during the second half of the sixteenth century it became fashionable to adorn vessels of this form with bust-length figures in antique armour and emblems in medallions at the centre of the bowl (fig. 13). The Armoury cup (cat. 1) is one of the best examples of this form. Seventeenth-century manuscript inventories and the published inventory of the Armoury of 1884–93 describe the vessel as a *razsolnik*, a Russian term reflecting the fact that in northern Europe the bowl was used not for wine but to hold sweets, fruits and other delicacies (*raznosol*).[5]

The font-shaped cup is a clear example of how Renaissance style was applied to three-dimensional objects. Its composition is clearly readable, thanks to the precise, carefully conceived separation of bearing and supported parts: the marked horizontal articulation differs strongly from the upward-soaring, more monolithic forms of Gothic plate, with its clear alternation of horizontal and vertical elements in both construction and decoration. Smooth or flower-patterned elongated *laminae* or lobes possibly appeared under the influence of vessels made from ivory plaques. The unusual stocky form with a heavy stem and the nature of the ornament (with its strapwork and low-relief chasing of the tendrils) are evidence of the cup's English origin. It is worth noting that among the designs that Hans Holbein the Younger produced for vessels for the wedding of Henry VIII and Jane Seymour in 1536 (now in the Ashmolean Museum, Oxford) are antique profiles in medallions and arabesque ornament similar to the decoration on the Armoury cup.

Objects produced during the second half of the sixteenth century were characterized by the flat treatment of ornamental motifs that cover the whole of the object's surface. Many pieces were adorned with engraving. A livery pot of 1594–5 (cat. 5) is covered with elegantly engraved grotesque spiral tendrils, heads of fantastical beasts and birds, large palmettes, shells and rosettes. This type of ornament, consisting of a complex combination of grotesques, was developed by the engraver Niçaise Roussel, who arrived in England from Flanders in 1563.[6] His compositions became widely known to English silversmiths, especially with the later publication of a book of Roussel's grotesques in 1623, which was reissued twice in the seventeenth century.

Among the Armoury's nine livery pots are some extremely interesting pieces dating from 1585 to 1663. All of them are *Hansekanne*, Hanse-type pots, with the exception of the Baroque livery pots of 1663 (cat. 34). *Hansekanne* are cylindrical and have elongated proportions, unlike the conical tankards of the Elizabethan age. They were generally used for beer and ale, although they might also be kept in churches. They were very popular in the sea towns of the Baltic region linked via the Hanseatic League – Riga, Lübeck, Rostock and Hamburg – where they continued to be made into the middle of the eighteenth century. The name *Hansekanne* appears in English documents of 1526 and the inventory of the royal Tudor plate compiled in 1574, and is repeated a dozen times in the list of objects in the Jewel House compiled in 1649.[7]

A superb example of late Tudor or early Stuart silverwork is found in a livery pot of 1613–14 (cat. 21). It is chased with images of Neptune and tritons on dolphins, the heads of winged cupids beneath baldachins, winged sirens with fish tails, a coat-of-arms and shells. The combination of convex decorative elements (the shells and a row of large *ovae* on the base) with flat strapwork and relief images creates a play of light and shadow that reinforces the overall stress on plastic effect that is typical of late Renaissance silver.

Cups occupied an important place among ambassadorial gifts and usually featured at the head of the list of gifts. Large gilded cups with covers, up to 35⅜ in. (90 cm) high, were specially chosen or made for such ceremonial purposes. They were not generally used, but placed on display buffets or stepped cupboards. More modest cups of 16–20 in. (40–50 cm) were a common gift in England during the late sixteenth and early seventeenth centuries, and often head the lists of new year's gifts in surviving inventories of the royal plate of the later Tudors. They were also given as presents by the livery companies, colleges and all kinds of societies.

13. View into the bowl of the Deane Cup (detail), possibly by Robert Danbe, 1551–52, silver, partly gilded. Willis Museum, Basingstoke

14. Title page of John Parkinson's *Paradisi in Sole Paradisus Terrestris*, engraved by Christopher Switzer, London, 1629. Beinecke Rare Book and Manuscript Library, Yale University

The rich collection of English cups in the Armoury reflects their variety of form and decoration and allows us to trace their evolution. One type frequently found has an ovoid bowl and characteristic ornament of Tudor roses in strapwork, with hops, pears, daisies, pinks, lilies-of-the-valley or harebells spread evenly across the whole surface. Such ornamental motifs give English silver its national flavour. We gain some idea of the favourite flowers of the time from a book by the apothecary and botanist John Parkinson (1567–1650), *Paradisi in Sole Paradisus Terrestris* (1629; fig. 14), where a depiction of the earthly paradise on the title page is accompanied by the text 'A Garden of all sorts of pleasant flowers which our English ayre will permitt to be noursed u[nt]o'.

Marguerites, or daisies, were the personal emblem of Lady Margaret Beaufort (1443–1509), mother of the first Tudor monarch, Henry VII. Five-petalled dog-roses formed the emblem of the dynasty, the famous Tudor roses (cat. 8).[8] The double Tudor rose represents the symbolic union of the houses of Lancaster and York. We know from the poetry of Edmund Spenser and Richard Barnfield, and the painted works of Nicholas Hilliard (c.1547–1619) that five-petalled dog-roses were, in the minds of contemporaries, the flowers of Queen Elizabeth.[9]

In addition to floral decoration, ovoid cups – as we can see from two items in the Armoury – might also contain images of beasts. The treatment of hunting subjects on one of these (cat. 20; fig. 15) is of markedly English character. Unlike the classically idealized hunting scenes on German silver, English silverwork is dominated by a desire for realistic action and naturalistic depictions of animals. Animation and a more personal, emotional expression is achieved through the unexpected introduction of somewhat naive details, such as the frog seated on a dragon (fig. 16). Some extremely rare heraldic cups in the Armoury are adorned with lions, unicorns and griffons. One is decorated with a typical English heraldic symbol, a striding *opinicus*, a composite beast, part dragon, part lion, amid heavenly orange trees (cat. 22; see p.102).

Another specifically English vessel form is the globular or thistle cup. This appeared in the late sixteenth century, though with a flatter form than was to be seen later. Like the Italian *tazza*, it was initially used as a wine-bowl. There are eight known globular cups produced between 1604 and 1615 using the diamond faceting technique.[10] The spread of this technique (imitating the faceting of precious stones) in European silverwork, notably among the works of Dutch and Augsburg silversmiths, was linked to the fashion for Venetian glass, imitating the *vetro de trina* pattern. On English vessels, however, there was a link not only with Venetian glass but also with the traditional depiction of the thistle (see cat. 8).[11]

A new form of vessel made its appearance at the start of the seventeenth century. It had a high stem with a baluster and loops on the foot. Two globular cups of this type in the Armoury, dating from 1605–6 and 1608–9 (cat. 15), are the sole examples to survive with their steeple covers intact. Such cups came to be used more extensively and were presented as gifts by livery companies, colleges and various societies. They also formed part of the range of diplomatic gifts. With their steeple covers they might be set out on general display on sideboards ranged along the walls or in the middle of tables, and they were often used when a single cup was passed around the table for all to drink, as during ceremonies related to the election of the head of a guild.

15. Cat. 20, detail

16. Cat 20, detail

The steeple or pyramid structure on the top was an unusual image of the might of the Tudor and Stuart dynasties and emphasized the specific symbolism of such cups. Pyramids have long been associated with majesty and strength. The glorification of the ruling dynasty that ran throughout English art of this period led naturally to the pyramid occupying a special place in the visual repertoire of the sixteenth and seventeenth centuries. Small pyramids formed part of the decoration of both secular and religious structures, whether adorning the façades of palaces and noble mansions, the interiors of colleges at Cambridge and Oxford, or church pulpits and monumental tombs.[12] As landscaping developed under Dutch influence throughout the seventeenth century, trees trimmed in pyramidal shapes became a characteristic feature of English parks and gardens. In silver, pyramids were widespread throughout the last quarter of the sixteenth and first quarter of the seventeenth century, and featured on cups of all kinds and on salts.[13]

Some forms were borrowed from German silver. Yet while bell-shaped and grape cups (cat. 16) directly repeat the shapes of German prototypes, gourd-shaped cups are clear examples of local masters applying a 'national' interpretation to a form introduced from elsewhere.[14] Hollowed gourds had been used as vessels for storing and transporting liquid from ancient times, certainly during the ancient Romans' campaigns in Greece and then during the Crusades. Depictions of gourds of all kinds are found in the celebrated book of emblems by Geoffrey Whitney published in London in

1586 (fig. 17) and the natural form of the *cucurbita lagenaria* or bottle gourd was repeated by craftsmen making silver plate. Prints by Albrecht Dürer (1471–1528), Hans Brosamer (1500–54), Johann (Hans) Sibmacher (d.1611) and other German engravers also feature images of gourd cups.[15]

Even though the form borrowed from German masters still represents a specific type of gourd, there are clear differences in the English works. German gourd cups have a stem in the form of a slender tree, often wound round with vines or silver spiral. Usually by the tree, or indeed on the trunk itself, there are figures of a woodcutter or of Adam and Eve.[16] By comparison, English vessels have a stem of much heavier proportions, a sturdy stump with shoots lacking any figures. English and German cups of identical form thus produce very different impressions, the elegance and whimsy of the decoration of German cups contrasting with the expressive simplicity of the English.

Two gourd cups in the Armoury differ in their manner of decoration. A standing cup of 1589–90 (cat. 3) is adorned with typical English flat-chased ornament of quatrefoils and multi-petalled rosettes in ovals and circles linked by strapwork. Another cup of similar form (cat. 10; fig. 18) employs motifs characteristic of Netherlandish ornament, the sirens and tendrils ending in dolphins' heads of the kind widespread in, for instance, the prints of Theodore de Bry (1528–98) and Marcus Gheeraerts (1530–90).[17]

17. 'A Mighie Spyre', from Geoffrey Whitney,
The Choice of Emblemes and other devises, London, 1586.
Cambridge University Library

18. Cat. 10, detail of the engraved decoration

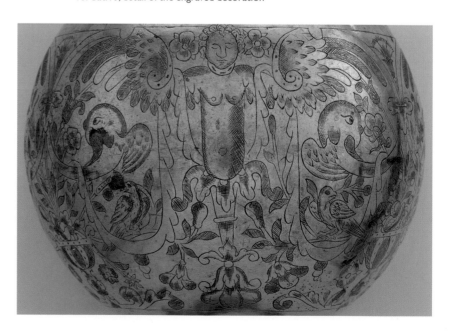

Fashion and innovation

Works of decorative and applied art were closely tied to everyday life and changing fashions. New types of vessel appeared during the English Renaissance, among them lavabo sets of richly adorned, often chased, ewers and basins. They enjoyed a huge popularity. The tradition of offering ewers with scented rosewater for washing one's hands between courses and after a meal grew in part out of the lack of forks and the need to eat one's food with one's fingers, but also out of the more sanitary, elegant habits of a new age. The most widespread type of ewer was oval, with an S-shaped handle and a mascaron (grotesque face or mask) on the neck beneath the spout. Surviving drawings by Italian masters show just such ewers in a manner that imitates Classical examples.[18]

The Armoury's ewer of 1652–3 (cat. 29) is just such a classicizing vessel. Its bowl is divided into two unequal parts by a horizontal band, and the decoration combines Italian Renaissance ornamental motifs (acanthus leaves, shells and mascarons) with typically English elements (sea creatures in oval medallions). Characteristically, a paired ewer and dish would have been adorned with similar ornament, its imagery usually linked with the sea.

Another characteristic English precious vessel that became popular in the Renaissance is the flagon, commonly called a pilgrim bottle because its shape derives ultimately from the flagons carried by pilgrims on their way to the Holy Land. Numerous prints, drawings and paintings depict such flagons, including a series of Bible illustrations by Hans Holbein the Younger. At the end of the sixteenth century globular and oval flagons were produced in both England and France[19] and descriptions of flat, oval flagons occur in the inventory of Tudor silver compiled in 1574.[20] English silversmiths also created special miniature flagons to hold aromatic essences.[21]

Six large flagons dating from between 1580 and 1663, measuring from 17⅜ to 19⅝ in. (44–50 cm) and densely covered with decoration, are in the Armoury collection.[22] With the exception of a Baroque flagon of around 1663 (cat. 33), they form the only known group of plate of rare conical form with elongated necks on a high base. They were extremely impressive and thus highly suitable for use as diplomatic gifts. Usually produced in pairs, this kind of object came to be a favourite commemorative gift in the following century, its popularity continuing right up to the nineteenth century.

The decoration of the oldest flagon in the collection (cat. 2; fig. 19), dating from 1580–1, takes the form of elegant Netherlandish engraved birds and hanging drapery combined with the flowers and sea creatures in rectangles so beloved of English craftsmen of the age. A later flagon of 1619–20 (cat. 27) is adorned with characteristic English flat-chased strapwork with clusters of fruit and sea creatures in oval medallions with shells (fig. 20).

Not surprisingly, the applied art of England – an island nation with a powerful navy – made extensive use of decorative elements on the theme of water: shells, dolphins, sea creatures, mythological tritons, hippocampi.

19. Cat. 2, detail

20. Cat. 27, detail of a sea monster

Indeed, depictions of sea creatures were popular in decorative art across northern Europe during the sixteenth and seventeenth centuries. Among the sources well known in many European centres of production, including those in England, was a book on monsters and prodigies by French scholar Ambroise Paré, one chapter of which was devoted to monsters of the sea.[23] Descriptions of all kinds of monsters also featured in the works of the English cleric Edward Topsell: *The historie of foure-footed Beastes* (1607) and *The Historie of Serpents* (1608).[24]

The iconographical sources for sea monsters and fish on English silver were undoubtedly Netherlandish prints. The majority of the dolphins adorning objects such as flagons and livery pots derive from identical images in prints

21. Adriaen Collaert, *Design for a Tazza*, Antwerp, late 16th century. Victoria and Albert Museum, London

by Erasmus Hornick (fl. 1565–83) or Adriaen Collaert (1560–1618). Silversmiths also frequently made use of the decorative frames from engravings, which included images of sea creatures (figs. 20, 21).[25]

In addition to the ovoid and globular (thistle) cups, font-shaped bowls and high-necked flasks, England produced another characteristic vessel in the large standing salt. English silversmiths designed all kinds of original salts during the sixteenth and seventeenth centuries.[26] Salt itself was rare and expensive, and the silver vessels used to hold it were richly prized. Books on the education of children carefully set out the rules for using salt.[27] Thus the salt cellar itself occupied one of the most important places in tableware, a particular symbol of the wealth and status of the host; it played an important role that was both functional and social. As ceremonial pieces, such salts were traditionally used in London's livery companies and at the colleges of Oxford and Cambridge, and frequently feature in lists of royal gifts.

By the middle of the sixteenth century two clearly defined kinds of large pillar-like salts were common, one cylindrical, the other having four straight sides. Both are represented in the Armoury's collection of English silver. The square salt (cat. 4) is an extremely interesting example of English silverware that might almost be described as a symbol of Elizabethan culture. Here characteristic features of many different kinds of art – prints and drawings, wood carving, textiles, even literature and the theatre – were brought together into a single whole. Elements of Netherlandish ornament in the engraving (snails on suspended draperies), the proportions of the figures reminiscent of English wood carving, the hunting scenes so widespread on tapestries, the depictions of gods that recall the costumed characters of sixteenth-century pageants – all combined to create an inimitable picture suffused with the very air of the late Tudor period. By contrast, the smooth cylinder (cat. 18) strikes us with its restrained simplicity and expressiveness amid the varied forms of English Renaissance silver. It is dominated by the smoothly polished metal surface accented by the steeple on the cover, the profiles and grotesque loops.

Among the jugs and pots, a considerable number are of the 'bellied' type, with a spherical body and S-shaped handle which imitated ceramics, notably German stoneware. Such silver vessels with their very low base appeared in England around 1555.[28] At the start of the seventeenth century, these vessels came to have a tall, smooth stem with a more convex cover, and the overall dimensions increased noticeably. A number of decorated ewers illustrate another of the main principles guiding the disposition of ornament in the work of English craftsmen (cats. 9, 17): a symmetrical geometric framework was constructed of strapwork and then filled with all kinds of images – dragons, sea creatures, shells, daisies, Tudor roses. One livery pot (cat. 13) features vines covering the whole surface, a completely new ornamental approach.

Particular mention must be made of a group of unique items, among them two pairs of large water pots of 1604–5 and 1615–16 and a pair of huge leopards of 1600–1 that have come to symbolize the Moscow collection (cats. 7,

8, 25). United by their common provenance, these outstanding examples of English silverwork once formed part of the English royal treasury known as the Jewel House. They are described in the list of plate forming the 'Great Guilt Cubberd of Estate' sold to the royal jeweller John Acton in 1626. The earlier water pots and leopards are mentioned among eighty-two items with an overall weight of 20,011 Troy ounces (622.4 kg): 'Two watter-pots gilt, chased in flames, with snake handles, per oz. 732 oz. [22.8 kg]' and 'Two leopards gilt and enamelled, with chaines, per oz. 1184 [36.8 kg]'.[29] Those same water pots are also mentioned in an earlier document of 1604–7, a list of plate received by Sir Edward Carey, Master of the Jewel House, from the King's goldsmith, John Williams, as a replacement for plate presented to the Constable of Castile by James I in 1604: 'Twoo Water pottes of silver guilte chased wth flames of fier and bodies of Roses and thistles, the handles like snakes, the Spoutes like dragons winged, poiz. 733 oz. [22.8 kg]'.[30]

Both pairs of water pots and the leopards were brought to Russia by the agent of the Muscovy Company, Fabian Smith (Ulyanov), as a gift for Tsar Mikhail Romanov in 1629. A note in the archive of the Treasury Office for 4 May 1629 records:

> On that same day by personal decree of the sovereign Tsar and grand duke Mikhail Fyodorovich of all Russia taken into the sovereign's treasury to the Treasury Court from the English merchant from Fabian Ulyanov silver vessels: 2 leopards silver gilded standing on their back legs on their haunches, pressing their tails under themselves, heads screwed on, in their paws fanciful shields, with chains of silver, gold, chain-mail, one weighing one *pood* 34 pounds 77 *zolotniki* [around 67½ modern lbs (30.6 kg)], the other weighing one *pood* 31 pounds [64 lbs (29 kg)], 4 ewers, silver, gilded, forming one with their covers, one weighing 28 pounds 21 *zolotniki* [(25⅜ lbs (11.5 kg)], the other 27 pounds 72 *zolotniki* [25 lbs (11.4 kg)], the third weighing 20 pounds 51 *zolotniki* [18½ lbs (8.4 kg)], the fourth weighing 20 pounds 24 *zolotniki* [18¼ lbs (8.30 kg)].[31]

The leopards also appear in the later inventory of the treasury of Mikhail Fyodorovich for 1635, while the water pots feature in the Armoury Inventory of 1640.[32]

Such water pots are unknown in any other collection of English silver, with nothing comparable either in terms of their notable height or their ornamentation. Both share common features – identical ovoid bowls, almost cylindrical necks, spouts in the form of a dragon's head with wings spread, complex handles in the form of a snake curled into a ring with jaws stretched wide. The nature of the ornamentation differs, however, and illustrates the features of two different national schools. The ornament on the water pots of 1604–5 is typically English. It consists of Tudor roses and thistles, while the base, upper part of the bowl and lid are chased with tongues of flame framed by woven ornament of the kind common in late Tudor silver. The German ornamental tradition – with its sense of dramatic tension, the pulsating and somewhat nervous treatment of form, its interest in plastic effects – is felt in the sirens with widespread wings and the abundance of applied details (lizards and frogs), as well as the overall density of decoration on the water pots of 1615–16.

English Baroque silver

Later English silver in the Armoury includes several works in the Baroque style. The group includes two cups, a flagon, a perfuming pot, fruit dishes, a pair of tankards and a pair of candlesticks, all made in 1663 and brought as gifts from Charles II for Tsar Alexey Mikhaylovich by the embassy of Charles Howard, 1st Earl of Carlisle. They arrived in Russia the following year. All of them, with the exception of the perfuming pot, are adorned with flowers and illustrate one of the leading trends in mid-seventeenth-century silver decoration.

European silver of the 1650s and 1660s quickly reflected the rapid spread from Holland of the *Blumenmode* or fashion for flowers. England too fell under the sway of the flower, and objects came to be covered with very large, naturalistic flower ornament, mainly double tulips and poppies, and leaves. The dense decoration in which the contours of the different elements flow naturally into one another created an illusion of movement and was ideally suited to the all-over surface adornment of English silver. This new approach not only made the individual elements larger, but brought out the dominant feature of Baroque silver: the whole surface was now covered with identical patterns linking together the different parts (in contrast to Renaissance objects on which decoration was divided into different zones, each with its own type of ornament).

22. Cat. 30, detail

To judge by the pieces in the Armoury, one specifically English feature in this fashion for flowers lay in the incorporation of all kinds of animals within the ornamental vegetation. Moreover, the works are remarkable for their impressive size, the cups (cat. 32) reaching 28¾ in. (73 cm) in height. Unlike the ovoid cups of the first half of the seventeenth century, with their ornamented balusters and loops, these have an almost cylindrical bowl and smooth or pounced balusters on the stem. A favourite Baroque technique was high-relief chasing, the careful alternation of chased and smooth surfaces creating a variety of effects of light and shade which emphasized the silver's full plastic potential. This is clearly seen in a standing cup (cat. 32) with a smooth stem and conical cover, all the remaining parts covered with chasing, and in a fruit dish (cat. 31). With its round, flat form, the fruit dish is similar to German and Dutch platters of the second half of the seventeenth century used for particular delicacies – fruit or oysters, or a glass of wine or lemonade – and placed on tables or passed to guests. Here the specifically English feature lies in the broad high stem. Such dishes were often made in England paired with a porringer (two-handled bowl), when they served as trays or stands. They might be used to serve fruit, as was the dish in the Kremlin, which is adorned with animals neatly fitted into the flower ornament to form a unified whole. All the ornamental elements are united by a circular movement – expressed in the poses of the animals and the smooth winding of the stems – that is in keeping with the vessel's form.

The censer or perfuming pot (cat. 30)[33] brought by Carlisle makes magnificent use of *Knorpelwerk* or auricular style (fig. 22). The term takes its name from the word *Knorpel*, the German for ear lobe, and the style made itself felt in English silverwork in the middle of the seventeenth century. It was Dutch master Christian van Vianen (*c.*1600–67), employed at the court of Charles I, who was responsible for introducing the auricular style into English silver. Around 1650 he published *Modelles artificiels*, an album of engravings based on his own works and those of his father, Adam van Vianen, showing all kinds of silver plate and *Knorpelwerk*. The designs were intended to be used as models by others.[34]

Knorpel is an abstract form of ornament which incorporates smoothly flowing outlines, grotesque masks and animal faces, with curls that recall the lobes of an ear. It is a striking feature of European Baroque silver. Variously modelled, this style dominates the perfuming pot, which is decorated with flowing grotesque masks on the walls and cover of the two-handled bowl, stylized dolphin feet with smoothly flowing lines, and openwork ornament of stars and circles. This last feature was extremely rare in seventeenth-century English silverwork, and was usually linked with Hispano-Portugese silver. It came into its own in England only considerably later, on Rococo silver. The unique elegant decoration of the perfuming pot, a rare example of the use of *Knorpelwerk* by an English craftsman, reminds us of the rarity and unparalleled importance of the English silver preserved in the Armoury collection.

Notes

1 The collection in the Victoria and Albert Museum in London has 144 pieces dating from the sixteenth and seventeenth centuries.

2 Goldberg 1954, p. 438.

3 Jones 1909, p. xix.

4 Versions of such cups are published in Penzer 1958.

5 Armoury Inventory 1884–93, part 2, book 2, no. 1325.

6 Glanville 1987, p. 211; Oman 1978b, p. 2.

7 Collins 1955, p. 43.

8 This ornamental motif, so widespread in English applied arts, featured on weaving and embroidery, wooden carving and all kinds of stucco work. It was an inalienable part of the decoration of English silver, playing a variety of different functions. Tudor roses might be the main organizing element in an ornamental composition (cat. 13) or fine bands might be used to accentuate details, such as the upper and lower part of the cylindrical salt (cat. 18); or yet again, as on the stem of the globular cup (cat. 15), they might form a frieze with *ovae*, occupying the place usually given on European silver to egg-and-dart and thus playing an important role in attributing English metalwork.

9 R. Strong, *The Cult of Elizabeth* (London, 1977), pp. 47–8, 68–71.

10 With the exception of one, dated 1641 (see Penzer 1960a, p. 106).

11 A favorite motif in English art as early as the Anglo Saxon period, the thistle appears on surviving silver *fibulae* from the mid- to late tenth century, being fashioned with those same diamond facets: see C. Jackson, *An Illustrated History of English Plate, Ecclesiastical and Secular* (London, 1911), figs. 83–4. During the later medieval period Gothic furniture was also carved with thistles, usually in the firm of circles with a rhomboid pattern framed by leaves: see M. Dean, *English Antique Furniture, 1450-1850* (London, 1976), pl. 1b. Identical treatment of the thistle is seen on two water pots with snake handles in the Armoury (cat. 8).

12 N. M. Penzer, 'The Steeple Cup. Part I', *Apollo*, December 1959, pp. 161–6.

13 An early gold cup with a pyramid steeple on top is mentioned in the inventory of Elizabeth I's precious goods; it was a gift from Sir Nicholas Bacon in 1573 (see Collins 1955, p. 542). Cups and salts with a variety of steeple tops feature in the Armoury collection (Goldberg 1954, ills. 18–21, 46).

14 Goldberg 1954, ills. 14–15, 36, 58 61.

15 On the influence of prints and drawings by Albrecht Dürer on silver, see Markova 1976. English publications of the 1570s (Thomas Tusser, *Five Hundreth Pointes of Good Husbandrie*, 1573; Raphael Holinshed, *Chronicle*, 1577–8) provide evidence that gourds were grown and used in England, among them the bottle gourd.

16 G. A. Markova, *Nemetskoe khudozhestvennoe serebro XVI-XVII vv.* ['German Artistic Silver of the Sixteenth to Seventeenth Centuries'] (Moscow, 1975), pl. 32.

17 State Hermitage Museum, St Petersburg, inv. nos. OG 3311, 329728, 329773.

18 Hayward 1976, nos. 12, 14.

19 F. Davies, *French Silver, 1450–1825* (London, 1970), pl. 18.

20 Collins 1955, nos. 687–8. In the author's opinion flasks of this form were used to carry alcoholic drinks from the cellar into the house.

21 Collins 1955, nos. 712–21; Glanville 1987, pl. 1.

22 Goldberg 1954, ills. 52–5.

23 See *Les Oeuvres d'Ambroise Paré … avec les figures … et de plusieurs monstres …* (Paris, 1579); *Opera chirurgica Ambrosii Paraei …* (Frankfurt, 1594).

24 E. Topsell, *The historie of foure-footed beastes* (London, 1607); *The Historie of Serpents* (London, 1608).

25 Silversmiths also took whole subjects and individual motifs from ornamental designs that were often inspired by the naval charts that depicted all kinds of sea creatures. Christopher Saxton's *Carta Marina* (1583) was particularly influential. The maps were decorated not only with ships, but with dolphins, marvelous fish and barrels. Dolphins scattered freely among the waves frequently occur on English silver in the first half of the seventeenth century, as on a flask in the Armoury (cat. 14).

26 Although new forms of salts developed in England were little known outside the country, there is a drawing of a salt 'in the English manner' by the celebrated Hamburg goldsmith Jacob Mores the Elder (1578–c. 1609): see Hayward 1976, p. 308.

27 See *The Babees Book* (c. 1475) and *The Young Children's Book* (c. 1500).

28 Goldberg 1954, ills. 2, 4.

29 Cited in Oman 1961, pp. 58, 60. Oman suggests that the enamelled decoration was removed before being sent to Russia. The system of measurement here is Troy weight (standard for precious jewels and metals), not avoirdupois pounds and ounces; one Troy ounce is equal to 31.1035 grams. The correlation between the weights given by archival records and current weights is frequently inexact.

30 Cited in Oman 1961, p. 60.

31 Documents published in Smirnova and Shumilov 1961, pp. 224–8. One Old Russian *pood* equals modern 36 lbs 2 oz (16.4 kg); one Old Russian pound equals modern 14⅜ oz (410 g); one *zolotnik* equals ⅛ modern oz (4.3 g).

32 Armoury Inventory 1884–93, part 2, book 3, no. 1922.

33 Described in British documents as a censer (cited in Oman 1970, p. 58).

34 C. van Vianen, *Modelles artificiels* (Utrecht, c. 1650).

Magnificence was a royal obligation. Princes in Baroque Europe competed in the sheer scale of their deployment of silver. For his chapel at Frederiksborg Christian IV King of Denmark, encased the altar and pulpit in sheets of chased silver, and his throne at Rosenborg Palace in Copenhagen is flanked by life-size silver lions.[12] When Henrietta Maria's dowry plate was being prepared in France in 1625, it required 2,315 ounces (72 kg) of gold (partly for the gilding) and 31,380 ounces (976 kg) of silver for a set of liturgical plate, gilded tableware and a toilet set. At the Louvre, Anne of Austria's winter chamber had a silver balustrade protecting her bed alcove.[13] In Madrid, a set of twelve silver lions holding the arms of Aragon was commissioned for the throne room of Philip IV's new palace of Buen Retiro in 1634 (although these were melted down within a decade).[14] Neither James I nor Charles I, however, commissioned silver of this flamboyance and indeed they had contrasting views of goldsmiths' work.

Under James, silver furniture and sconces glittered as the backdrop to state occasions at Whitehall, Denmark House and Hampton Court. His court admired fantastic mounted rock-crystal vessels, extravagant jewels and silver furniture such as the Queen's fire-dogs crowned with cupids, and he showed Christian IV with pride the contents of the secret Jewel House, his most private assemblage of state treasures at the Tower. When James's daughter Elizabeth married Prince Frederick, Elector of Bohemia, in 1613, her gift from the States General of Holland was a large mirror of embossed and enamelled silver. Weddings of James's courtiers saw the exchange of lavish gifts of gold ewers and basins and jewelled cups.[15] Charles himself, however, grave and austere, with a strong preference for decorum, disliked lavish display – as is shown in his revision of the household ordinances in 1633. The ewer and basin Henrietta Maria brought from France at her wedding (cats. 35–6) are chased with scenes emblematic of her challenging role as a Roman Catholic bride at a potentially hostile Protestant court: ten Muses with musical instruments evoke the harmony of a good marriage, while the basin depicts the fate of Scylla, daughter of Nisus, who betrays her father and city for love of their enemy Minos, King of Crete, and is punished by the gods. This suited Charles' taste for Mannerist plate, laden with messages to be decoded by viewers, and exemplified by Rubens' design for a basin and ewer made for the King (see p. 50). Charles' disdain for his inherited Great Gilt Cupboard of Estate makes sense when this picturesque jumble is compared to the symmetrical buffet displays of richly chased allegorical silver fashionable at the French court.[16]

John Williams and John Acton, royal goldsmiths, supplied a flow of goods from gold chains to tableware. Even when the King was short of money, he had to act in a princely manner. In 1623, a warrant for the Jewel House noted: 'There is a great defect and want of necessary store of plate … whereby the Kings service … at festival times and for entertainment of ambassadors suffers much dishonour.' The Great Gilt Cupboard of Estate, a mixture of massive pots, flagons and fountains reflecting early Tudor court taste, was set up for the entertainment of the new Queen Henrietta Maria at Canterbury in June and for the Duc de Chevreuse's reception at the

Banqueting House, Whitehall, in 1625. John Acton supplied 133 ells of Holland linen (500 feet; 152 m) to cover two great cupboards of estate (dressers or buffets) to display this ancient royal plate. Dressed with massive, thickly gilded ancient objects, their sole purpose was to impress.[17] Across northern Europe ambassadors were lent plate while on mission, while incoming embassies expected to be provided with gilt plate and sent away with presents. In 1638 John Merrick bequeathed to William Russell, his brother-in-law and fellow ambassador to Russia, 'my Kovsh of silver double gilt sett with stones given me by the Emperor of Russia, also his picture of gold with his title about it', fruit of his many embassies.[18]

Under James I, the Jewel House had to be restocked. Already depleted in 1600 – when Elizabeth sent a fifth of its contents to the Mint after a series of bad harvests and her draining war with Spain – it was the source of major gifts of historic plate in 1604 when James signed the Treaty of London with Spain. Ancient treasures of the Crown such as Jane Seymour's gold ewer and basin (perhaps designed by Hans Holbein), the Royal Gold Cup (a masterpiece of medieval French enamel work now in the British Museum) and other exceptional Tudor pieces were presented to the Constable of Castile.[19] A conscious choice was made (based on the works' associations) in compliment to their Spanish recipients, just as Henrietta Maria's Parisian silver was selected as appropriate for the embassy to Russia in 1663–4.

Silver-gilt buffet plate weighing more than 25,400 ounces (790 kg) was presented to the four Spanish ambassadors, far more than the customary allowance of 1,500 or 2,000 ounces (47 or 62 kg) apiece.[20]

A lover of antiquities, James I commissioned drawings of the plate which had travelled with the Spanish delegates to honour his Tudor ancestors (fig. 25), 'answerable in weights and fashion according to the several patterns thereof taken'. Various goldsmiths then made 14,000 ounces (435 kg) of new plate for the Great Gilt Cupboard of Estate, some chased with Stuart thistles. These historical pieces reproduced objects which had belonged to Henry VIII; the original pots might even have come from Spain with Catherine of Aragon in 1501. Two objects were copies of Tudor table fountains, oversized toys with taps and barrels for perfumed sprays which cost a hefty thirteen shillings and fourpence an ounce.[21]

We gain a sense of the evolving personal tastes of the Stuarts for decorative and furnishing silver through the inventory made of the property of Anne of Denmark in 1619, Abraham van der Doort's list of Charles I's works of art in the 1630s and Henrietta Maria's possessions formerly at Somerset House in the 1660s.[22] It is hard, however, to envisage the sheer weight of practical plate, particularly tableware, drinking vessels and light fittings of all kinds. In 1634 a single officer, the Sergeant of the Scullery, was responsible for more than 1,000 pounds (375 kg) just in plain serving plate, 283 dishes for meat and salad, chargers and platters replacing vessels lost in the Firth of Forth when a ferry carrying chests of the King's dining silver capsized in 1633.[23]

Fashions in food presentation were changing after 1600 (fig. 26). The Stuarts were eating with forks by 1620 – and probably long before. Their personal cutlery, plates and drinking vessels were of gold, of which Charles I's tiny toothpick case in the Harley Collection is the sole survivor. More complex objects now appeared: cruets, potage pots (precursor of the tureen), chafing dishes, sugar boxes, dishes for artichokes and salad, salts with branches for candles (forerunners of the *surtout* or centrepiece) and the 'kettle with a ladle to wash glasses' left by Frances, Duchess of Richmond and Lennox in 1639. These refinements were to drive out the large sets of open platters and dishes.[24] Perfume burners appear in aristocratic inventories and in 1650 were considered a fitting gift from the City of London to Oliver Cromwell. Virtually no fashionable aristocratic silver survived the Commonwealth, although the new French way of presenting a meal in a sequence of dishes and of entertaining at suppers influenced goldsmiths' wares in the late 1650s.[25]

25. *Design for Silver for James I,* anonymous German designer, before 1620.
The British Museum, London

26. Gerrit Houckgeest, *Charles I, Queen Henrietta Maria and Charles, Prince of Wales, Dining in Public,* 1635.
The Royal Collection, Her Majesty Queen Elizabeth II

Unlike the Valois kings of France, who set up ateliers for privileged gold-smiths and related trades at the Louvre and the Tuileries, free from the restrictions of the Paris guild, the Stuarts did not establish royal work-shops.[26] Nonetheless, James I, Charles I and Charles II all protected for-eigners who supplied designs, brought in skilled workmen and negotiated purchases of art works. Specialists trained in the workshops of Paris, Cologne, The Hague or Antwerp came to London either to widen their experience as part of a *Wanderjahre* or to make a career.[27]

Resentment of these aliens recurs through the late sixteenth and seven-teenth centuries. Yet court contractors needed their superior skills to devise fashionable ornament, such as designs for James I attributed to a German. A typical example is Theodore (Derick) Loockemans, a Dutch goldsmith-jeweller and maker of a mirror given to Princess Elizabeth in 1613 (described in her list of wedding presents). He was in London around 1609–13, during which period his mark, 'TvL' conjoined, appears on distinc-tive filigree-ornamented objects. His workshop at The Hague supplied the Stadtholder's court for two generations.[28] In 1643, after the Parisian gold-smith Claude Villiers created an *ex voto* of a ship with a figure of the Virgin as a thanks offering for the Queen's survival in a January storm in the North Sea, she appointed him her goldsmith. He worked in London for her between 1662 and 1665.[29]

Under pressure from the London artisans, the Lord Mayor and Privy Council demanded the names of aliens in 1593, 1615, 1622, 1639, 1653 and in the early 1660s. Suppliers to the Crown recur. Among 206 'strangers' listed by the company in 1615 were Sir John Spilman from Lindau and Arnold Lulls from Antwerp, both resident since the 1580s and jewellers to Queen Anne; Christian van der Passe, royal engraver and medallist; Isaac Oliver the miniaturist; and Nicaisius (Niçaise) Roussel, another engraver who had been in London for more than forty years and also supplied goldsmiths' wares to Anne of Denmark. In January 1641 the working jewellers of London petitioned against an influx of 'alien strangers', of whom there were 'above 140' compared to the fifty native jewellers free of the company.[30]

Silver under Charles I

Gold and silver of a new refined Mannerist style featured prominently in Charles I's collections, particularly in his 'new erected Cabonett roome' off the Privy Gallery at Whitehall.[31] Under the Earl of Arundel's guidance he commissioned Peter Paul Rubens to design a basin and ewer chased with the Triumph of Neptune (fig. 27).[32] He acquired silver plaques exquisitely chased by Theodore Rogiers of Antwerp and Paulus Van Vianen as well as others 'done hir by viano' that is Christian, Paulus' nephew. Paying a pension

27. Peter Paul Rubens, *The Birth of Venus*, c. 1632–33. The National Gallery, London

28. Opposite: Wenceslaus Hollar, 'The Inthronization of the King and the High Altar of Westminster Abbey', from John Ogilby, *The Entertainment of His Most Excellent Majestie Charles II in his passage through the City of London to his Coronation* …, London, 1662. Dean and Chapter of Westminster

to Christian to draw him over from Utrecht, the King ensured him prestigious commissions, notably a set of richly chased altar plate he made in the 1630s for the Order of the Garter at Windsor, stolen by Captain Fogg in 1642.[33]

Although Charles' reign has been described as disastrous for English silver because so much was melted down during the Civil War, families and institutions regularly renewed plate 'in the new fashion'. Plate, after all, defined status. As Elizabeth Smythe advised her son in the 1630s, 'money spent on strong substantiall plate will doe you more service and credit than in your purse'.[34] Orders for new styles demanded the melting of old objects to provide the raw silver. Objects 'battered, bruised and unfit for service' were unsentimentally recycled and monarchs raided their plate reserves in times of need. In 1600 Queen Elizabeth disposed of 14,029 ounces (436.4 kg) of old plate and in 1620 James I selected more that was 'unserviceable and unfit to be preserved'.[35]

Innovation as much as financial need swallowed old silver. From centrepieces to forks, from 'hottwater cups' for brandy to vases for flowers, from casters and cruets to scollop dishes for serving fruit, inventories and bills show novel forms of domestic plate driving out obsolete objects. For purchasers the expense lay in the weight of metal, not the workmanship, unlike the situation today, when silver is so cheap that it hardly counts as a precious metal. Silver's advantage was its known value. When Charles I was desperate for coin to pay his staff at the siege of Newark in 1645–6 and had no access to the Mint, plates and dishes were simply cut up into rough 'shillings', some even retaining traces of the royal stamp which identified his 'vessell'.[36]

We know more about the silver holdings of Henry VIII and Elizabeth than those of the Stuart kings. Records disappeared during the turbulent years 1642–60, presumably because the Master of the Jewel House, Sir Henry Mildmay, was afraid of later repercussions. He (or his heirs) would have been held responsible for any losses of plate from the holdings of the Crown and so needed to destroy the paper trail. Forty years ago, Charles Oman regretted that Jewel House records kept by Carew Mildmay, Sir Henry's nephew and Groom of His Majesty's Jewels and Plate, had vanished. Some, however, have now reappeared. Although fragmentary, these papers document normal plate transactions at court such as repairing, 'colouring' and burnishing the Great Cupboard of Estate for Charles' coronation in April 1625 (fig. 28), issues to the royal children in the 1630s and 1640s and to officers of state (Sir Henry Mildmay, Master of the Jewel House since 1618, had 3,400 ounces (105 kg) for his personal use) and customary presents. The silver matrices of the great seal of James I, a perquisite of office for Thomas Coventry, Lord Keeper of the Great Seal, were converted into his tall gilt cup in 1626.[37]

Obligations included new year's gifts of gilt plate graded by rank from a few spoons to large cups. Two hundred and thirty-five members of James's household received gifts. As the Mildmay papers show, Charles gave plate at the new year to some 192 recipients even when struggling financially in the

1640s. This custom was finally abandoned by Charles II.[38] Mildmay lists a total of 4,500 pounds (1,680 kg) given away 'casually' by James and Charles between July 1618 and April 1641. This long-lost archive also includes the first draft of what was to be sold in September 1626, a list which sheds new light on the desperate financial circumstances in which silver from Charles I's Jewel House ended up in Moscow.[39]

As early as the autumn of 1625 Charles' scramble for money was a matter of diplomatic gossip. Why did he pawn his mother's gold tableware, as well as Jane Seymour's Cup and other Jewel House treasures from the time of Henry VIII, a mere six months after coming to the throne in March? War consumed silver. Bubonic plague disrupted the economic life of the city, so that Charles' coronation had to be deferred until February 1626. His first Parliament, having urged the war against Spain and support for 12,000 English soldiers in Holland led by the German mercenary Count Ernest von Mansfield to recapture the Palatinate, refused to vote funds to carry out these costly military adventures. Charles had to sustain four regiments in the Low Countries, find £1,500 a month for his exiled sister Elizabeth and, from December 1626, pay his uncle Christian IV £30,000 a month towards the campaign to reinstate Frederick and his wife (Charles' sister Elizabeth of Bohemia 'The Winter Queen') to the Palatinate. Lord Keeper Thomas Coventry pointed out to an obdurate Parliament in March 1627–8 how many sacrifices Charles had made to carry out their desired but costly foreign policy: 'the example the King hath set you, for his lands, his plate, his jewels are under sale for the supply of the wars; so that what the people have proferred … the king on his part hath willingly performed.'[40]

Negotiations with Moscow always had plate as an adjunct. As Charles Oman suggests, Cromwell's attempt to reopen trade relations with Moscow in 1654–5 probably explains the presence of large German display pieces on the London market in 1660, bought for that failed embassy.[57] An entwining of silver and trade goods characterized the Earl of Carlisle's embassy in 1663–4 too. Gifts included 'a great quantity of Cornish tynne and a hundred piggs of lead'.[58] Simon Digby's mission in 1635 was furnished with plate (Richard Blackwell marked one of the cups) and carried two propositions: one that 100,000 cloths a year be exported to Russia, and the other the deployment of 100,000 Crimean Tatars to rescue the Palatinate from Roman Catholic rule. Neither proposal flourished and Digby became enmeshed with the curious affair of John Cartwright and the Tsar's silver.[59]

From early 1632 Cartwright had a contract approved by the king to export to Russia 2,000 muskets and bandoliers and 5,000 swords. A 'privileged merchant' of the Russia Company from 1633, he then bought tobacco from the Tsar, paid for in part by munitions and in part by plate 'from beyond the sea' worth 4,530 rubles 'for the Tsar his use'. This is more than the sum paid to Fabian Smith in 1629 for the former Jewel House plate. Unhappily Cartwright, instead of exporting the tobacco, took it to the English House in Moscow and began to sell it to the locals. In 1635 the Tsar had the store sealed; his silver had not yet arrived. Cartwright was still seeking redress in 1639, when silence fell.[60]

By the 1630s Charles was in a better situation. The papers of Carew Mildmay show that royal orders for plate flowed. England was prosperous and at peace. The King's 1633 journey to Scotland for his belated coronation attracted gifts en route such as a ewer and basin 'fairly adorned' from the town of Leicester. In 1632 the Earl of Arundel brought over the talented Utrecht silversmith Christian van Vianen and in 1639 the latter's Westminster workshop employed nine Dutchmen and three Frenchmen, more skilled workmen than any London goldsmith.[61]

When the political scene darkened in 1642 and the king retreated from London, plate was called in to the Guildhall for melting and the Assay Office instantly registered a drop in business. It handled a mere 4,000 pounds (nearly 1,500 kg) of new plate in 1642–3 and as little as 88 pounds (33 kg) the following year.[62] Parliament closed the City's goldsmiths' shops in August 1643. Bartholomew Fair had no goldsmiths' stalls, only a milliner selling 'wares of goldsmithery', including a pair of scissors, enamelled rings and cast medals. In an atmosphere of gathering unease and public disorder, the Goldsmiths Company re-equipped its armoury with muskets, bandoliers and swords. Demands from Parliament for plate to pay for soldiers bore heavily on both private individuals and institutions. Although the company decided not to sell plate in October 1643 because the next Lord Mayor, Sir John Wollaston, was a member of the Goldsmiths Court and needed to borrow for his official entertaining, he was lent far less than in former mayoralties.[63]

In October 1644 Sir Henry Mildmay, Master of the Jewel House, released 'to pay the soldiers at Abingdon' by order of Parliament 500 pounds (187 kg) of gilt plate, 'rare pieces' which included the royal font and four sets of massive flagons weighing up to 1,500 ounces (47 kg) a pair, plus six great candlesticks which Charles had brought back from Madrid. A growing sense of history and the significance of these royal treasures as part of a national heritage stimulated objections from the House of Lords.[64]

At 9,000 pounds (3,360 kg) the total of plate assayed in 1647–8 was healthier than in 1643–4, although an August search in Westminster shops by the Goldsmiths Company produced only small wares, such as tobacco stoppers, seals, buttons and fan handles. No goldsmith was risking offering for sale larger objects.[65]

Ordered by his uncle Sir Henry Mildmay, Carew Mildmay gave up his keys in 1649 when more plate (worth £16,496) was taken from the Tower and a modest £848 from the Jewel House at Whitehall Palace. In 1653–4 the plate assayed had risen again, to 29,000 pounds (10,824 kg). Confidence had returned, although most objects of the 1650s are markedly plain: after all, if they had to be sacrificed, little money would have been wasted on fashion.[66]

'The fashion is worth so much'

In this silver-loving society, every social encounter was graced with a ceremonious display of gilded plate. The plate added prestige, spoke of wealth and tradition and was central to ritual toasts and handwashing. The halls of the twelve great livery companies held large sets of gilded flagons and standing cups to display on the buffet, ewers and basins for the washing of hands, voider baskets for clearing broken meats and hundreds of drinking vessels and spoons. Fancy objects such as the Lutma Salt at the Fishmongers Company or the Bowes Cup and Gibbons Salt at the Goldsmiths Company (both treasured in the company halls today) were preserved for their associations and their 'fashion' or workmanship through all the crises of the mid-seventeenth century, but otherwise plate was unsentimentally remade as required.[67]

Plate holdings grew by gift, bequest or fine for avoiding office. Wealthy merchants such as alderman Ralph Freeman and Sir John Merrick left money for ewers and basins to their livery companies and the twelve 'great companies' lent silver to the Lord Mayor or sheriff in a display of competitive pride.[68] In 1611 the young Lombard Street retailer William Terry lent 296 items from stock, including 'forty nest of bowls and goblets' plus standing cups, altogether 136 drinking vessels alone for Sir James Pemberton's first dinner as Lord Mayor.[69]

Plate also acted as a reserve of cash. In 1620 the Merchant Taylors Company sold old plate from their holdings of some 6,000 ounces (187 kg), their contribution towards a City loan to James I for the 'defence of the Palatyne country'.[70] In 1627 the Goldsmiths Company sold plate worth £400 to make up another City loan to the King and a further 1,500 ounces (47 kg) of gilt plate went in 1637, when they were completing their new hall designed by Nicholas Stone. A ewer and basin of 1610–11 chased with their badges was bought by the refiner William Gibbs, who passed it on to the second-hand market. The sheer weight of metal locked up in these institutional holdings was an easy target for the City and Parliament when loans of cash were needed, as in 1642 and 1644.[71]

Identifying marks in this period, a focus of silver research since the 1860s, is not straightforward. Marks do not identify artistic responsibility; merely the man sponsoring plate at the assay office, who might be neither the maker nor the retailer. In the 1630s van Vianen as a foreigner was not allowed his own mark. If clients insisted on the reassurance of a hallmark, as the Earl of Salisbury in 1636 did, a 'stranger' had to pass his wares through the assay office under the mark of an Englishman, such as the deputy assay-er Alexander Jackson.[72] A search through the Minute Books of the Goldsmiths Company for the owner of the mark 'IH', found on plate from the 1590s to around 1620, turned up over 40 possible names. Fines for mis-working in the court minutes of the Goldsmiths Company are the key to assigning names to marks, coupled with a chain linking the careers of mas-ters and their apprentices. For example, Thomas Vyner (fig. 31), financier to the Crown and the Commonwealth, had been apprenticed to William Terry, a retailer supplying the court.[73]

Marks identified with certainty include the partnership of John Middleton and Francis Brown which began in 1614, the year Middleton became free of his master, the royal supplier John Acton. Their joint mark, 'IM' over 'FB' appears on a steeple cup In the Armoury (cat. 22). Simon Owen's speciality of ewers and basins identifies the 'SO' mark as his, struck on the set he sup-plied to the company in 1610. The mark of Clement Punge, 'CP' over a rose, is struck on a pulley salt of 1639. He got into trouble for clogging the base with too much solder, which increased the weight but misled the buyer. Most silver was valued by weight, with little allowance for the workman-ship, as Samuel Pepys ruefully commented on 19 October 1667. His richly chased gilt flagons, a recent gift, were weighed and valued at £50: 'They judge the fashion to be worth above 5s per ounce more. Nay, some say 10s an ounce the fashion …yet am sorry to see the fashion is worth so much and the silver come to no more.'[74]

A father and son, both suppliers to the Stuart court over more than fifty years, were freemen of the Merchant Taylors Company, not the Goldsmiths (a misunderstanding that obscured their identity until recently, since their names were being sought in Goldsmiths Company apprentice lists, where they did not appear). Richard Blackwell the elder used the 'RB' conjoined mark, found on an 'Almain' style cup taken to Moscow by Merrick's 1620 embassy (Moscow Kremlin Museums), as well as a salt of 1611–12 (cat. 18) and the two 1615 water pots (cat. 25). The younger, also Richard, is the intriguing 'hound sejant maker', so-called from his mark; he was active in London from the mid-1640s to the 1660s and was known for producing sophisticated and costly plate. Research by David Mitchell for the Goldsmiths Company is establishing attributions for other Stuart plate workers.[75]

31. Gerard Soest (attrib.), *Sir Thomas Vyner*, c. 1660. The Goldsmiths' Company, London

1628; UK National Archives, PRO, Indexes to Privy Council Registers 1628–33, 20 Feb 1627/8 to Dec 1628, PC 2/38(581), House to be provided; 24 Dec 1628 to 31 May 1630, PC 2/39(217), Pass for his return.

51 Calendar of State Papers, Venetian, vol. 19, p. 534, Contarini to Doge, 11 Sept 1626.

52 Somerset County Record Office, Mildmay Papers, Box 19, item 108d.

53 H. Ottomeyer, *Die Öffentliche Tafel: Tafellzeremoniell in Europa 1300-1900*, Deutsches Historisches Museum exh. cat. (Berlin, 2002), pls. 30–2.

54 Listed Sotheby's, London, Silver Sale, 10 June 1993; one is in the Victoria and Albert Museum, London.

55 Glanville 1990, ch. 5, 'The Market for Imported Plate'. Disputes over Nuremburg plate recur in the Goldsmiths Company Minute Books from 1605.

56 Wilson 1927; Forbes 1999, pp. 108–9; Oman 1961, p. 59; Bencard and Markova 1988, pl. 31.

57 C. Oman, 'The Civic Gifts to Charles II: The Failure of a Mission', *Proceedings of the Silver Society* 2 (1973), pp. 3–4; The Exeter Salt (Glanville 1990, fig. 48) and the Plymouth Fountain are in the Jewel House, Tower of London, with Nuremburg tankards purchased for the 1660 Coronation. The fountain compares in scale and form to the Hamburg sweetmeat stand presented by the Swedish ambassador to the Tsar in 1647: see Gifts to the Tsars 2001, pp. 270–1.

58 Carlisle 1669, p. 144.

59 UK National Archives, PRO, State Papers, SP 91/3, f. 9, undated [1635].

60 UK National Archives, PRO, State Papers, SP9/1, f. 181, 9 Nov 1631, Charles to Tsar; f. 206, 1 Jan 1631–2, Charles to Patriarch; S P 91/2 f. 221; SP 91/3, f. 37, March 1638, Tsar to Duke of Holstein about Cartwright; SP 91/3, f. 45, undated [1639], Cartwright to Charles.

61 Glanville 1990, p. 95.

62 Forbes 1999, p. 129.

63 Goldsmiths Company Minute Book W, ff. 91, 96.

64 Somerset County Record Office, Mildmay Papers, Box 19, 1644 sale.

65 Goldsmiths Company Minute Book X, f. 235, Search for substandard wares; Book Y, f. 9.

66 Somerset County Record Office, Mildmay Papers, Box 19, 1649; Oman 1970, e.g. pls. 51a, 59a.

67 Glanville 1990, ch. 6, 'Civil War and After'; Glanville 1987, p. 53.

68 Will of Sir Ralph Freeman, Alderman of Saint Michael Cornhill, City of London, April 1634, UK National Archives, PROB 11/165; will of John Merrick, see note 18.

69 Goldsmiths Company Minute Book P, part 1, f. 36, 14 October 1611.

70 T. M. Fry and R. S. Tewson, *Silver Plate of the Merchant Taylors Company* (London, 1929), pp. viii–ix.

71 For sales by the Goldsmiths Company, see W. S. Prideaux, *Memorials of the Worshipful Company of Goldsmiths*, 2 vols. (London, 1896–7), vol. 1, pp. 8–11.

72 Glanville 1990, pp. 88–9.

73 Forbes 1999, p. 135; Goldsmiths Company Apprenticeship Books.

74 Taylor 1984, pp. 97–9; S. Hare, *Touching Gold and Silver: 500 Years of Hallmarks* (London, 1978), pp. 53, 56. The Librarian at Goldsmiths Hall records confirmed identifications as well as misattributions.

75 Smith 2003, pp. 19–45.

76 David Mitchell, personal communication; D. Mitchell, '"To Alderman Backwell's for the candlesticks for Mr Coventry": The manufacture and sale of plate at The Unicorn, Lombard Street, 1663–72', *Silver Society Journal* 12 (2000), pp. 111–24 for the post-1663 trade.

77 Oman 1970, p. 5, citing assay figures for 1653–62, emphasizes that these understate the totals of plate made, because of private orders and Assay Office misconduct. Nor were royal orders included in Assay Office totals. This was a boom time for goldsmiths.

78 A. Grimwade, 'New Light on English Royal Plate', *Silver Society Journal* 7 (1995), pp. 369–80.

79 Bimbenet-Privat and D. Mitchell, 'Words or Images: Descriptions of Plate in England and France 1660–1700', *Silver Society Journal* 15 (2003), pp. 47–62; P. Glanville, 'Feather Flagons of the Order of the Garter', *Society of Friends of St George Annual Report* (2003–4), pp. 221–7.

33. Opposite: cat. 1, view of inside

English Silver

1

Font-shaped cup

London, 1557–8
Silver; cast, chased, engraved, gilded

Height 6⅛ in. (15.7 cm); bowl diameter 7⅛ in. (18 cm);
weight 31¼ oz (894.7 g)

Marks: city, assay, year (Jackson 1989, p. 49),
maker (erased)

Provenance: historic collection of the Armoury

Moscow Kremlin Museums inv. no. MZ–650

Published sources: Armoury Inventory 1884–93,
part 2, book 2, no. 1325

Literature: Jones 1909, p. 2, pl. 1; Bartenev 1912–16, vol. 2,
ills. 202–3; Goldberg 1954, p. 472, ill. 12; Penzer 1958,
p. 48, figs. 6–7; Armoury 1958, no. 283; Oman 1961,
pp. 22, 64, pls. 42–3; Smirnova 1964, p. 225; Markova 1988,
p. 226, pl. 153; English Silver 1991, no. 92, pp. 92–3;
Elizabeth 2003, no. 179, pp. 163–4; Russia–Britain 2003,
no. 94, p. 128

Font-shaped cups such as this rare example were widespread in the Tudor period. They were characterized by their shallow, broad bowls and the presence of vertical decorative elements, in this case flat-chased *laminae* (lobes). This stemmed cup is gilded and has low sides adorned with creeping floral ornament between strapwork frames. In the bottom centre is the chased profile of a classical warrior wearing a helmet surrounded by a frieze of acanthus leaves with large fruit. The remainder of the interior surface is covered with radiating *laminae* alternately blank and with stylized floral ornament. The same *laminae* appear on the broad faceted stem between a projecting horizontal ring and a twisted ring. *Laminae* on the foot are supplemented by a frieze with female profiles against a background of tendrils.

Penzer cites the Deane Cup, created in 1551–2 by Robert Danbe (Daube), as a close analogy for the cup's medallion with its profile and the stem with its twisted projecting ring. He attributes the Kremlin bowl to the same master (Penzer 1958, p. 48, fig. 5; Danbe's mark: Jackson 1989, p. 92). A medallion with the profile of a Roman warrior inside is a typical feature of Italian wine-bowls. Such wine-bowls are frequently mentioned in the inventory of royal Tudor vessels compiled in 1547 (Collins 1955, nos. 445, 449, 456).

Goldberg argues that the cup was among objects brought by Anthony Jenkinson for Tsar Ivan IV some time between 1561 and 1571, while Oman places it with a group of objects not linked with any particular embassy. No reference to the presentation of such an object to Ivan IV by Elizabeth I or her diplomats has been found in any known documents relating to the Moscow Palace Offices.

N.A.

2

Flagon

London, 1580–1

In the royal Jewel House, London, during the reign of James I

Monogrammist TF

Silver; cast, chased, engraved, gilded

Height 17¼ in. (44 cm); weight 104 oz (2,972.5 g)

Marks: city, assay, year (Jackson 1989, p. 50),
maker – monogrammist TF (Jackson 1989, p. 97)

Provenance: historic collection of the Armoury

Moscow Kremlin Museums inv. no. MZ–657

MS sources: Treasury Inventory 1634, f. 83v; Treasury
Inventory 1663–6, f. 149v; Armoury Inventory 1835, no. 1365

Published sources: Armoury Inventory 1884–93, part 2,
book 2, no. 1538

Literature: Jones 1909, p. 4, pl. 2, no. 1; Goldberg 1954, p. 500,
ill. 53; Oman 1961, pp. 30, 72, pl. 11; Armoury 1958, no. 284;
English Silver 1991, no. 94, pp. 140–3; Gifts to the Tsars 2001,
no. 57, p. 235; Russia–Britain 2003, no. 95, p. 129; Elizabeth
2003, no. 180, p. 164

This flagon mixes the English ornamental tradition (with its wild pinks
and rosettes) with a Netherlandish one. It is influenced by ornamental
prints such as those of Marcus Gheeraerts the Elder (1530–90), whose
compositions include the same framework, hanging draperies and birds
(e.g. State Hermitage Museum, St Petersburg, inv. nos. OG 331138–9,
288389–90).

It is one of a pair of gilded flasks with a high neck adorned with
Renaissance floral ornament and sea monsters (the other Moscow
Kremlin Museums inv. no. MZ–656). The body is divided into three parts
by friezes of laurels. In the upper part are chased sea monsters in
rectangular panels and clusters of fruit; the middle part has engraved
leaves, wild pinks, rosettes and the arms of James I; the lower part has an
applied plate with chased bunches of fruit and strapwork. On the sides
are lion's-head masks with rings, linked by chains. An engraved pattern
of alternating clusters of fruit and birds on hanging drapery covers the
neck. The cover is topped with cast grotesque spirals to which a chain is
attached. The base is ornamented with *ovae* in decorated frames, a frieze
of rhombuses and clusters of fruit.

Goldberg links this pair of flasks with records of an embassy in 1604
(see also Oman 1961, p. 30; Arel and Bogatyryov 1997, p. 452). Among
the gifts from James I to Tsar Boris Godunov delivered by the embassy
of Thomas Smith in 1604 there was indeed a pair of flasks. So much
greater, however, is their weight as recorded in the list of the gifts sent
from the Treasury Office to the Ambassadorial Office on 12 October
1604 and entered in the Ambassadorial Book, that we are convinced
they should not be identified with the flasks today in the Armoury.

N.A. / I.Z.

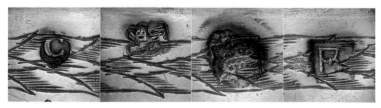

3

Gourd-shaped cup

London, 1589–90

Presented by the States General of Holland
to Tsar Alexey Mikhaylovich in 1647

Monogrammist K

Silver; cast, chased, gilded

Height 13¾–14½ in. (35–7 cm);
weight 47¾ oz (1,363.5 g)

Marks: city, assay, year (Jackson 1989, p. 50),
maker – monogrammist K (not listed by Jackson)

Provenance: historic collection of the Armoury

Moscow Kremlin Museums inv. no. MZ–636

MS sources: Ambassadorial Book 1647–8, f. 165;
Book of Receipts 1647–8, ff. 119v–120

Published sources: Armoury Inventory 1884–93, part 2,
book 2, no. 1139

Literature: Goldberg 1954, p. 474, ill. 14; Markova 1976, no. 7,
p. 147; English Silver 1991, no. 95, pp. 144–5; Russia–Britain
2003, no. 96, p. 131

This gilded standing cup would once have had a cover. The cup was the first item in a list of goods sent by the government of the States General of Holland and presented by the head of the embassy, Conrad Burch, a week before the audience granted him on 20 July 1647 in the Gold Chamber of the Kremlin Palace. An engraved inscription on the smooth part of the base notes that on 16 June 1647 the cup was a gift from the Dutch rulers to the Russian state, and gives the weight of the vessel. The cup was also the first of the objects to be entered in the Book of Receipts of the Treasury Office (Ambassadorial Book 1647–8; Book of Receipts 1647–8). All the silver items presented during this trip from Holland were adorned with the Russian arms before they left Dutch soil (Markova 1990, nos. 47–51, 54–70, 149–59) and we know from documents that they also appeared on the now lost cover of this cup.

This was the only object of non-Dutch origin among all the goods presented at that time. It is, moreover, the only known piece of English silver to bear (or have borne) the Russian state arms. It is one of a group of English silver works in which the influence of German silver – here in the form of the bowl and stem – is clearly visible, despite the characteristically English decoration. The broad upper part of the bowl is decorated with four-petalled flowers in large strapwork frames and multi-petalled rosettes in ovals against a ground of floral ornament. The lower part of the bowl is smooth and without decoration, the stem taking the form of a twisted trunk with a stump, knots and snails. On the high base are clusters of fruit and *rollwerk* cartouches; the top is smooth.

N.A. / I.Z.

4

Salt

London, 1594–5

Monogrammist AS

Silver; cast, chased, engraved, gilded

Height 16⅛–16⅜ in. (41–41.5 cm);
weight 46½ oz (1,325.2 g)

Marks: city, assay, year (Jackson 1989, p. 50),
maker – monogrammist AS (not listed by Jackson)

Provenance: historic collection of the Armoury

Moscow Kremlin Museums inv. no. MZ–651/1–2

Published sources: Armoury Inventory 1884–93,
part 2, book 2, no. 1491

Literature: Filimonov 1893, p. 20, no. 44; Artistic
Treasures 1902, p. 256, pl. 110; Jones 1909, p. 14,
pl. 7, no. 1; Bartenev 1912–16, vol. 2, p. 245, ill. 269;
Goldberg 1954, p. 492, ill. 45; Armoury 1958, nos.
285–8; Oman 1961, p. 65, pl. 45; English Silver 1991,
no. 97, pp. 148–51; Russia–Britain 2003, no. 97,
pp. 132–3

This gilded four-sided salt has the figure of a warrior on the cover and stands on ball-shaped feet clasped in claws. On the body are chased figures of Venus, Diana, Mercury and Mars with their attributes framed by fantastical columns. In the upper part are lion's-head masks in *rollwerk* cartouches, winged horses and decorative vases. The smooth gilded salt-holder has a hemispherical dip in the middle. On the convex surfaces of the base are scenes of deer, boar, unicorn and lion hunts. The rounded top is crowned with a figure of a Roman warrior with a shield and spear and has a chased procession of gods: Saturn, Ceres, Jupiter, Juno and Apollo. Engraved along the edge of the cover are snails, bees and linen-fold ornament. On the bottom of the base in an engraved seventeenth-century inscription indicating the weight.

The salt belongs to the type of large four-sided Tudor salts, similar in proportion and decorative scheme to a salt of 1569–70 belonging to the Vintners Company (Jackson 1921, frontispiece). In the treatment of its figures, with the proportions and overall composition far from classical perfection and balance, the images on the salt recall English Renaissance wood-carving. It is possible that the hunting scenes and animals were borrowed from English weaving or embroidery of the same period. Certainly, similar scenes appeared in borders along the edge of tablecloths and various decorative textiles (e.g. Bradford table carpet, c.1600, Victoria and Albert Museum, London; reproduced in *A Picture Book of English Embroideries* (London, 1933), vol. 2, p. 31).

Engraved snail and bee decoration derives from the Netherlandish ornamental tradition, notably the prints of Theodore de Bry (1528–98; State Hermitage Museum, St Petersburg, inv. no. OG 329749). Some of the devices are so archaic that the only close analogies to be found are in medieval manuscript illuminations, such as the depiction of an arrow being released from its bow and simultaneously hitting the deer (see Millar 1926, pl. 100).

Gerald Taylor of the Ashmolean Museum, Oxford, has suggested (personal communication) that the maker's mark may be that of Augustine Soday.

N.A.

5

Livery pot

London 1594–5

Brought to Russia by the embassy of John Merrick in 1614–15 (?)

Maker with the mark of a gryphon's head

Silver, glass; chased, cast, engraved, gilded

Height 15⅛ in. (38.5 cm); weight 93¾ oz (2,679.8 g)

Marks: city, assay, year (Jackson 1989, p. 50), maker – gryphon's head (half-erased)

Provenance: historic collection of the Armoury; formerly belonged to Patriarch Philaret (included in the inventory of his property for 1637 with the note 'from the English gifts of 1615', Goldberg 1954, p. 496)

Moscow Kremlin Museums inv. no. MZ–664

Published sources: Armoury Inventory 1884–93, part 2, book 2, no. 1686

Literature: Filimonov 1893, p. 20, no. 47; Goldberg 1954, p. 496, ill. 47; Jones 1909, p. 10, pl. 5, no. 1; Oman 1978a, pl. 14a, p. 32; Oman 1978b, p. 6, pl. 5; Markova 1988, no. 158, p. 231; English Silver 1991, no. 96, pp. 146–7; Russia–Britain 2003, no. 98, pp. 133–4

This gilded cup of the *Hansekanne* type (see p. 37) has an S-shaped handle and flip cover. It was formerly one of a pair. The body is decorated with finely engraved grotesque ornament consisting of tendrils with the heads of fantastical beasts, palmettes and shells. In the lower part is an applied twisted band with three small winged heads. The base with its profiled edge is adorned with ovae and circles in strapwork frames. The cover is adorned with grotesque engraved ornament and a round medallion with green glass in the middle; the pull for the cover is in the form of a two-sided figure of a winged siren. On the handle is engraved floral ornament, with an applied winged head on the end. On the bottom is an engraved seventeenth-century inscription recording the weight.

The pot is one of a small group of items with grotesque ornament developed by Niçaise Roussel (fl. 1580–1620; see Oman 1978b, pp. 4–8; examples of Roussel's ornament are published in Warncke 1979, pp. 265–70). The decoration of the Kremlin's livery pot is similar to one engraved by Roussel dating from 1587 and belonging to the Church of St Mary Woolnoth in London (Oman 1978a, p. 47), but no analogies have been found for the finial.

As a rule, livery pots, jugs and flasks were brought in pairs from London. Until 1930, the pair to this pot, which had yellow rather than green glass in the cover, was also in the Armoury, but it was then allocated to *Antikvariat* (a Soviet government foreign trade organization) for sale at auction. Goldberg notes that the livery pot still in the Kremlin features in the documentation relating to the Patriarch's vestry, described as a gift in 1615, and it seems correct to suppose, therefore, that these two pots arrived from London among the gifts brought by John Merrick from James I to Mikhail Fyodorovich.

N.A. / I.Z.

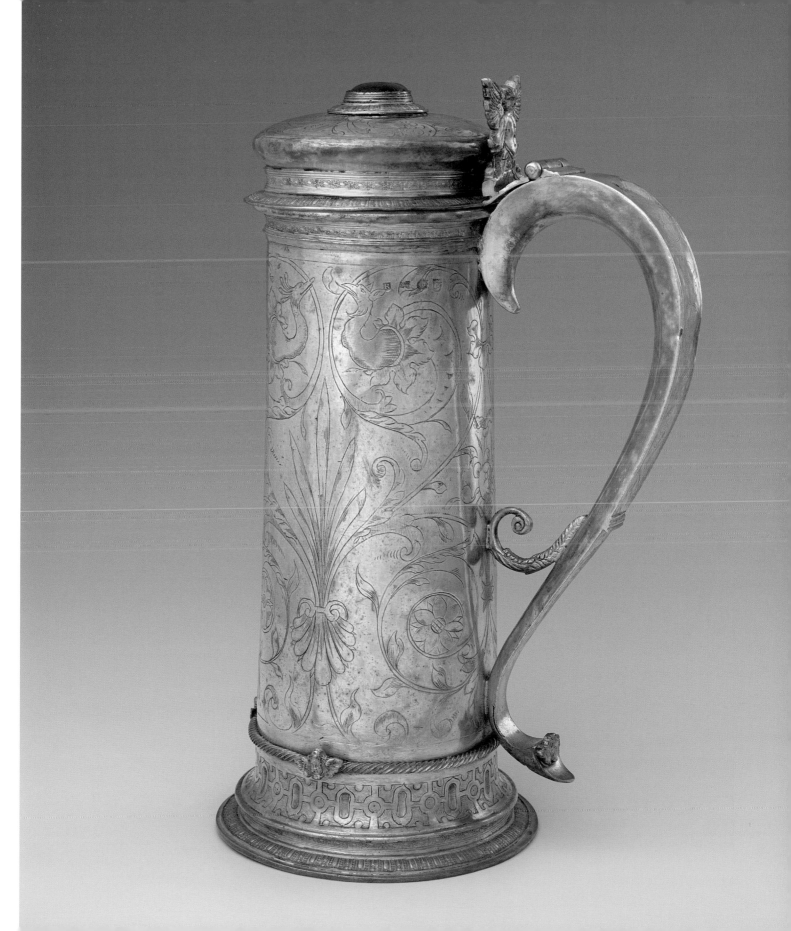

7

Leopard vessel

London, 1600–1

Brought by Fabian Smith of the Muscovy Company
for the treasury of Tsar Mikhail Fyodorovich in 1629.
Possibly a former gift to Elizabeth I, it may have derived
from the English monarchy's Jewel House and formed
part of the 'Great Guilt Cubberd of Estate' of 1626

Maker with the mark of a triangle with two crosses

Silver; cast, chased, gilded

Height 37 in. (94 cm); weight 1,026¼ oz (29,322.7 g)

Marks: city, assay, year (Jackson 1989, p. 51),
maker – triangle with two crosses (Jackson 1989, p. 105)

Provenance: historic collection of the Armoury

Moscow Kremlin Museums inv. no. MZ–693

Published sources: Armoury Inventory 1884–93, part 2,
book 2, no. 1922

Literature: Filimonov 1893, p. 20, no. 49; Bartenev 1912–16,
vol. 2, p. 271, ill. 316; Goldberg 1954, p. 466, ill. 1; Oman 1961,
pp. 58–9; Smirnova and Shumilov 1961, pp. 92–5; Smirnova
1964, p. 226; Great Britain, USSR 1967, no. 13, p. 13;
Hernmarck 1977, vol. 1, pp. 95, 111, 259; Nenarokomova
and Sizov 1978, pp. 82–3; Treasures 1979, no. 93, pp. 125,
209; Trésors 1979–80, no. 93, p. 190; Markova 1988, no. 157,
p. 230; English Silver 1991, no. 98, pp. 152–3; Russia–Britain
2003, no. 100, pp. 136–7; Elizabeth 2003, no. 178, p. 163

This unique example of English silver sculpture of the turn of the
sixteenth and seventeenth centuries is an outstanding piece. One of a
pair (the other Moscow Kremlin Museums inv. no. MZ–694), the leopard
is in fact a cast and gilded decorative vessel. Standing on a high, square
base, it supports a heraldic shield between its front paws and has a
removable head. The whole of the figure's surface is covered with fine
pounced linear ornament imitating fur. On his shoulders are applied
lion's-head masks with rings linked by a massive chain, to which is
attached a finer chain descending from the leopard's head. On the
shield is chased Renaissance strapwork ornament, with an applied cast
female head on the side. The profiled base has rows of convex and flat-
chased *ovae*, the upper part being decorated with clusters of fruit. In the
lower part, on the curl of the shield, is an engraved seventeenth-century
inscription indicating the weight.

Heraldic lions and leopards were not uncommon in the English applied
arts. They feature in interiors as carved wooden figures flanking staircases
and on furniture. In silver, they usually appeared as finials on vessels and
the ends of spoons (see Hackenbroch 1969, p. 8, nos. 13, 66).

N.A.

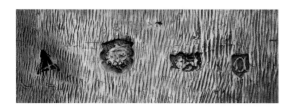

9

Livery pot

London, 1604–5

Presented by James I, via the embassy of John Merrick, to Patriarch Philaret in 1620 (?)

Monogrammist IH

Silver; chased, cast, gilded

Height 20 in. (51 cm); weight 133¾ oz (3,823.1 g)

Marks: city, assay, year (Jackson 1989, p. 5), maker – monogrammist IH (Jackson 1989, p. 99)

Provenance: historic collection of the Armoury

Moscow Kremlin Museums inv. no. MZ–645

MS sources: Ambassadorial Book 1620–1, ff. 570, 574v; Armoury Inventory 1835, no. 845

Published sources: Armoury Inventory 1884–93, part 2, book 2, no. 1183

Literature: Goldberg 1954, pp. 469–70, ill. 9; Oman 1961, p. 35, pl. 22; Russia–Britain 2003, no. 102, pp. 139–40

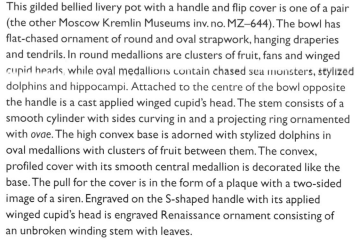

This gilded bellied livery pot with a handle and flip cover is one of a pair (the other Moscow Kremlin Museums inv. no. MZ–644). The bowl has flat-chased ornament of round and oval strapwork, hanging draperies and tendrils. In round medallions are clusters of fruit, fans and winged cupid heads, while oval medallions contain chased sea monsters, stylized dolphins and hippocampi. Attached to the centre of the bowl opposite the handle is a cast applied winged cupid's head. The stem consists of a smooth cylinder with sides curving in and a projecting ring ornamented with *ovae*. The high convex base is adorned with stylized dolphins in oval medallions with clusters of fruit between them. The convex, profiled cover with its smooth central medallion is decorated like the base. The pull for the cover is in the form of a plaque with a two-sided image of a siren. Engraved on the S-shaped handle with its applied winged cupid's head is engraved Renaissance ornament consisting of an unbroken winding stem with leaves.

On the bottom of the base is an engraved inscription indicating that the water pot belonged to the Patriarch's treasury in 1620 and recording its weight. This vessel differs in its particularly large size and densely packed decoration from other examples in collections around the world, the height of which varies between 12 and 15¾ in. (30–40 cm).

Goldberg suggests that the other water pot in this pair was a personal gift from the ambassador John Merrick, presented to Tsar Mikhail Fyodorovich on 15 December 1620 (Goldberg 1954, p. 470). Certainly the treasury notes of the Ambassadorial Book record two vessels of similar weight presented by Merrick, one to the Tsar and the other to the Patriarch. Merrick's 'signs of respect' included a *bolvanets* weighing 18 *grivenki* 24 *zolotniki* (just over 8 modern lbs; 3.8 kg), while he paid his respects to the head of the Russian Church with a 'silver gilded *stopa*' weighing 18 *grivenki* 39 *zolotniki* (just over 8 lbs; 3.8 kg). Treasury Office documents might call such a vessel either a *bolvanets* or a *stopa*, and the weights indicated in the documents accord with those engraved on the bottom of each vessel. It thus seems correct to identify the vessels in the Armoury today with those presented by Merrick.

N.A. / I.Z.

10

Gourd-shaped cup

London, 1604–5

Silver; cast, chased, engraved, gilded

Height 18½ in. (47 cm); weight 48¾ oz (1,394.1 g)

No marks

Provenance: historic collection of the Armoury

Moscow Kremlin Museums inv. no. MZ–634/1–2

Published sources: Armoury Inventory 1884–93, part 2, book 1, no. 1137

Literature: Goldberg 1954, p. 475; Oman 1961, p. 65, pl. 47; Russia–Britain 2003, no. 103, pp. 141–2

English gourd-shaped cups such as this one were brought to Moscow on a number of occasions among royal gifts and personal ambassadorial presents. There is a reference to one, for instance, among gifts presented by the men of rank who took part in an audience with Tsar Mikhail Fyodorovich on 15 December 1620: a 'cup of silver, gilded gourd-shaped, with a cover' of relatively light weight and modest dimensions (Ambassadorial Book 1620–1, f. 571). Likewise a pair of gourd-shaped cups was presented to Mikhail Fyodorovich by Simon Digby, envoy from Charles I, in the name of his King on 3 January 1636/7 during an audience in the Gold Chamber (Book of Receipts 1645–6, f. 142).

The upper part of the gourd-shaped bowl has grotesque ornament: engravings of sirens, tendrils terminating in dolphins' heads, clusters of fruits in vases, hanging draperies and birds. The smooth lower part is framed by four large applied gilded acanthus leaves. The stem is shaped like a curving tree trunk with five shoots and a stump with two scrolled brackets and snails. On the convex base with its smooth convex transition in the middle and profiled edge are chased winged cupids' heads and clusters of fruits in cartouches. The convex cover that forms a single shape with the bowl has three engraved cartouches containing running dogs, foxes, deer and clusters of fruit. The finial takes the form of a smooth cylinder on top of which stands a small cast figure of Ceres.

Goldberg judged the cup to be English by analogy with two cups in the Armoury bearing a full set of marks (Moscow Kremlin Museums inv. nos. MZ–633, MZ–635).

N.A. / I.Z.

11

Steeple cup

London, 1605–7

Presented by the Prior of the Monastery of the Nativity in Vladimir to Tsar Alexey Mikhaylovich in 1645

Monogrammist LB

Silver; chased, cast, gilded

Height 21⅝ in. (55 cm); weight 47½ oz (1,356.8 g)

Marks: city, assay, year (Jackson 1989, p. 51), maker – monogrammist LB (Jackson 1989, p. 106)

Provenance: historic collection of the Armoury

Moscow Kremlin Museums inv. no. 629/1–2

MS sources: Book of Receipts 1645–6, f. 142; Armoury Inventory 1835, no. 611

Published sources: Armoury Inventory 1884–93, part 2, book 1, no. 1132

Literature: Filimonov 1893, no. 1132; Jones 1909, p. 18, pl. 9, no. 1; Goldberg 1954, p. 476, ill. 21 (incorrect date); Oman 1961, p. 52, pl. 34b; Russia–Britain 2003, no. 104, pp. 142–3

The base of this cup has an engraved inscription which notes, in addition to the cup's weight, that it was presented to the sovereign, Tsar Alexey Mikhaylovich, by the administration of the Monastery of the Nativity in Vladimir on 29 September 1645.

Between September 1645 and February 1646 the new Tsar Alexey Mikhaylovich received courtiers, members of the government offices, leading merchants and heads of Russian towns and monasteries in the Gold Chamber of the Kremlin Palace and at his country palaces in the villages of Pokrovskoe and Kolomenskoe. The gifts presented to the young ruler from clerical visitors tended to be silver cups (mainly of German work), precious textiles and bundles of sables. This English cup that featured among these tokens of respect from the monarch's subjects (Book of Receipts 1645–6) was a great rarity.

It is a gilded ovoid cup on a stem with a high base and pyramid-shaped finial (steeple) on the cover. Both the bowl and the cover are adorned with the same chased images of vines and bunches of grapes. On one side, in place of hops, is a chased coat-of-arms with an erased image, the monograms 'FL' and 'OLB' (for which Oman proposed a German origin; Oman 1961, p. 52) and the date 1634. The hemispherical cover, convex with a smooth overhanging edge, is crowned with a three-sided steeple finial standing on three curved grotesque feet. At the very top of the steeple are scrolled brackets and a smooth ball to which is attached a cast dragon and the feet from a now lost figure of St George. The baluster stem has three scrolled brackets. The high bell-shaped base with profiled edge is adorned with large acanthus leaves.

N.A. / I.Z.

12

Steeple cup

London, 1606–7

Presented by the boyar Prince Fyodor Ivanovich Sheremetev to Tsar Alexey Mikhaylovich in 1645

Monogrammist M

Silver; chased, cast, gilded

Height 22⅜ in. (57 cm); weight 55 oz (1,569 g)

Marks: city, assay, year (Jackson 1989, p. 51), maker – monogrammist M (Jackson 1989, p. 101)

Provenance: historic collection of the Armoury

Moscow Kremlin Museums inv. no. MZ–628/1–2

MS sources: Book of Receipts 1645–6, f. 24

Published sources: Armoury Inventory 1884–93, part 2, book 2, no. 1131

Literature: Goldberg 1954, p. 478, ill. 20; Oman 1961, p. 54, pl. 34a; Russia–Britain 2003, no. 105, pp. 144–5

This gilded ovoid cup is a characteristic example of the most widespread type of English Renaissance cup. It has a striking pyramid-shaped finial or steeple on the top. The bowl and convex cover are chased with hanging pears against a pounced ground, with the lower part of the bowl decorated with *ovae* in strapwork frames. The cover has a smooth profiled edge crowned with a steeple adorned with openwork scales, grotesque brackets with gryphons' heads below and lions' heads above. Six grotesque brackets are attached to the cast smooth baluster stem. The high bell-shaped base with a profiled edge is ornamented with *ovae*, large acanthus leaves and pomegranates within. On the bottom of the base is an engraved inscription noting that the cup came to the royal treasury from the boyar (high-ranking Russian noble) Fyodor Ivanovich Sheremetev, as well as its weight.

Among the first courtiers seeking an audience to pay their respects in the immediate wake of Alexey Mikhaylovich's accession to the throne in 1645 were the young Tsar's uncle, Prince Nikita Ivanovich Romanov, and his tutor, Boris Ivanovich Morozov. The next to present his gifts to the sovereign was Prince Fyodor Sheremetev, *de facto* head of government during the last years of Mikhail Fyodorovich's reign. One original item among his gifts was a gold chain, the rest being composed of the traditional silver cup, precious textiles and fur. According to custom the cup was presented first (Book of Receipts 1645–6).

N.A. / I.Z.

13

Livery pot

London, 1606–7

Presented by James I, via the embassy of John Merrick,
to Tsar Mikhail Fyodorovich in 1615 (?)

Monogrammist TS

Silver; chased, cast, gilded

Height 15⅛ in. (38.5 cm); weight 69¼ oz (1,979.1 g)

Marks: city, assay, year (Jackson 1989, p. 51),
maker – monogrammist TS (Jackson 1989, p. 105)

Provenance: transferred from the Patriarch's vestry in 1920

Moscow Kremlin Museums inv. no. MZ–701

Literature: Goldberg 1954, p. 471, ill. 10 (incorrect marks);
English Silver 1991, no. 100, pp. 160–1; Treasures 1998,
no. 53, p. 83; Gifts to the Tsars 2001, no. 58, p. 236;
Russia–Britain 2003, no. 106, pp. 145–6

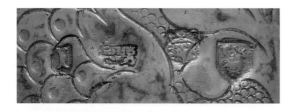

This livery pot combines a remarkable harmony of form and decoration
with the extremely careful execution typical of English Renaissance silver.
This is most notable in the bands of egg-and-dart framing the cover and
base, alternating with stars and quatrefoils, as well as the pull and the
engraved ornament on the handle.

The gilded bellied livery pot on a high base has a flip cover. The bowl is
chased with smooth tendrils forming circles and rhombuses containing
bunches of grapes, marguerites and Tudor roses. The centre of the
bowl bears the engraved arms of James I, evidence that this piece once
belonged to the royal buffet. The upper part of the base is a smooth
cylinder and the lower part is adorned like the bowl; the same chased
ornament appears on the convex profiled cover. The pull of the cover
has the form of a decorative plaque with profile masks to the sides and
a shell with acanthus tendrils in the middle. Engraved Renaissance floral
ornament features on the S-shaped handle. Along the edge of the base
a seventeenth-century engraved inscription notes the weight.

Goldberg suggests that the livery pot was among gifts presented to Tsar
Mikhail Fyodorovich (Goldberg 1954, p. 471). Certainly royal presents to
the Tsar included two similar vessels (Ambassadorial Book 1614–17, f. 57),
but a comparison of the weight indicated there has made it possible
to identify that entry with two other vessels in the Armoury. The
Ambassadorial Book recording John Merrick's visit in 1615 makes no
mention of any other pair of vessels – which might be variously described
according to the terminology of the seventeenth to nineteenth century.
It therefore seems unlikely that we can identify this livery pot with any
particular diplomatic gift.

N.A. / I.Z.

16

Cup

London, 1609–10

Maker John Wardlaw (?)

Silver; cast, chased, gilded

Height 12–12¼ in. (30.5–31 cm);
weight 28¼ oz (806.1 g)

Marks: city, assay, year (Jackson 1989, p. 51),
maker – John Wardlaw (?) (Jackson 1989, p. 108)

Provenance: historic collection of the Armoury; formerly
belonged to boyar Prince Yury Yansheevich Suleshev,
stol'nik (middle-ranking Russian noble) under Tsars Boris
Godunov and Vasily Shuysky

Moscow Kremlin Museums inv. no. MZ–615

MS sources: Armoury Inventory 1835, no. 644

Published sources: Armoury Inventory 1884–93, part 2,
book 2, no. 1085

Literature: Goldberg 1954, p. 504, ill. 57; Oman 1961,
p. 55, pl. 37

An English maker here imitated a German grape cup of the sort
widespread among Nuremberg masters in the first half of the seventeenth
century. The Armoury has the largest collection of Nuremberg silver in
the world, including a number of such grape cups (Moscow Kremlin
Museums MZ–273/1–2, MZ–1037/1–2; see Markova 1980, nos. 86, 142).

Grape cups are so named for the rows of round projections on the oval
bowl. This cup also has a cast figure of a woodcutter with a staff on the
stem. The base consists of a cylinder with convex walls with three
brackets and a row of round projections in the lower part. On the bottom
of the base is an engraved inscription noting that the cup belonged to Yury
Yansheevich Suleshev.

N.A.

18

Salt

London, 1611–12

Presented by James I, via the embassy of John Merrick,
to Tsar Mikhail Fyodorovich in 1615 (?)

Maker Robert Blackwell

Silver; chased, cast, engraved, gilded

Height 17½–17¾ in. (44.5–45 cm);
weight 44¾ oz (1,280.5 g)

Marks: city, assay, year (Jackson 1989, p. 51),
maker – Robert Blackwell (Smith 2003, p. 41)

Provenance: historic collection of the Armoury

Moscow Kremlin Museums inv. no. MZ–652

MS sources: Ambassadorial Book 1614–17, ff. 57–58v;
Treasury Inventory 1640, f. 25; Treasury Inventory 1663–6,
delo 151; Treasury Inventory 1676, ff. 214v–215; Armoury
Inventory 1835, no. 1317

Published sources: Philaret Inventory 1876, p. 932; Armoury
Inventory 1884–93, part 2, book 2, no. 1493

Literature: Viktorov 1877–83, p. 20; Kologrivov 1911, p. 20;
Goldberg 1954, p. 493, ill. 46; Armoury 1958, pls. 285–8;
Oman 1961, p. 32, pl. 16; Great Britain, USSR 1967, no. 17,
p. 13; Gifts to the Tsars 2001, no. 59, p. 237; Russia–Britain
2003, no. 109, pp. 150–1

The gilded silver salt is cylindrical and stands on three feet in the form of spheres. During the first quarter of the seventeenth century there were two kinds of smooth cylindrical salt. Although decorated in the same manner, they differed in the number of bowls for the salt, which could be single or double. A salt of analogous form but with two bowls, also bearing the mark of the monogrammist RB (possibly Robert Blackwell), is in the Victoria and Albert Museum in London (Glanville 1987, no. 95, p. 462).

The salt has a pyramid-shaped finial (steeple) on the cover. Another similar salt in the Armoury (Moscow Kremlin Museums inv. MZ–653) is missing its steeple. The cylindrical body is smooth and profiled, with edges turned out, and with two convex rims, the upper and lower parts adorned with friezes of alternating *ovae* and rhombuses, with Tudor roses and *ovae* on the rims. Widening towards the bottom, the cylindrical base has a profiled edge resting on three spherical feet clasped in bird's claws. The smooth bowl is hemispherical. On the round, smooth convex cover is a steeple attached to the body by four scrolled brackets. The removable finial is in the form of a four-sided pyramid on four grotesque loops with a smooth baluster at the top. On the base is an engraved seventeenth-century inscription noting the weight.

Among the royal gifts brought to Mikhail Fyodorovich by John Merrick in 1615 we find reference to a 'gilded salt with cover' (Ambassadorial Book 1614–17, f. 57v), but no indication of weight for the silver objects appears in the documents of the Treasury or Ambassadorial Offices. Goldberg sees a reference to this item in the inventory of the private treasury of Patriarch Philaret Nikitich which mentions a salt weighing 5 *grivenki* 16 *zolotniki* (nearly 2¼ modern lbs; just over 1 kg), but this weight differs from that engraved on the base of the salt by some 8 oz (200 g), so the inventory reference is likely not to be to this object.

N.A. / I.Z.

19

Standing cup

London, 1613–14

Presented by James I, via the embassy of John Merrick, to Tsar Mikhail Fyodorovich in 1620

Monogrammist TC

Silver; chased, cast, gilded

Height 20–20½ in. (51–2 cm);
weight 71¼ oz (2,033.1 g)

Marks: city, assay, year (Jackson 1989, p. 51),
maker – monogrammist TC (Jackson 1989, p. 107)

Provenance: historic collection of the Armoury

Moscow Kremlin Museums inv. no. MZ–619

MS sources: Ambassadorial Book 1620–1, f. 169r,v;
Armoury Inventory 1835, no. 592

Published sources: Armoury Inventory 1884–93, part 2,
book 2, no. 1122

Literature: Jones 1909, p. 38, pl. 19, no. 1; Treasures 1998,
no. 54, p. 84; Russia–Britain 2003, no. 110, pp. 151–2

John Merrick brought items from James I that were not entirely standard seventeenth-century gifts from English royalty. They included not only silver plate and textiles, but also items of semi-precious stones (more characteristic of gifts made during the second half of the sixteenth century), as well as silver sculpture (more typical of gifts from continental states). Nor was the order in which the silver was presented the regular one: the cups were not presented first (as was usual) but only after a crystal salt, a jasper cup in a gold mount and table sculptures of a unicorn, lion and ostrich (Ambassadorial Book 1620–1, f. 169r,v; see also Goldberg 1954, pp. 448, 450–1).

This standing cup employs the form and decorative system most widespread in England during this period. Three groups of harebells are a standard feature of silver cups in the first quarter of the seventeenth century. There are three similar cups, albeit of lesser size, in the Armoury (Moscow Kremlin Museums inv. nos. MZ–627, MZ–630, MZ–631).

The whole of the bowl of this gilded high-stemmed ovoid cup is chased with ornament and divided into two parts by large smooth *ovae*. In the upper part are stems and harebells grouped in threes and growing out of strapwork; in the centre is an empty shield; in the lower part large pomegranates and acanthus leaves. The bottom of the bowl is framed by applied acanthus leaves cut from ungilded silver. The cast stem consists of two cylinders and a smooth knop with grotesque brackets between them. On the base with its wide profiled edge are long *ovae* alternating with bands of scaly ornament below, with large acanthus leaves framing shells above. In the upper part of the base and on the bottom are engraved seventeenth-century inscriptions recording that the object was in the imperial treasury and noting its weight.

James I also sent cups for the Patriarch. They feature among the gifts from the ambassador and nobles for both the Patriarch and his son, the Tsar (Ambassadorial Book 1620–1, ff. 170v–174v). In the list of values that features in the Ambassadorial Book, the cup is noted as weighing 14 *grivenki* 16 *zolotniki* (about 6½ modern lbs; 3 kg) (Ambassadorial Book 1620–1, f. 567). This accords with the weight engraved on the bottom of the base. It is this cup, in the opinion of Goldberg, which was then described in detail in the Book of Receipts 1620–1 (Goldberg 1954, p. 482).

N.A. / I.Z.

20

Standing cup

London, 1613–14

Monogrammist TC

Silver; chased, cast, gilded

Height 22½–23 in. (57–58.5 cm);
weight 83¾ oz (2,395.9 g)

Marks: city, assay, year (Jackson 1989, p. 51),
maker – monogrammist TC (Jackson 1989, p. 107)

Provenance: historic collection of the Armoury

Moscow Kremlin Museums inv. no. MZ–618/1–2

Published sources: Armoury Inventory 1884–93, part 2,
book 2, no. 1121

Literature: Filimonov 1893, p. 23, no. 73; Jones 1909, p. 40,
pl. 20, no. 1; Goldberg 1954, pp. 482–3, ill. 22; Oman 1961,
p. 66, pl. 50; English Silver 1991, no. 102, pp. 164–5;
Russia–Britain 2003, no. 111, pp. 153–4

This English piece with its depictions of animals is a rare seventeenth-century example. Only three silver cups of this form decorated in this way are known (see Penzer 1960b, p. 177), two of which are in the Armoury (the other is cat. 22). The decoration reveals the influence of textiles such as tablecloths of the late sixteenth and early seventeenth centuries.

Dogs attack a boar and lions in the hunting scene depicted on the cover of this gilded ovoid cup. The top of the cover is cylindrical with traces of a lost pyramid finial. The upper part of the bowl is decorated with dogs chasing a boar, a leopard attacking a lion and a scene of battle between a sea creature and a dragon; the lower part has large acanthus leaves with fruits and shells. The baluster stem has three grotesque brackets while the bell-shaped base is adorned with acanthus leaves with shells and harebells. Engraved seventeenth-century inscriptions on the upper part of the base and on the bottom record that the cup belonged to the Tsar's treasury and note its weight.

N.A.

21

Livery pot

London, 1613–14

Presented by Charles I, via the embassy of Simon Digby, to Tsar Mikhail Fyodorovich in 1636

Monogrammist WR

Silver; chased, cast, gilded

Height 16⅛ in. (41 cm); weight 85¾ oz (2,449.2 g)

Marks: city, assay, year (Jackson 1989, p. 51), maker – monogrammist WR (Jackson 1989, p. 107)

Provenance: presented by Tsar Alexey Mikhaylovich to Patriarch Iosif and kept in the latter's treasury; transferred from the Patriarch's vestry in 1920

Moscow Kremlin Museums inv. no. MZ–699

MS sources: Ambassadorial Book 1635–6, f. 56; Book of Receipts 1636–7, ff. 33v–34

Literature: Jones 1909, p. 30, pl. 15, no. 1; Goldberg 1954, pp. 496–7, ill. 49; Oman 1961, p. 36, pl. 26a; English Silver 1991, no. 103, pp. 166–9; Russia–Britain 2003, no. 112, pp. 154–5

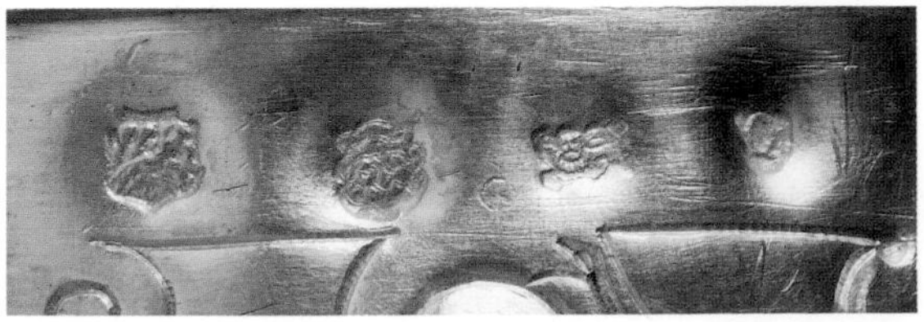

This livery pot is a gilded *Hansekanne* or Hanse cup (see p. 37). It has an S-shaped handle and a flip cover. A triton and Neptune playing instruments are set in oval strapwork, with shells in circles, winged heads beneath baldachins and sirens with dragonfly wings and snakes' tails chased on the body. The base has a frieze of concave *ovae*. On the lid are chased shells in round medallions and a winged head. Floral ornament is engraved on the S-shaped handle. On the bottom is an engraved seventeenth-century inscription recording that the livery pot belonged to Patriarch Iosif and noting its weight.

The careful execution of all the details – including the cast pull for the lid with its two-sided image of a siren, in itself an important work of art – demonstrates the great skill of English silversmiths. The sirens with dragonfly wings and the sea gods playing instruments reveal a superb knowledge of Netherlandish ornament. Behind the image of a triton playing a horn, for instance, lies a detail from an engraving by Adriaen Collaert, *Arion with a Lyre Riding a Dolphin* (see Hollstein 1949, vol. 4, no. 408).

A pair of livery pots of similar weight and description features among the royal objects presented to Tsar Mikhail Fyodorovich by the envoy Simon Digby at an audience in the Gold Chamber on 3 January 1636/7 (Book of Receipts 1645–6, ff. 33v–34). In the order of presentation they came after a pair of cups – the cups having been presented first, as was usual. The plate that featured among the royal gifts on that occasion was traditional: in addition to the cups and tankards or livery pots, the King sent paired flasks, single candlesticks and a lavabo set (Ambassadorial Book 1635–6, f. 56; see also Goldberg 1954, p. 451).

N.A. / I.Z.

Standing cup

London, 1614–15

Makers John Middleton and Francis Brown

Silver; chased, cast, gilded

Height 17⅝ in. (44.6 cm); weight 42¼ oz (1,208.7 g)

Marks: city, assay, year (Jackson 1989, p. 51),
maker – IM over FB (Jackson 1989, 109; mark identified
by Gerald Taylor, Taylor 1984, p. 99, no. 14))

Provenance: historic collection of the Armoury

Moscow Kremlin Museums inv. no. MZ–626

MS sources: Armoury Inventory 1835, no. 803

Published sources: Armoury Inventory 1884–93, part 2,
book 2, no. 1129

Literature: Goldberg 1954, p. 483; Oman 1961, pp. 78–9,
pl. 51; Russia–Britain 2003, no. 113, pp. 156–7

A chased garland of laurel divides the bowl of this gilded ovoid cup into two parts. The upper part is decorated with deer pursued by a dog, a lion and a gryphon among trees. In one of the trees is the coat-of-arms (a later addition) of Mildmay Fane, Earl of Westmorland (c. 1600–66). Fane was a relative of Sir Henry Mildmay who, from 1618, was Master of the Jewel House, where this cup originated. Above the coat-of-arms are the remains of a poorly preserved inscription: (interpreted by Oman as 'The city of York to its patron, Thomas Howard, Earl of Suffolk'). In the lower part of the bowl are chased acanthus leaves with large pomegranates in between. The cast stem is in the form of a baluster with three scrolled brackets. Long acanthus leaves and pomegranates alternate on the upper part of the high bell-shaped base. In the lower part are two lions and a unicorn between trees. On the bottom of the base an engraved seventeenth-century inscription notes that the object belonged to the Tsar's treasury.

The cup's decoration combines common hunting scenes with a deer and dogs with the typical English heraldic striding *opinicus*, a composite beast which was part dragon, part lion. To contemporary minds there was a natural unity between mythological beasts (such as the unicorn, gryphon or *opinicus*) and the real animals they knew.

N.A.

23–4

Beakers (only one illustrated)

London, 1615–16

Monogrammist IR

Silver; chased, cast, engraved, gilded

MZ–704: Height 4½ in. (11.5 cm);
weight 9½ oz (273.5 g)

MZ–707: Height 4½ in. (11.5 cm);
weight 9 oz (259.5 g)

Marks: city, assay, year (Jackson 1989, p. 51),
maker – monogrammist IR (Jackson 1989, p. 109)

Provenance: belonged to boyar Prince Afanasy Vasilevich
Rostovsky; transferred from the Patriarch's vestry in 1920

Moscow Kremlin Museums inv. nos. MZ–704, MZ–707

Literature: Goldberg 1954, pp. 493–4, ill. 32; Oman 1961,
pp. 54, 66, pl. 36; Russia–Britain 2003, no. 114, p. 157

The arabesque decoration on this cup was widespread in western
European ornament during the second half of the sixteenth and first
half of the seventeenth century. It is frequently found on designs for
book bindings by Hans Holbein the Younger (see Pakhomova 1989,
no. 83, p. 193).

These partially gilded cups are two of nine similar beakers in the
Armoury (Moscow Kremlin Museums inv. nos. MZ–704 to MZ–712).
The smooth cups have a profiled base, and the gilded rim is separated
from the body by a profile and adorned with a frieze of engraved
arabesque. On the bottom of the base, an engraved seventeenth-century
inscription records that the beakers belonged to the boyar Prince
Afanasy Vasilevich Rostovsky (Lobanov; elevated to the rank of boyar
1627, died 1629).

N.A.

25

Water pot

London, 1615–16

Brought by Fabian Smith of the Muscovy Company for the treasury of Tsar Mikhail Fyodorovich in 1629. Derived from the English monarchy's Jewel House and formerly part of the 'Great Guilt Cubberd of Estate' of 1626

Maker Robert Blackwell

Silver; cast, chased, gilded

Height 24⅜ in. (62 cm); weight 290 oz (8,283 g)

Marks: city, assay, year (Jackson 1989, p. 51), maker – Robert Blackwell (Smith 2003, p. 41)

Provenance: historic collection of the Armoury

Moscow Kremlin Museums inv. no. MZ–640

MS sources: Treasury Inventory 1640

Published sources: Armoury Inventory 1884–93, book 2, part 2, no. 1163

Literature: Artistic Treasures 1902, p. 257, pl. 3; Goldberg 1954, p. 487, ill. 40; Oman 1961, p. 60; Smirnova and Shumilov 1961, pp. 94–5; Hernmarck 1977, vol. 2, p. 95, pl. 257; Russia–Britain 2003, no. 115, pp. 158–9

The gilded water pot has an ovoid body that widens towards the top. The pot is adorned with chased grotesque ornament consisting of a complex interweaving of tendrils, clusters of fruit, winged sirens and convex cast heads and fantastical beasts. The spout takes the form of a winged dragon with a cylindrical horn in its mouth and a cast figure of a fantastical beast on top of its head; the handle is composed of a snake curled into a loop with an applied figure of a lizard. The round profiled base with a convex upper part is decorated with large chased pumpkins or gourds framed by acanthus leaves and openwork ornament. The tall cylindrical neck with profiled edges and the round convex cover with a smooth medallion in the middle are adorned like the body. The provenance of the object was established by Smirnova (Smirnova and Shumilov 1961).

N.A.

26

The Warwick Cup

London, 1617–18

Presented by James I, via the embassy of John Merrick, to Tsar Mikhail Fyodorovich in 1620

Maker F. Terry

Silver; chased, cast, gilded

Height 18¾ in. (47.8 cm); weight 63 oz (1,797.8 g)

Marks: city, assay, year (Jackson 1989, p. 51), maker – F. Terry (Jackson 1989, p. 106)

Provenance: historic collection of the Armoury

Moscow Kremlin Museums inv. no. MZ–623

Published sources: Armoury Inventory 1884–93, book 2, part 1, no. 1126

Literature: Goldberg 1954, p. 484, ill. 31; Oman 1961, pp. 75–6, pls. 18–19

This cup, known as the Warwick Cup, is of particular historical interest. It would seem to be one of only two surviving gifts of those made to James I in 1617 during his traditional tour of his lands. The presence of James I's arms pounced on a plate on the cup are evidence that it was in the royal treasury or Jewel House, while the device of the city of Warwick allows us further to identify the cup's origin.

Oman suggests that the cup was a gift to the King from Sir Fulke Greville, Chancellor of the Exchequer (to whom James had granted Warwick Castle). James I visited Warwick in 1617, some time after 3 September when he visited Coventry, where he was presented with a gold cup filled with gold coins to the value of £100 (the cup is lost, but a design for it survives in the Coventry City Archives: see Oman 1961, p. 75, pl. 8). In the castle gates Greville greeted the King on his entrance to the city with a speech in Latin and then met him again in the hall of Leicester Hospital. Oman judges that the cup was presented to him during that meeting (Oman 1961, p. 76). If his theory is correct, and it certainly seems likely, then we can trace the history of this marvelous cup from Warwick in September 1617, through the Jewel House in London where it was kept until 1620, to Russia, where it featured as an ambassadorial gift for Tsar Mikhail Fyodorovich and was added to the Tsar's treasury.

The cup is adorned with three chased winged sirens, clusters of fruit, tendrils and the engraved arms of James I in the upper part of the bowl. The lower part of the gilded ovoid cup's bowl is decorated with large acanthus leaves, fruit and shells. The tall bell-shaped base is divided into two parts, like the bowl, by a garland of laurels and adorned with acanthus leaves and shells above and clusters of fruit and tendrils below. On the bottom is an engraved seventeenth-century inscription noting that it belonged to the Tsar's treasury and recording the weight. Attached beneath the foot is a smooth plate with the engraved device of the city of Warwick. The cup would once have had a cover (now missing).

N.A.

27

Flagon

London, 1619–20

Presented by James I, via the embassy of John Merrick, to Tsar Mikhail Fyodorovich in 1620

Monogrammist IS

Silver; chased, cast, gilded

Height 18⅞ in. (48 cm); weight 101¾ oz (2,908.7 g)

Marks: city, assay, year (Jackson 1989, p. 51), maker – monogrammist IS (not listed by Jackson)

Provenance: historic collection of the Armoury

Moscow Kremlin Museums inv. no. MZ–654

MS sources: Ambassadorial Book 1620–1, ff. 169v, 568v; Book of Receipts 1620–1, f. 33

Published sources: Armoury Inventory 1884–93, part 2, book 2, no. 1535

Literature: Filimonov 1893, p. 25, no. 87; Goldberg 1954, p. 501, ill. 55; Oman 1961, p. 35, pl. 23; Great Britain, USSR 1967, no. 21, p. 14; English Silver 1991, no. 104, pp. 170–3; Russia–Britain 2003, no. 116, pp. 159–60

This high-necked gilded flagon is one of a pair (the other Moscow Kremlin Museums inv. no. MZ–655). The flask is a characteristic example of English silver from the start of the seventeenth century, with the much loved flat-chased decoration covering the whole of the surface. The central part of the body is decorated with chased images of sea creatures in oval strapwork frames, the upper part filled with clusters of fruit and large acanthus leaves with fruits, the lower with shells. Attached to the sides of the body are lions' masks with rings linked by a chain. The neck has acanthus leaves, clusters of fruit and shells. The lid is topped with grotesque tendrils to which a chain is attached. Sea creatures in oval frames with clusters of fruit adorn the base. On the bottom of the base is an engraved inscription recording that the flagon belonged to the Tsar's treasury in the seventeenth century and noting the weight.

John Merrick brought the pair of silver flagons to Moscow on behalf of James I. After works of semi-precious stones, silver sculpture and cups, the *okol'nichiy* (noble) Nikita Vasilyevich Godunov presented Tsar Mikhail Fyodorovich with the next royal gift, 'two flasks of gilded silver'. In the list of values in the Ambassadorial Book these are given as 'silver flasks gilded to one pattern', with the weight for the two together of 27 *grivenki* 24 *zolotniki* (nearly 12½ modern lbs; 5.6 kg) (Ambassadorial Book 1620–1; see also Goldberg 1954, p. 448). Their description and the weights cited in the Book of Receipts for 1620–1 (see Goldberg 1954, p. 501) accord with those engraved on the base.

N.A. / I.Z.

28

Candlestick

London, 1624–5

Maker with a trefoil mark

Silver; cast, chased, gilded

Height 9 in. (23 cm); weight 22½ oz (644.8 g)

Marks: city, assay, year (Jackson 1989, p. 51),
maker – trefoil mark (Jackson 1989, p. 98)

Provenance: transferred from the Archangel Cathedral
in the Moscow Kremlin

Moscow Kremlin Museums inv. no. MZ–716

Literature: Goldberg 1954, p. 490, ill. 41; Oman 1961, p. 61,
pl. 41; English Silver 1991, no. 105, pp. 174–5; Russia–Britain
2003, no. 117, pp. 160–1

This gilded candlestick is the only known example of its kind dating from
the English Renaissance. It is remarkable for its harmony of form and
decoration. Taking into account the high skill and beauty of the piece,
Oman suggests that it may have formed part of the group of objects from
the Jewel House sold in 1626 (Oman 1961, p. 61).

The single candlestick on a high base has no projection to catch wax.
Its cast cylinder has vertical openings and is chased with acanthus leaves
and suspended draperies. The knop has three herm brackets and is
adorned with strapwork, clusters of fruit and lions' masks. On the round
base with a smooth transition and profiled edge alternate egg-and-dart
pattern with rosettes in circles. The convex part of the base has winged
heads beneath a baldachin, with strapwork and floral ornament.

N.A.

29

Ewer

London, 1652 3

Monogrammist WB

Silver; chased, gilded, cast

Height 18¼ in. (46.2 cm); weight 97½ oz (2,766 g)

Marks: city, assay, year (Jackson 1989, p. 52),
maker – monogrammist WB (not listed by Jackson)

Provenance: transferred from the State Valuables Store
in 1925; formerly in the collection of the Princes Yusupov

Moscow Kremlin Museums inv. no. MZ–718

Literature: Goldberg 1954, p. 492, ill. 44 (incorrect maker's
mark); Oman 1961, pp. 65, 80 note 1, pl. 46; Russia–Britain
2003, no. 118, pp. 161–2

This ewer's unusual nature lies in the form of the bowl which is divided
into two parts. A lavabo ewer of 1606 of similar design can be found in
Sidney Sussex College, Cambridge. The abundance of masks and their
placing on the body, the S-shaped handle and overall composition are
evidence of a good knowledge of Italian prototypes, such as drawings
in the manner of Giulio Romano dating from the second half of the
sixteenth century (see Hayward 1976, no. 72). It is possible that the year
mark for 1652–3 was a later addition to the ewer and does not reflect
the date it was produced.

The gilded ewer on a high base has an elegant spout and S-shaped handle.
The bowl is divided into two uneven convex parts by a smooth profiled
band. The upper part has sea monsters in oval strapwork frames, clusters
of fruit and an applied Cupid's head; the lower has large acanthus leaves
and pomegranates. The base is chased with shells with smooth strapwork
frames, the spout adorned with clusters of fruits and mascarons. A female
figure tops the S-shaped handle and there are lions' masks where it joins
the neck and body.

N.A.

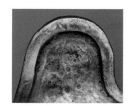

The Embassy of Charles Howard, 1st Earl of Carlisle

Irina Zagorodnaya

All of which was sent before to the pallace, the plate being carried by four and twenty men, the cloth by threescore, ten men carried the Velvets Sattins and Damask, six and twenty the stufs and table linning, and ten more the Gun, the Pistols, the Watches, and the Clocks …

—Description of the Earl of Carlisle's embassy to Moscow, 1663–4 (see cat. 80)

Warrant from the Lord Chamberlain for the issue of gifts to be taken to Russia by the Earl of Carlisle

These are to signifye unto you his Ma^ty pleasure that you forthwith prepare & deliver to the Right Honble the Earle of Carlisle for his Ma^ty Agent to the Emperor of Russia, one Bason & Ewer, a pr. of flagons, a pr. of bottles, a pr. of standing bowles, & covers, a pr. of candlesticks, & one p[er] fuming pot, six fruite dishes, all large & curiously enchased & gilt, the whole to amount in weight to two thousand ounces or thereabouts, with case of leather gilt, Also twelve knives with Agatt hafts & gilt heades; and an embroidered case to them, and this shall be your Warrant. Given under my hand this 26th day of June, 1663, in the 15th year of his Ma^ty reigne. MANCHESTER.

—UK National Archives, PRO, LC5/107, p.100, and LC5/137, p.144.

The embassy to Tsar Alexey Mikhaylovich led by Charles Howard, 1st Earl of Carlisle (1628–85), lasted from September 1663 to June 1664. To judge by the records of the Ambassadorial Office in Moscow (Ambassadorial Book 1663–4), Russian officials found themselves facing a situation unique in their experience.

Carlisle, an intimate of the recently restored Charles II, arrived at the mouth of the River Dvina in two ships. His vast suite consisted of some 120 people, including his wife and son. The politician and poet Andrew Marvell was secretary to the embassy. Their journey to Moscow was complicated by the weather and they were only able to travel once the roads had frozen over, which meant that their arrival in the capital was delayed until February 1664. As they passed along the roads, the group was accorded much honour in the larger towns. They were greeted with speeches on behalf of the local governors and supplied with all necessary means of transport and provisions – although the Earl was forced to pay for some items of food and for repair to the transport out of his own pocket (see Carlisle 1669).

On the Tver Road in Moscow, not far from the *Zemlyanoy val* or 'earth rampart' that surrounded the city, the ambassador was greeted on 4 February by two high-ranking officials, the *dumnyy dvoryanin* (nobleman of the boyars' council) Ivan Pronchishchev and *d'yak* (secretary) Grigory Bogdanov, in full accordance with the accepted rules for greeting diplomats of such high status. Thence they passed through the city streets, across Red Square to Pokrovka Street and the residence of a Dutch merchant known in Russia as Davyd Mikolaev. He enjoyed the trust of the government of Muscovy and frequently made his rich apartments available to house diplomatic missions.

On the day of his royal audience, 18 February, some two weeks after his arrival in the capital, Carlisle was received in the Faceted Chamber. He was accompanied by his Muscovite *pristav* or bailiff and the *okol'nichiy* (court officials charged with greeting foreigners) Vasily Semyonovich Volynsky, Pronchishchev and Bogdanov. The procession was magnificent: the gifts from the King and the ambassador alone required a hundred *streltsy* (members of an elite military corps) to carry them. One hundred officials of the state offices or ministries walked ahead of the ambassadors dressed in brightly coloured robes, while the ambassador's own suite consisted of thirty-three men mounted on richly caparisoned horses. Emerging from his sledge onto Cathedral Square at the very heart of the Kremlin, the ambassador, followed by his son and suite, moved towards the audience chamber. Along the way they were 'greeted' three times with speeches by courtiers of princely rank: the *stol'niki* Andrey Ivanovich Khilkov, Nikita Ivanovich Sheremetev and Ivan Alexeevich Vorotynsky.

All went exactly as it should at the audience. At the end the gifts from Charles II were presented to the Tsar, his sons and wife, after which came the presentation of the ambassador's own gifts, with unusual and touching speeches. Unlike most official visitors to Tsar Alexey, Carlisle was considered worthy of an invitation to dinner on the first day of negotiations with the commission of boyars, which took place on 19 February.

The embassy's purpose – the return of the English merchants' trading privileges – was unrealistic from the start. Russian merchants had by this time so established their own position that they too had begun to be aware of their own commercial interests. Growing conflicts between them and the English and Dutch overflowed in collective petitions to the Tsar in 1646 and 1649, as well as speeches on their behalf in 1648–9 at sittings of the *Zemskiy sobor* or Assembly of the Land. Alexey Mikhaylovich and his government went some way to meet their demands and took measures to limit the activities of foreign merchants. Taking advantage of the formal excuse of the execution of Charles I, Russia annulled the privileges of the Muscovy Company in 1649, putting an end to more than one hundred years of duty-free purchase and sale of goods across Russian territory. That same year a decree was issued exiling the English from the inner regions of Russia and leading to the liquidation of the Muscovy Company's letters of patent. Henceforth, English merchants were to be permitted to trade only in Archangel. No subsequent monarch of the United Kingdom was able to convince the Russian government to return their former privileges. The rules for exacting duties also changed, and in 1653 new customs regulations were introduced, increasing the amount of duty paid by foreign merchants.

These reasons were all explained to Carlisle during his first meeting with the commission of boyars, but he continued to insist on full restitution and an apology for what he saw as insults to him from Russian officials.

His obstinacy increasingly irritated the staff of the Ambassadorial Office but even so, in April he was granted a personal meeting with the Tsar in order to discuss 'secret matters'. To mark the passing of the ambassadorial cortege through the Kremlin on the occasion of Carlisle's visit to the Terem Palace, where the Tsar and his family had their private chambers, *streltsy* were posted with rifles, banners and drums. On the stairs and passageways of the palace itself stood *streltsy* commanders and *sokol'niki* in 'coloured kaftans with halberds', while the entrance to the antechamber was guarded by the very highest military officials, among them a man from Tsar Alexey Mikhaylovich's closest circle, Artamon Sergeevich Matveev, who would later head the Ambassadorial Office.

In the Tsar's private apartments, the walls from the porch to the sovereign's study were 'hung with velvets and satins and Persian carpets with gold thread … the porch was spread with carpets and the porch adorned and the canopy and the front were adorned'. But the spring rain spoiled all the decorations and the precious textiles had to be covered over with 'coarse crimson cloth'. At the end of the secret talks, which brought Carlisle none of the results he had hoped for, there was a light meal. The Tsar drank the King's health in *Romany* from a cup, and the ambassador in his turn drank the health of the Russian monarch. Rhenish wine was served to members of the ambassadorial suite and boyars present in the chambers.

By June 1664 all subjects for negotiation had been exhausted. The Ambassadorial Office sought to put an end to Carlisle's visit in accordance with the accepted rules of diplomacy – reimbursing his personal financial outgoings on the road to Moscow, if such there had been, and presenting him with a gift 'for his visit and his presents'. But it did not prove possible to carry out this plan in full. Firstly the ambassador was dissatisfied with the form of compensation, which was made in sable furs. He declared that he was no merchant and therefore had no need of furs, but preferred money, on which he insisted, getting his own way in the end. Secondly, he refused to accept the Tsar's gift, stating that he had not been able to carry out his mission and therefore did not deserve such favour. So scandalous a declaration was intended to demonstrate to the Muscovites not only the importance of Carlisle's visit and the significance of the Tsar's decision, but also to make clear the English grandee's personal ambitions. The Ambassadorial Office sought to convince the indomitable Earl to accept the sables in exchange for the wonderful silver – a basin and ewer and three dishes – which he had brought as his personal gift to the Tsar but to no avail. In light of his refusal, his personal gifts were returned to him. Russian documents record that in the course of yet another conversation with his *pristav*, Vasily Semyonovich Volynsky, Carlisle – presumably seeking to soften the by now tense situation – stated that he preferred 'to keep them [the silverware] as a souvenir, since he had presented them to such a great sovereign and they had been with his imperial majesty in his chambers a long time, and then given back to him, and would always remind him of this'.

Carlisle's visit to Moscow caused a stir which no previous embassy ever had. The 'exchange of pleasantries' and to-ing and fro-ing of gifts wrought confusion in the Ambassadorial Office, where the event was cited thereafter as an example of mutual failure. Moreover, the ambassador set an example of provocative behaviour that was to be followed by a number of his successors, the English merchants who visited Moscow during the second half of the seventeenth century.

34. Sir Godfrey Kneller, *Charles Howard, 1st Earl of Carlisle*, c.1675, the Castle Howard Collection, Yorkshire

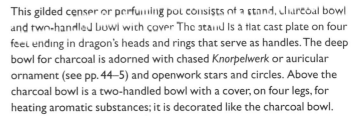

*English Silver
brought by the Earl of Carlisle*

30

Perfuming pot and stand

London, *c.*1663

Presented by Charles II, via the embassy of Charles Howard, Earl of Carlisle, to Tsar Alexey Mikhaylovich in 1664

Monogrammist IN

Silver; cast, chased, gilded, openwork carving

Height 17¾ in. (45 cm); weight 202¼ oz (5,774.9 g)

Marks: maker – monogrammist IN (Jackson 1989, p. 125; Oman thinks this is not the maker's mark but that of the assay master, placed upon works by foreign craftsmen: Oman 1970, p. 27)

Provenance: historic collection of the Armoury

Moscow Kremlin Museums inv. no. MZ–695/1–4

MS sources: Ambassadorial Book 1663–4, ff. 201v, 284

Published sources: Armoury Inventory 1884–93, part 2, book 2, no. 1937

Literature: Goldberg 1954, p. 472, ill. 11; Armoury 1958, no. 301; Oman 1961, p. 40, pl. 31; Great Britain, USSR 1967, no. 22, p. 14; Oman 1970, pl. 73; English Silver 1991, no. 108, pp. 184–5; Russia–Britain 2003, no. 119, pp. 162–3

This gilded censer or perfuming pot consists of a stand, charcoal bowl and two-handled bowl with cover. The stand is a flat cast plate on four feet ending in dragon's heads and rings that serve as handles. The deep bowl for charcoal is adorned with chased *Knorpelwerk* or auricular ornament (see pp. 44–5) and openwork stars and circles. Above the charcoal bowl is a two-handled bowl with a cover, on four legs, for heating aromatic substances; it is decorated like the charcoal bowl.

This censer is clearly based on the traditional English porringer or two-handled bowl. But the ornament that covers its surface must surely be one of the most outstanding examples of auricular decoration on English silver. This is a unique work in an English context, both in its type and decoration, combining chased auricular style with openwork ornament.

On 18 February 1664 the Earl of Carlisle, sent to Russia by the recently restored English monarch Charles II, was received by Tsar Alexey Mikhaylovich. In addition to the more traditional kinds of English plate he presented (cats. 31–4), there were more unusual pieces, among them this perfuming pot (Ambassadorial Book 1663–4, f. 201v; see also Goldberg 1954, pp. 455–6). In the list of values recorded in the Ambassadorial Book, it is described as a 'table porringer with a cup and lid, silver gilded', with a weight of 14 pounds 24 *zolotniki* (over 12¾ modern lbs; 5.8 kg), which accords with the figures engraved on the censer itself (Ambassadorial Book 1663–4, f. 284; see also Goldberg 1954, p. 472). Unlike other diplomatic gifts from London, the silver plate presented by Charles II has Russian seventeenth-century inscriptions on the bottom that record not only the weight but also the date and place of presentation, as well as the names of the giver and receiver. This censer is an exception in having no mark to record that it was a gift.

N.A. / I.Z.

31

Fruit dish

London, 1663

Presented by Charles II, via the embassy of Charles Howard, Earl of Carlisle, to Tsar Alexey Mikhaylovich in 1664

Monogrammist TH

Silver; chased, gilded

Height 3⅜ in. (8.5 cm), diameter 16¾ in. (42.5 cm); weight 64 oz (1,828.5 g)

Marks: city, assay, year (Jackson 1989, p. 52), maker – monogrammist TH (not listed by Jackson)

Provenance: historic collection of the Armoury

Moscow Kremlin Museums inv. no. MZ–648

MS sources: Ambassadorial Book 1663–4, ff. 202, 284

Published sources: Armoury Inventory 1884–93, part 2, book 2, no. 1286, pl. 233

Literature: Filimonov 1893, p. 26, no. 111; Jones 1909, p. 48, pl. 24, no. 2; Goldberg 1954, p. 491 (incorrect mark); Oman 1961, p. 40, pl. 32; Oman 1970, p. 58, pl. 18b; English Silver 1991, no. 106, pp. 176–9; Russia–Britain 2003, no. 120, pp. 164–5

The silver gifts presented on behalf of Charles II included six fruit bowls 'on stands silver gilded' (Ambassadorial Book 1663–4, ff. 202, 284; UK National Archives, PRO, LC5/107, p. 100, and LC5/137, p. 144). Such fruit dishes had never before been included in royal gifts to Russia. They were all of roughly the same weight and had similar decoration, though there were differences in the selection of chased animals. Three more survive in the Armoury (Moscow Kremlin Museums inv. nos. MZ–646, MZ–647, MZ–649).

The fruit dish on a short broad stem is round and gilded. The smooth inside is surrounded by a frieze with high-relief poppies, tulips and a deer, dog, horse and boar. On the bottom of the base is a note of the dish's weight and a seventeenth-century inscription recording that the dish was sent to the sovereign by the English King in 1664.

In England, such objects served as an early type of platter and were intended to hold fruit. They might be made as a pair to a two-handled bowl. In Russia, however, such bowls were used for marinated berries and fruits and all kinds of pickles (*raznosol*), and was thus known as a *razsolnik*.

N.A. / I.Z.

32

Standing cup

London, *c.*1663

Presented by Charles II, via the embassy of Charles Howard, Earl of Carlisle, to Tsar Alexey Mikhaylovich in 1664

Maker Francis Leake (fl. 1655–83)

Silver; cast, chased, gilded

Height 28¾ in. (73 cm); weight 142½ oz (4,073.5 g)

Marks: maker – Francis Leake (Jackson 1989, p. 123; the lack of other marks may be due to the possible lapse of general rules for marking silver in the 1660s; certainly there are cases when only maker's marks were placed on silver pieces produced on commission: see Oman 1970, p. 7)

Provenance: historic collection of the Armoury

Moscow Kremlin Museums inv. no. MZ–621/1–2

MS sources: Ambassadorial Book 1663–4, ff. 201v, 284; Treasury Inventory 1690, f. 55v; Treasury Inventory 1721, f. 59v

Published sources: Armoury Inventory 1884–93, part 2, book 1, no. 1124

Literature: Jones 1909, pp. 40–1, pl. 20, no. 2; Goldberg 1954, p. 486, ill. 24; Oman 1961, p. 39, pl. 29; Oman 1970, p. 2b; English Silver 1991, no. 107, pp. 180–3; Gifts to the Tsars 2001, no. 63, p. 242; Russia–Britain 2003, no. 121, pp. 165–6

The decoration on this gilded cup is a superb example of the floral style in English silver, with animals set naturally within the floral motifs. The cup has a cylindrical bowl and is one of a pair (the other Moscow Kremlin Museums inv. no. MZ–620/1–2). The bowl is decorated with tulips with luxuriant leaves and birds, deer and a dog.

In the middle of the smooth composite stem is a large knop. The base is decorated with images of a hare and dog amid large leaves and tulips. A deer and a dog appear among flowers on the cover, which has a conical point with a finial in the form of a rider wearing classical armour and a helmet and carrying a spear. On the bottom is a note of the weight and an engraved inscription recording that the cup was sent to the sovereign by the English King in 1664.

N.A.

33

Flagon

London, c 1663

Presented by Charles II, via the embassy of Charles Howard, Earl of Carlisle, to Tsar Alexey Mikhaylovich in 1664

Maker Robert Smythier (fl. 1660–86)

Silver; cast, chased, gilded

Height 15 in. (38 cm); weight 150¾ oz (4,308.7 g)

Marks: maker – Robert Smythier (Jackson 1989, p. 126; Smythier's marks are found on many works, including some belonging to the royal family, from the period 1664–86)

Provenance: historic collection of the Armoury

Moscow Kremlin Museums inv. no. MZ–659

MS sources: Ambassadorial Book 1663–4, ff. 201v, 284; Treasury Inventory 1676, f. 53v

Published sources: Armoury Inventory 1884–93, part 2, book 2, no. 1540

Literature: Antiquities 1849–53, section 5, pl. 37; Artistic Treasures 1902, p. 256, pl. 110, nos. 9–10; Jones 1909, p. 52, pl. 26, no. 2; Goldberg 1954, p. 501, ill. 52; Oman 1961, p. 39, pl. 28; Gifts to the Tsars 2001, no. 64, p. 243; Russia–Britain 2003, no. 122, pp. 167–8

This silver gilded flask has a high smooth neck, an oval bowl and chains. The oval bowl is adorned with high-relief chased leaves and flowers, amid which we see a unicorn and a boar with a piglet. On the sides are mascarons (grotesque faces or masks) with rings linked by a massive chain. The smooth lid has a ring from which hangs a small chain supporting the large chain. On the bottom is a note of the weight and an engraved inscription recording that the silver gilded flask with a weight of 10 pounds 60 *zolotniki* (over 9½ modern lbs; 4.4 kg) at 8½ rubles per pound was a gift to the sovereign from the English King on 11 February 1664.

N.A.

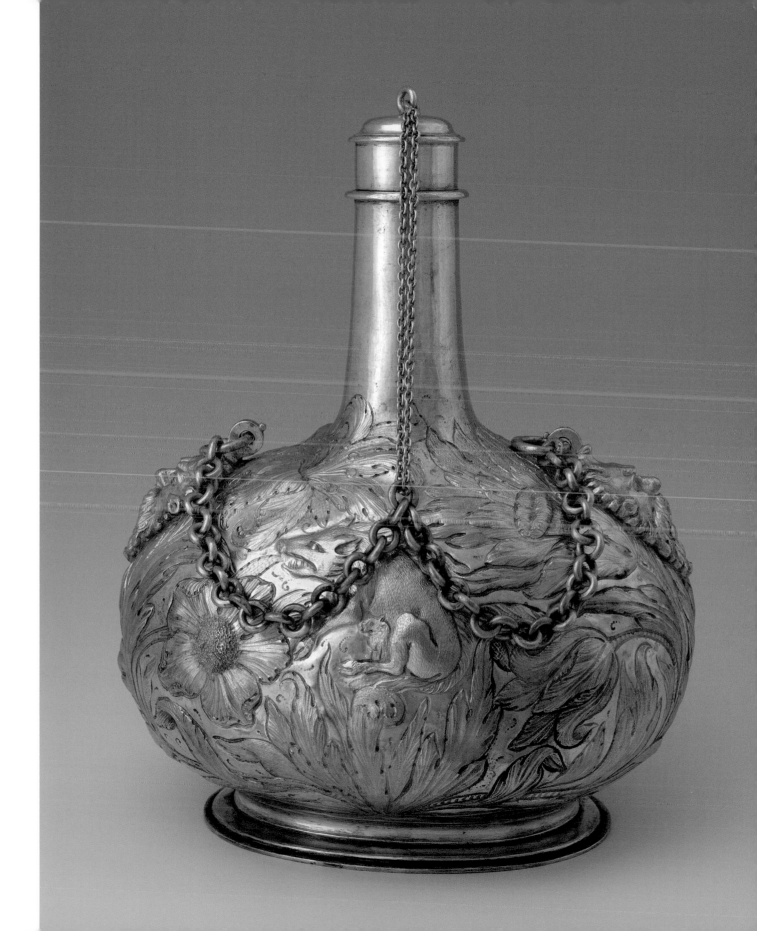

34

Livery pot

London, 1663

Presented by Charles II, via the embassy of Charles Howard, Earl of Carlisle, to Tsar Alexey Mikhaylovich in 1664

Maker Henry Greenway (fl. 1648–65)

Silver; cast, chased, gilded

Height 15¾ in. (40 cm); weight 169¼ oz (4,835 g)

Marks: city, assay, year (Jackson 1989, p. 52), maker – Henry Greenway (Jackson 1989, p. 121)

Provenance: historic collection of the Armoury

Moscow Kremlin Museums inv. no. MZ–660

MS sources: Ambassadorial Book 1663–4, ff. 201v, 283v

Published sources: Armoury Inventory 1884–93, part 2, book 2, no. 1679

Literature: Jones 1909, p. 52, pl. 26, no. 2; Goldberg 1954, p. 499; Oman 1961, p. 39, pl. 27; Russia–Britain 2003, no. 123, pp. 168–9

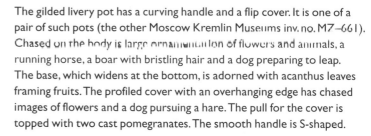

The gilded livery pot has a curving handle and a flip cover. It is one of a pair of such pots (the other Moscow Kremlin Museums inv. no. MZ–661). Chased on the body is large ornamentation of flowers and animals, a running horse, a boar with bristling hair and a dog preparing to leap. The base, which widens at the bottom, is adorned with acanthus leaves framing fruits. The profiled cover with an overhanging edge has chased images of flowers and a dog pursuing a hare. The pull for the cover is topped with two cast pomegranates. The smooth handle is S-shaped.

On the bottom an engraved inscription records that the livery pot belonged to the Tsar's treasury. It indicates that the pot weighs 11 pounds (nearly 10 modern lbs; 4.5 kg) valued at 8½ rubles per pound and was sent to the sovereign by the English King on 11 February 1664.

N.A.

French Silver
Brought by the Earl of Carlisle

35–6

Basin and ewer

Paris, 1624

Presented by Charles II, via the embassy of Charles Howard, Earl of Carlisle, to Tsar Alexey Mikhaylovich in 1664

MS sources: Ambassadorial Book, 1663–4, ff. 201v, 283v

Published sources: Armoury Inventory 1884–93, part 2, book 2, nos. 1217, 1467, pl. 255

Literature: Veltman 1844, ill. 255; Armoury 1958, ill. 355; Smirnova 1964, p. 249; Seizième siècle en Europe 1965–6, pp. 90–1, ill. 117; URSS 1974, no. 524; Hernmarck 1977, vol. 1, p. 244; vol. 2, pl. 661; Rashkovan 1988, pp. 290–2, ills. 203–4; Versailles 1993–4, p. 37; Applied Art of France 1995, pp. 34–5, nos. 21–2; Markova 1996, pp. 44–5, ills. 39–40; Gifts to the Tsars 2001, pp. 246–9, no. 66a,b; Temps d'exubérance 2002, pp. 256–8, no. 146a,b

Basin

Maker Antoinette Marqueron

Silver; cast, chased, gilded

Diameter 29½ in. (75 cm); weight 355½ oz (10,156.7 g)

Marks: Paris year (Bimbenet-Privat and de Fontaines 1995, no. 119), maker – Antoinette Marqueron

Moscow Kremlin Museums inv. no. MZ–1780

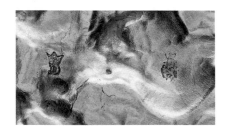

Ewer

Maker René Cousturier

Silver; cast, chased, gilded

Height 17¾ in. (45 cm); weight 154¼ oz (4,408 g)

Marks: Paris year (Bimbenet-Privat and de Fontaines 1995, no. 119), maker – René Cousturier

Moscow Kremlin Museums inv. no. MZ–1781

This unique ewer and basin represent some of the best work of French silversmiths of the first quarter of the seventeenth century. Each was the work of a different master, although they were intended as a single set. According to research by Michèle Bimbenet-Privat in the National Archives in Paris, they formed part of the trousseau of Princess Henrietta Maria of France and were taken to England when she married Charles I in 1625. They remained in the Jewel House until 1664 when they were sent to the Russian Tsar as a gift from Charles II.

Russian documents record that the royal gifts brought to Russia by the Earl of Carlisle included a basin weighing 25 pounds (over 22½ modern lbs; 10.3 kg) and a jug weighing 10 pounds 78 *zolotniki* (over 9¾ modern lbs; 4.4 kg). Both were passed to the treasury where they were valued at 8½ rubles per pound, around 300 rubles for the two together (Ambassadorial Book 1663–4; first published by Irina Zagorodnaya of Moscow Kremlin Museums in Gifts to the Tsars 2001, pp. 246–9).

The heavy cast basin, completely gilded, was intended for decorative purposes and not for actual use. In the centre, framed by a garland, is a high-relief chased composition with numerous figures, the subject of which has been variously interpreted. Some have suggested that it comes from Torquato Tasso's 1581 narrative poem *Jerusalem Delivered* (Applied Art of France 1995, p. 34). A similar composition is found in *View of the Crusaders' Camp Beneath the Walls of Jerusalem*, a painting by the Flemish artist Ambroise Dubois (1543–1614/15) produced for the Cabinet de la Reine at Fontainebleau (inv. no. 84 B). Bimbenet-Privat interprets it as a scene from Ovid's *Metamorphoses* relating the story of Scylla, daughter of Nisus (Temps d'exubérance 2002, p. 256). The broad rim is adorned with alternating herms and large convex smooth *ovae* and eighteen grotesque masks in a manner influenced by the auricular style, against a matt pounced ground. The lobed edge has a narrow border of small convex *ovae* which serve to emphasize the overall decorative effect.

In form the ewer is close to classical models of the kind seen in Italian Renaissance ornamental prints by such masters as Agostino de Musi (c.1490–c.1536) and Enea Vico (1523–67). The ewer's body has eight facets on each of which stands a dancing Muse with a different musical instrument. Symbols of universal harmony – in turn the basis for a harmonious married life – the Muses were very fitting on a ewer produced for the royal trousseau. The figures of the Muses are framed with bands of *Knorpelwerk* with rams' heads above the edges of the facets; on the neck are abstract masks. Various elements of the highly plastic auricular style are used in different ways to decorate the ewer.

On the reverse of the basin and on the bottom of the ewer are engraved inscriptions with numbers, weight, date and value set out in letters, as well as information regarding how the objects arrived in the royal treasury.

N.A.

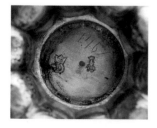

2

English Firearms in Moscow

The whole consisted in Vessels of gold and silver, in cloth, velvets, satins, and damaske of divers colours; there was also great quantities of stufs, and table linnen, two gold-watches, three clocks, two pair of Pistols, one gun, and two carabins, besides six pieces of cast Canon, a great quantity of Cornish tynne, and a hundred piggs of lead. All of which was sent before to the palace ...

—A Relation of the Three Embassies from His Sacred Majestie Charles II to the Great Duke of Muscovie ... Performed by the Right Honorable the Earle of Carlisle in the Years 1663 & 1664 (London, 1669)

Seventeenth-Century English Firearms in the Kremlin

Elena Yablonskaya

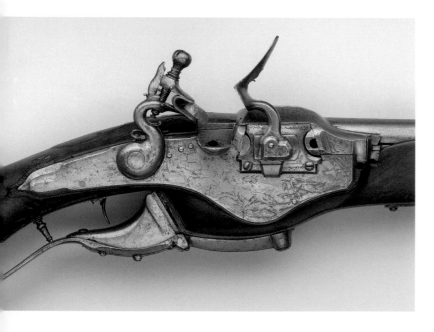

35. Cat. 50, detail

English seventeenth-century weapons occupy a considerable place within the Armoury of the Moscow Kremlin Museums. The English weaponry consists entirely of firearms, with the sole exception of one early crossbow. Among these firearms, however, are works by outstanding gunsmiths – Thomas Southwick, Henry Burrows, William Martindall, Thomas I. Saunders and others – as well as works by craftsmen who came from continental Europe to work in England and gained fame there: Warner Pin, Caspar Kalthoff and Haerman Barnevelt (Harman Barne). Such migration of masters among leading European armoury centres was not unusual in the seventeenth century.

The collection of arms reflects the general picture of relations between Russia and England during this period. The main body of English seventeenth-century firearms, some thirty-two items, is from the first quarter of the seventeenth century, the period of closest Anglo-Russian contacts. Only a few items date from the second half of the century when English weapons (with the exception – albeit an important one – of the gifts brought by the Earl of Carlisle's embassy of 1663–4) ceased to arrive in Russia via diplomatic channels. By no means all seventeenth-century English firing technologies are represented in the Armoury. As one might expect, a royal treasury contained mostly rare works of parade, presentation and hunting weaponry, pieces intended to illustrate the high level, both technical and artistic, achieved by English gunsmiths throughout the seventeenth century.

Economic contacts between Russia and England were closely linked to military interests. Goods vital to the English fleet and army – rope, wax, tar, hemp, saltpetre – played a major role in determining the structure of Anglo-Russian trade in the late sixteenth and early seventeenth centuries, as did those essential to Russia – brimstone, lead, tin and weapons, including parts and ammunition. From the second half of the sixteenth century, regular visits were made to Moscow both by royal ambassadors and by agents of the Muscovy Company, which had been established in London in the wake of the English discovery of a northern sea route to Russia. Firearms were always appreciated as gifts, and the repertoire of objects presented to the Tsar, his family and courtiers frequently included richly adorned weaponry. English presentation guns were certainly to be found in the armouries of Ivan IV, Fyodor Ivanovich and Boris Godunov. An inventory compiled in 1589 of the 'Attire, weapons, military armour and equestrian items of Tsar Boris Godunov' mentions an English heavy spear and ten 'English helmets inlaid with gold leaf on alternate facets'.[1]

Weaponry continued to appear among gifts brought by the English. An embassy to Moscow in 1604 was led by the head of the East India Company, Sir Thomas Smith. No Ambassadorial Books for 1604 survive, but documents relating to the work of the Ambassadorial Office, the Russian government body responsible for receiving foreign diplomats, record that the gifts presented to Tsarevich Fyodor Borisovich by the ambassador included 'two short self-shooters'.[2] The notice confirms the original English list of gifts, which records that Smith's personal presents to the Tsarevich included 'One case of pistolles'.[3] Unfortunately the documents provide no further description of the items, and so it has not proved possible to identify them among the many objects that survive today.

We know of one instance when weapons were presented to a Russian ambassador in England. Fyodor Andreevich Pisemsky was sent to London in 1582. Pisemsky performed all the tasks set by his sovereign and was well received by Queen Elizabeth. Among other magnificent sights, he was shown naval ships and the firing of ships' cannon; when he visited the celebrated Arsenal at Greenwich, Pisemsky received a gift of weapons. All this was described in his report: 'they went into the Armoury and the Queen's adviser Christopher Hatton presented Fyodor [Pisemsky] with a short self-shooter, and a sword, and Neudach [d'yak or secretary of the Ambassadorial Office, who was accompanying Pisemsky] with a short self-shooter; and said "As the Queen's Armoury stores are under my command, I make present of weapons from it".'[4]

During the Time of Troubles – the time of uncertainty and civil war between the death of Boris Godunov in 1605 and the establishment of a new ruling dynasty, the Romanovs, in 1613 – the Kremlin treasuries, including the Armoury, were robbed. At the same time, there was a break in Anglo-Russian relations. After Mikhail Fyodorovich Romanov was elected to the throne in 1613, however, once more centralizing all power, English diplomats and merchants travelled to Russia once more. They came requesting that the new ruler – known for his sympathy to the English – reaffirm those privileges they had enjoyed formerly.[5] The gifts they brought with them thus served not only a ceremonial purpose, but as a means of reminding the Tsar of their requests. The presentation of gifts was quite frequently accompanied by the presentation of petitions.

So it was that in December 1613, Fabian Smith, head of the Muscovy Company and known in Russian sources as Fabian (Fabin) Ulyanov, was received by Tsar Mikhail Fyodorovich. The Book of Receipts for 1613 contains the following entry:

> English merchant Fabin Ulyanov presented … a gilded silver cup, a basin and ewer, a piece of cloth … and a long gun, its barrel and lock and … [trigger guard] inlaid with gold and silver, the stock of pear wood, encrusted in it shells and ivory, copper set between them … the value of the gun withal thirty rubles; pair of short English pistols, the barrels and locks inlaid with gold, the stocks of apple wood with shells set into them; in an iron cage a parrot …[6]

These precious gifts were probably an offering of thanks for permits to trade on Russian territory granted in that year to Smith and nineteen other members of the Muscovy Company. A decade later, in 1625, Fabian Smith again made a gift to Mikhail Fyodorovich, to mark the young Tsar's marriage. Among the precious objects of gilded silver were two richly decorated Dutch muskets (cats. 47–8).[7]

By the end of the first quarter of the seventeenth century, the affairs of the Muscovy Company were in decline. The company was permitted to fit out no more than two ships in Russia each year, and there was a sharp reduction in the number of English merchants conducting trading operations in Russia.[8] From 1649, trading and economic relations between England and the Russian state were severed: on 1 June of that year, after news was received of the execution of Charles I, the order was given to expel the English from the inner reaches of the land.

It was fifteen years later, after the restoration of the Stuarts, that a representative of the new monarch, Charles II, arrived in Russia on a 'great' embassy. Among the numerous gifts brought by the ambassador, Charles Howard, Earl of Carlisle, were a gun that had once belonged to the executed Charles I and a pair of Charles II's own pistols. It is noteworthy that the first object to be carried and presented to Tsar Alexey Mikhaylovich was the gun. In his speech, Carlisle emphasized its commemorative significance: 'This Gun was delivered to me by his Majesties own hand, being excellent in its kind, the same which his Royal Father of blessed and glorious memorie used to shoot in, and which as a Relique of that renowned Prince he thought could not be better dedicated than to the hands of Your Imperial Majestie.' Then came the pistols: 'That pair of Pistolets (saith he) his majestie delivered me also with his own hand, commanding me to excuse their oldness, which he thought would not make them less acceptable, when You knew they were those, with which after so long adversity, He rid in His triumphant Entry into His Metropolitan City of London.'[9]

Russian documents describe the English ambassador's visit in detail. They give a list of all the gifts Carlisle brought,[10] but there is no precise description of the arms, and of the pistols it is said only that they had ivory butts. At the end of the list of gifts to Tsar Alexey Mikhaylovich we also find '100 poods of lead; 6 copper cannon', both clearly intended to hint that the new British monarch was prepared to aid Russia in her military affairs. Gifts to the heir to the throne, Tsarevich Fyodor Alexeevich, also included arms: a gun and a pair of pistols.[11] The weapons brought by the embassy are mentioned in a parchment roll in the Armoury archives, dated 12 February 1664:

> In this year 172 [1664] February on the 11th day the ambassador of the English King Carlus, Charles Howard, was at the reception in the Tsar's Court with the Great Sovereign … Tsar Alexey Mikhaylovich, and he presented as gifts from His Royal Majesty to the Great Sovereign a commemorative hand-held harquebus – fifteen rubles, a pair of bone-stocked pistols – twenty rubles, to the True-believer Sovereign Tsarevich and Grand Duke Alexey Alexeevich … a hand-held rifled harquebus – valued at twenty rubles, a pair of double-barrelled pistols – twenty rubles; to the True-believer Sovereign Tsarevich and Grand Duke Fyodor Alexeevich … a hand-held zatinnaya harquebus – twenty rubles.[12]

In the Armoury and Royal Treasury Inventory Book for 1686–7, two multi-shot magazine guns, then known as 'fast-shooters', are linked to the gifts from Carlisle's embassy.[13] Only one of these has been identified today, a gun of 1658 (cat. 50; fig. 35) which bears the engraved name of Charles II's court gunsmith, Caspar Kalthoff. To judge by the information provided in the 1686–7 inventory, this gun was one of those presented to Fyodor Alexeevich. Also in the Armoury is a multi-shot rifle made in London by another royal gunsmith, Harman Barne (cat. 51). Despite the lack of documentary evidence, it seems likely that this too arrived among the gifts of Carlisle's embassy.

English seventeenth-century guns made their appearance in the Tsar's Armoury not only via English merchants and agents, but also as gifts from the Russian nobility to members of the Tsar's family. The inventory for 1686–7 also provides the information that one pair of English pistols was presented to Tsar Mikhail Fyodorovich by the *d'yak* or secretary Zhdan Shipov (cats. 42–3). No date is given for the gift and we can only presume that these handsome foreign weapons were a mark of thanks from Shipov in 1613, when he was elevated to the prestigious rank of *d'yak*.

Design and decoration

Undoubtedly the most magnificent of the surviving firearms in the Armoury is a pair of presentation pistols of 1600–20 (cats. 37–8). Like the Armoury's other English firearms of the early seventeenth century, they are fitted with snaphaunce locks. Nearly all locks of this type and date on English arms had a safety catch mounted on the sideplate to prevent accidental shot. One notable feature of early versions of this English lock was that the safety had an external spring. The collection also has a pistol from the 1640s (cat. 49) with an English lock, a type which appeared in the early seventeenth century and became widespread during the following decades in England, where it may have been invented. This construction formed a transition from the Anglo-Dutch type to the French flintlock.

English rifles and pistols in the Armoury can be recognized by the design and finish of their barrels. English barrels, for instance, tended to have a specific bell-shaped muzzle (cat. 39; fig. 36), while the stocks of early English weapons had transverse bands and narrow raised bands with the sight notch at the breech end of the barrel. Sometimes a back-sight slit was cut into this ring, or even a large V-shaped sight. It is also important to note that the fore-end on early English pieces does not continue to the end of the muzzle. Most of the pistols in the Armoury collection were intended to be worn on a belt. They would have been attached by a long belt-hook mounted on the opposite side to the lock.

Gunsmiths used a variety of devices to adorn the metal details of weapons – the barrel, lock, trigger-guard, belt hook and barrel bands. Frequent use was made of a method popular in England in which the surface was encrusted with gold, a technique known as 'damascened gold' and often described as 'false' damascening. In some cases, an even more complex technique of relief carving against a pounced ground was used, the relief then being gilded. This technique was used in the making of the pair of presentation pistols of around 1600–20 (cats. 37–8).

Ornamental compositions on English arms from this period consist of arabesques or stylized foliage and flowers with three, four or five petals. Some barrels are decorated with 'candelabra' ornaments made up of stylized tendrils, vases, baldachins, masks, grotesque half-figures, griffons or two-headed eagles (cats. 37–40). The hunting scenes that were so common in English applied and decorative art occur in embroidery, on silver – and on weapons of all kinds.

36. Cat. 39, detail

One element of interest in the decoration of English arms during the first decades of the seventeenth century is the full-length figures that appear in oval medallions on the barrels of the guns. One pair of pistols in the Armoury is ornamented with medallions containing gilded figures (cat. 44; fig. 37). Such methods of adorning the barrel reflect the influence of the German firearms tradition. The sources were sixteenth-century German and Dutch prints. As in continental Europe, prints showing standard-bearers, drummers, pikemen, musketeers, officers and soldiers enjoyed great popularity in England over the course of many years.[14] Such subjects were engraved by many different artists, including the Dutchmen Hendrik Goltzius (1558–1617) and his student Jacques de Gheyn (1565–1629) whose *Exercise of Armes* was published in The Hague and Amsterdam in 1607 and in England the following year (fig. 38). Such prints were highly influential and it is well known that many anonymous European masters produced prints 'after Goltzius'.[15]

37. Cat. 44, detail

38. Page from Jacob de Gheyn's *The Exercise of Armes ...* , Amsterdam 1607. Beinecke Rare Book and Manuscript Library, Yale University

Among other possible artistic models for decorators of the barrels of English pistols may have been thirty plates showing the funeral procession of Sir Philip Sidney that were well known in England. The engravings were commissioned in 1586 from one of the best European artists of the age, the Flemish Theodore de Bry (1528–98), who was invited to London for the purpose. He depicted the thousands of participants in the procession, and the long scroll has engraved a vast number of tiny figures dressed in contemporary costume. The figures include young people marching three in a row bearing weapons, infantry and cavalry officers, honorary citizens of London and many others (fig. 39).[16]

39. Theodore de Bry, 'Muskaters, drumes and ffyfe', from Thomas Lant, *Funeral of Sir Phillip Sidney*, plate 25, London 1588. Christ Church Picture Gallery, Oxford

The decoration of wooden stocks and pistol handles developed under the influence of continental schools and cannot therefore be said to reflect any clearly expressed national character. Wooden details on English guns – like those on contemporary European guns – are richly adorned with bone inlay, frequently with guilloche ornament, little engraved plaques or mother-of-pearl shaped into stylized flowers or fruits, circles or more fancifully shaped insets. They might show birds or butterflies, serpent-like monsters, snails, and other real or fantastical beasts. Such images featured widely in the applied arts of Flanders, the influence of which on the decoration of English firearms was considerable, as was the influence of art from northern France and the Netherlands.[17] Rifle stocks frequently had as well an encrustation of silver or brass wire. Used to lay out winding tendrils, little stars and petals, the wire provided a rich ground for the mother-of-pearl insets. Several items in the Armoury collection serve as illustrations of the form given to rifle stocks during the earlier period: the stock of one carbine, for instance, has a flat, so-called musket butt with a thumb rest cut in the comb of the stock (cat. 46).

Undoubtedly, however, the collection of pistols provides a fuller picture of English seventeenth-century firearms, their decoration and variety of handle forms. Pistols appeared relatively early in England. They are mentioned as early as the 1547 inventory of the Arsenal of Henry VIII, where they are called 'dags' or 'tackes', terms which indicated wheel-lock pistols.[18] Despite a number of royal bans on the wearing and use of pistols, they became widespread during the second half of the sixteenth century; by

1600, and in the decades that followed, pistols with Anglo-Dutch snaphaunce locks were being produced in England for all kinds of purposes.

Pistol stocks in the first decades of the seventeenth century show a notable French influence. Handles were turned at a slight angle towards the fore-end rather than being almost straight, as was characteristic of German wheel-lock pistols of the late sixteenth century. The stock ended in a pommel in the form of an elongated apple with convex or spiral convex facets (cats. 37–8), sometimes with a flat surface, sometimes rounded. A number of pistols (cats. 42–3) have small cushions of velvet or thick silk attached to the handle by the lock plate, intended to protect the hand during firing (fig. 40). A rare English long-barrelled pistol was intended for use by cuirassiers or cavalry soldiers (cat. 41).

Firearm production in England and Russia

By the end of the sixteenth century, the production of guns took place not only in the armouries of the Tower of London but also in East Smithfield Minories.[19] Gunsmiths belonged to two guilds: the armourers and the blacksmiths. Even during this early period masters specialized in narrow fields of activity: there were barrel-smiths and lock-makers, stock-cavers and decorators who adorned their works with gold inlay, engraving and encrustation. Later the gunsmiths involved in the making of firearms formed the Gunmakers Company and in 1638 received a royal charter for the control of gun production. This company brought together only those masters living in London who were involved in making the metal details for and assembling firearms. Initially there were more than 120 members. Each year, on the first Thursday after the Feast of St Bartholomew on 24 August, they elected a new Master, two Wardens and the so-called Court of Assistants of ten members.[20]

The quality of products was checked through the use of control and city marks and the personal marks that craftsmen put on their works. According to the company's regulations, all firearms made, imported or sold in London itself and within a radius of ten miles (16 km) had to undergo control. At the company's assay stations, control marks were placed on weapons (the letter 'V' beneath a crown and 'P' beneath a crown) as evidence of the item's quality. As a rule the members of the Gunmakers Company had their own workshops where they produced commissions for both private clients and the state, including military orders for the Royal Ordnance.

During the first decades of the seventeenth century, English firearms in the 'Great State Armoury Treasury' often served as models for imitation by masters in the Armoury workshops. Among the descriptions of rifles and pistols by Armoury masters in archive documents we find records that certain Muscovy rifles or pistols had been executed 'to the English fashion' or that they had 'locks to the English fashion gilded and silvered'. Indeed, visible confirmation of such copying and imitation is found in the collection today: several works by Russian masters in Moscow were clearly produced under the influence of English models (cats. 52–5).

40. Cat. 42, detail

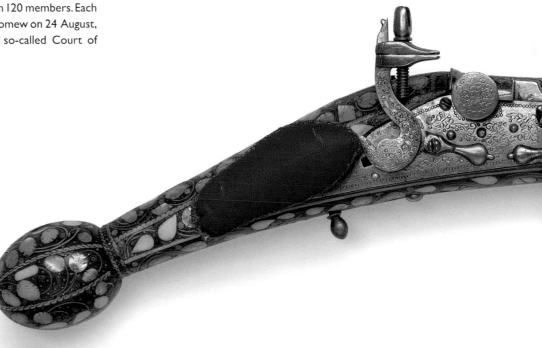

There is a type of flintlock known in Russian sources as *Aglinskaya* (English) or *Shkotskaya* (Scottish). Both the design and decorative finish of the flintlock's stocks and handles were clearly influenced by English firearms. As a rule those Russian masters who imitated the English model tended to use typical Russian ornament and subjects when decorating the weapon's metal parts. Such is the case, for instance, with a pair of pistols by Pervusha Isaev (cats. 52–3; fig. 41) and the hunting harquebus by Timofey Luchaninov (cat. 54). But there were also instances when a direct copy was produced, as is recorded in the Armoury and Royal Treasury Inventory Book for 1686–7: 'Pair of pistols, one smooth, made by Ivan Luchaninov, the other English, inlaid with gold along the barrel, locks carved English, one was gilded, stocks of beech with shells and with ivories … stocks with apples [apple-shaped pommels] … value four rubles'. The document suggests that one pistol was English, the other made to match it by Ivan Luchaninov, a master at the Armoury workshops.[21]

The practice of inviting professionals from outside to work in Russia was known from the end of the fifteenth century, and foreign craftsmen were to be found working in sixteenth- and seventeenth-century Moscow. That these included gunsmiths we know from an angry letter sent to Elizabeth I by the Polish King Sigismund II in 1568:

> We see that Muscovy, not merely a current enemy of our kingdom but also the age-old enemy of all free peoples, thanks solely to the recently established navigation, is abundantly supplied not only with weapons and ammunition … but we see that it is supplied also with important goods in no way a hindrance to it in its actions and even useful unto it, that it is supplied with artists, who unceasingly produce for it arms, ammunition and other similar things previously unseen and unknown in that barbarian land …[22]

From the first years of Mikhail Fyodorovich's reign the Russian government was interested in attracting foreigners not only to serve in the military but also to meet other state needs, among them all kinds of production (fig. 42). Envoys, messengers, resident representatives, commissars and foreign merchants were requested to engage masters to serve the Russian state. Detailed conditions were set for the selection of such servants: specialists were invited for a set period or for permanent residence, with those who agreed to come for a set period giving firm assurances that they would not linger after performance of all the necessary work (although they did not always keep their word). After the Time of Troubles the English were among those arriving to join the Russian service.

41. Cat. 52, detail

42. Johann Jacobi von Wallhausen, *Uchenie i khitrost' ratnago stroeniya pekhotnykh lyudey* (A Manual of Arms for Pikemen and Infantry), Moscow, 1647. Slavic and Baltic Division, The New York Public Library, Astor, Lenox and Tilden Foundations

Foreigners with specific skills and abilities might originally be taken on for military service and then, when they were no longer required, offer themselves to the Muscovite state as craftsmen. A good example of this is the Scotsman William Games (James), who spent many years in the extremely important post of 'viewer' at the Armoury. The archives contain many surviving petitions from Games in which he describes himself as an 'ensign of the making and patterning of arms'. The duties of the viewer included keeping a careful eye on the receipt and allocation of weapons to regiments as well as the stowing and storage of arms purchased abroad or made in Russia. The post was established in 1633.

Games worked as Viewer of Arms at the Armoury for nearly twenty years, between 1644 and 1662.[23] In 1663, after his death, his place was taken by his son William Vilimovich ('William, the son of William'), 'ensign of the cavalry service' who remained in the post until 1676. We know that in 1665 Games the Younger lived at the house of the port master David Artemyev in the *Novo-nemetskaya sloboda* or 'new foreigners' settlement'. Everything we know about the father and son, and indeed about many of the other foreigners who worked in the Armoury, derives from archive documents, where they are described simply as *nemtsy* (literally 'Germans', the word used to indicate all foreigners) or *inozemtsy* (people of other lands). Only in rare cases do we find their names written not in Cyrillic but using the Western alphabet, or a mention of the land from which they came. We can usually, therefore, only guess at the craftsmen's origins. Gunsmith 'Filipp Timofeev Ulyanov', for instance, might well have been English, since the master's full name as it appears on his works is given as 'Filipp son of Timofey Ulyanov', the English name William being frequently converted to 'Ulyanov' in Russian in the seventeenth century. The gunsmith's name might therefore have been Philip Williams, son of Timothy Williams.

We do know that Filipp Ulyanov was a notable figure among the foreign craftsmen working in Moscow in the last third of the seventeenth century. For many years he played a leading role among the workers, being a member of the council to assess the results of training and taking part in resolving administrative matters. In his decorative works Ulyanov followed the Russian tradition, using the gold inlay characteristically applied by the Muscovite school of armoury during the last third of the seventeenth century, a technique used by English gunsmiths throughout the century.

Another well-known European gunsmith who worked in Moscow was Caspar Kalthoff the Younger. The Kremlin owns his rifle of 1665 (cat. 55) which bears an inscription indicating that it was made in Moscow. According to Blackmore's *Dictionary of London Gunmakers*, he was the son of Caspar Kalthoff and worked from 1645 to 1658 in Holland and Dordrecht, and from 1661 with his father in London. Blackmore suggests that Kalthoff the Younger had arrived in Russia to work at the court of Tsar Alexey Mikhaylovich from 1664 to 1665.[24] No mention is found of Kalthoff among documents relating to the arrival of foreigners in Russia; it is therefore difficult to say exactly when he arrived, but it was surely not before 1661. If his first impressions of Muscovy were anything like those of the Scottish officer Patrick Gordon, then he would have been thinking only of how soon he

could leave the country. But departure was not as easy as one might have hoped, and was almost impossible without permission and a pass.

Kalthoff features prominently towards the end of Guy de Miège's description of the embassy of the Earl of Carlisle in 1664. He is described as having been forced to remain in Moscow despite the request of King Charles II that he be released and despite letters of intervention from Carlisle. Patrick Gordon's diary contains interesting evidence to suggest that the master was still in Russia in 1667. In that year, Gordon had an audience with Charles II on the eve of his return to Russia and the monarch entrusted him with the task of requesting that the Russian Tsar permit the gunsmith to return to England. Gordon recorded the King's verbal request in his diary.[25] Kalthoff's fate is not clear, but his name appears again in a letter sent by Charles to the Russian Tsar in February 1671 with the envoy George Holmes:

> …we have been told that there is another of our servants, by name Caspar Kalthoff, in the service of your Imperial Majesty, with regard to which we feel it right to ask Your Imperial Majesty, and that your Imperial Majesty allow him his freedom. That he might return to our Kingdom of Great Britain, where it is most needful to us that he resume his service as he did promise us … (your most loving brother Charles the King).[26]

In March 1671 Alexey Mikhaylovich sent a response via a courier, Ivan Khomonov, in which he firmly and unambiguously made clear his unwillingness to release Kalthoff to England: 'we do most lovingly inform you that your Kapert Kaltov now in the service of our great sovereign Imperial Majesty is in receipt of a generous payment and it is now impossible to release him to your Royal Majesty, but when the time shall come then Kashper Kaltov shall receive his release from our Imperial Majesty together with generous payment.'[27]

Kalthoff the Younger was never a salaried master at the Armoury and his name does not appear in the archive documents of the Armoury Office, and therefore almost nothing is known of the gunsmith's life and work in Moscow, or his further fate.

Notes

1 P. I. Savvaitov, *Opisanie starinnykh tsarskikh utvarey, odezhd, oruzhiya, ratnykh dospekhov i konskogo pribora* ['Description of Antique Imperial Utensils, Clothes, Weapons, Fighting Armour and Horse Caparison'] (St Petersburg, 1865), pp. 32, 35.

2 Russian State Archive of Ancient Acts, Moscow, fund 35, *opis'* 1, *delo* 3, ff. 141–5, *Priezd posla Fomy Shmidta* 1604 ['The Arrival of Ambassador Thomas Smith 1604'].

3 A. Maskell, *Russian Art and Art Objects in Russia* (London, 1884), p. 231.

4 Ambassadors' Travels 1954, p. 124.

5 Dyomkin 1994, issue 1, p. 44.

6 Book of Receipts 1613–14, ff. 36–7.

7 Book of Receipts and Allocations 1625, f. 34.

8 Dyomkin 1994, issue 1, p. 43.

9 Carlisle 1669, p. 182.

10 Ambassadorial Book 1663–4, ff. 22–5.

11 Ambassadorial Book 1663–4, f. 25.

12 Gifts Presented to the Tsar 1664, ff. 1–2.

13 Armoury and Royal Treasury Inventory Book 1686–7, f. 223.

14 A. Bartsch *et al.*, *The Illustrated Bartsch*, vol. 3: Hendrik Goltzius (New York, 1980), pp. 123–5, 187–90.

15 Bartsch, vol. 3, pp. 350–2, 381–91.

16 S. Colvin, *Early Engraving and Engravers in England, 1545–1645* (London, 1905), pp. 38–9.

17 Hayward 1960, p. 126.

18 Blackmore 1990, p. 5.

19 H. L. Blackmore, *English Pistols* (London, 1985), p. 5.

20 Blackmore 1986, p. 15.

21 Armoury and Royal Treasury Inventory Book 1686–7, f. 422.

22 Cited in Gamel 1865–9, p. 83.

23 Russian State Archive of Ancient Acts, Moscow, fund 396, *dela* 4141, 4929, 5091, 7944, 8224, 8755.

24 Blackmore 1986, p. 125.

25 Gordon 2002, p. 192.

26 'Gramota angliyskogo korolya Karla II tsaryu Alekseyu Mikhaylovichu, 1671 g.' ['Letter from the English King Charles II to Tsar Alexey Mikhaylovich, 1671'], Eighteenth-century translation from the English, Russian State Archive of Ancient Acts, Moscow, fund 35, *opis'* 2, *delo* 103, f. 2.

27 Russian State Archive of Ancient Acts, Moscow, fund 35, *opis'* 2, *delo* 103.

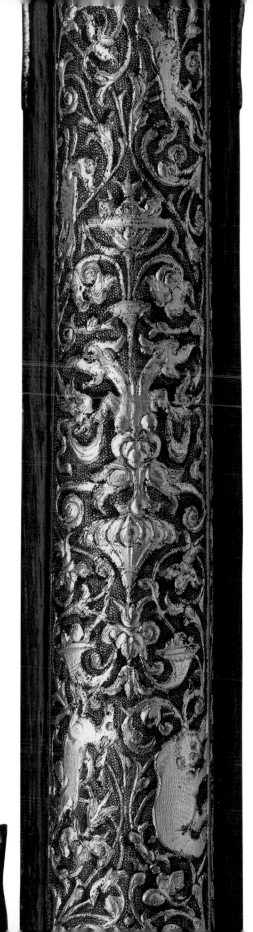

43. Cat. 37, detail (overleaf)

English Guns

37–8

Pair of belt pistols

London, 1600s–1610s

Barrel: Thomas Southwick (?)

Barrel and lock decorated by Stephen Russell (?)

Steel, wood, mother-of-pearl; wrought, carved,
gold damascening, engraved, encrusted, gilded

Overall length 28⅜ in. (72 cm);
length of barrel 18⅞ in. (47.8 cm);
calibre 0.5 in. (13 mm)

Marks: Barrel – heraldic lily and TS in a shield
(Blackmore 1999, p. 106)

Provenance: historic collection of the Armoury

Moscow Kremlin Museums inv. nos. OR–2800, OR–2801

MS sources: Armoury and Royal Treasury Inventory Book
1686–7, f. 399

Published sources: Armoury Inventory 1884–93, part 5,
book 4, no. 8243

Literature: Sobolev and Ermolov 1954, pp. 425–6; Eaves
1976, p. 284; Treasures 1998, no. 56; Yablonskaya 1999,
p. 50; Sovereign's Armoury 2002, no. 89; Russia–Britain
2003, nos. 149–50

The construction and decoration of these pistols are typical of English firearms of the late sixteenth and early seventeenth centuries. The barrels, whose breeches have five facets, have the bell-shaped muzzle typical of English arms. The surfaces of the barrels are adorned with gilded relief foliage on a dark pounced ground. On the sides are hunting dogs pursuing and attacking wild beasts. The upper facet of the barrels incorporates grotesque Mannerist figures, tents and vases. At the breech end of the barrel is a projecting band with a back-sight slit, a typical feature of English weapons of the time.

The pistols have Anglo-Dutch snaphaunce locks and the lock-plates are adorned with very fine arabesques damascened with gold. The safety mechanisms are mounted on the side of the butt opposite the locks, along with hooks for attaching the pistols to a belt. The walnut handles end in slightly elongated apple pommels with concave facets. Set into the handle are engraved mother-of-pearl plaques in the form of birds, butterflies, snake-like monsters, snails, stylized leaves and flowers – images characteristic of western European applied arts in the sixteenth and seventeenth centuries. As on *mille-fleurs* tapestries, the background is composed of elegant leaves on fine stems, here made of flattened silver wire. The contours of the handles are encrusted with straight mother-of-pearl bands covered with engraved woven ornament. The mounts are of iron and the barrel attachment plates are decorated with gold inlay, while the belt hooks and rectangular safety-catches are carved and gilded to match the barrel.

The mark stamped into the pistol barrels may be that of the barrel-maker Thomas Southwick, though he was unlikely to have been responsible for the carved and inlaid ornament and decorative subjects. It seems probable that this was done by Stephen Russell, gunsmith to the Prince of Wales. We know that Russell decorated a gun intended as a gift for the Danish King Christian IV in 1604, and scholars also suggest that he decorated weapons as part of a set of gifts presented to Philip III of Spain in 1608. In those works, Russell used the same rare technique of carving on a pounced ground and with gold relief, a technique that would seem to have been known to only a few skilled contemporary masters. The pistols in the Armoury are certainly of a very high level of execution (Blackmore 1999, pp. 102, 106).

Up to the end of the seventeenth century these unique examples of the gunsmith's skill remained in the sovereign's Armoury or arsenal, stored in extremely handsome holsters 'of colored velvet on a yellow ground … over the top crimson velvet with ornamental vegetation the belt of the holsters of crimson silken braid with three double silver buckles'. They were valued extremely highly at forty rubles for the pair in their holsters (Armoury and Royal Treasury Inventory Book 1686–7). While no mention is made of who might have presented such pistols to the sovereign or from whom they might have been acquired, it is clear that such luxurious objects could only have come from a wealthy person – someone such as Fabian Smith of the Muscovy Company, who certainly made a number of expensive gifts, including ceremonial arms, to Tsar Mikhail Fyodorovich in the period 1613–25.

E.Y.

39

Long-barrelled gun

London, 1600s–1610s

Possibly a gift from Fabian Smith of the Muscovy Company to Tsar Mikhail Fyodorovich in 1613

Steel, wood; engraved, gilded, damascened with gold

Overall length 68⅞ in. (175 cm);
length of barrel 51⅞ in. (131.8 cm);
calibre 0.6 in. (14.5 mm)

Marks: breech of the barrel and lock-plate – lily beneath a crown in a shield

Provenance: historic collection of the Armoury

Moscow Kremlin Museums inv. no. OR–2002

MS sources: Book of Receipts 1613, ff. 36–7; Armoury and Royal Treasury Inventory Book 1686–7, f. 222; Armoury Inventory 1835, f. 139, no. 6310

Published sources: Armoury Inventory 1884–93, part 5, book 4, no. 7478

Literature: Yablonskaya 1999, p. 52

An identical mark to the one found on this gun is stamped on the lock plate of a pair of English pistols, dated 1593, in the Habsburg Castle of Konopiště in the Czech Republic (Hayward 1960, pl. 38). It also appears on the lock-plate of an English long-barrelled gun with an Anglo-Dutch snaphaunce lock of the late sixteenth or early seventeenth century (British Royal Armouries inv. no. XII–1758). That gun also preserves its original stock, richly encrusted with engraved mother-of-pearl insets.

The barrel of the gun in the Armoury is smooth and broadens towards the muzzle. Its surface is engraved with a grotesque candelabra composition. The barrel has traces of gilding in places. In three places on the barrel are carved crosswise or vertical double bands characteristic of English barrels of this period, with luxuriant engraved acanthus leaves beside them. At the breech end of the barrel is a prominent ring but with no back-sight slit. A round foresight is attached to the muzzle. The Anglo-Dutch lock has an external safety. The lock-plate is adorned with stylized ornament using a superficial gold inlay; the ends are carved into fantastical dragon heads. The cocking-piece and steel support are also engraved.

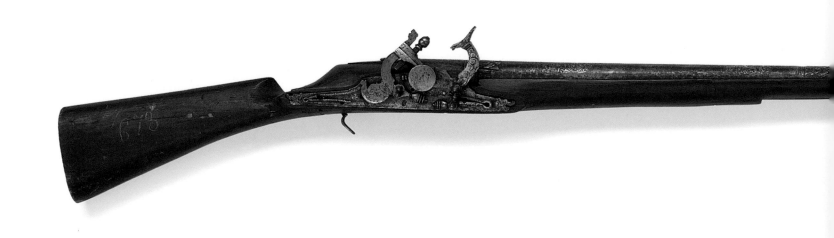

The Armoury Inventory of 1835 contains interesting information regarding the decoration on the gun. Today the barrel and lock bear only traces of gilding, but the 1835 description makes clear that the gun was both gilded and silver-gilded: 'English harquebus with six worn silver paired bands; between which along the length of the barrel chased vegetation, outlined in gold and silver, with a large English carved lock the plate of which is outlined in the middle in silver, and along the edges with a golden border, depicted on the cocking-piece are a dolphin's head and a satyr's mask. Stock of plain wood.' The birchwood stock was probably made in the Kremlin between 1808 and 1835 to replace the original worn stock.

E.Y.

40

Hunting gun

London, 1600s–20s

Gift from Fabian Smith of the Muscovy Company to Tsar Mikhail Fyodorovich

Steel, wood, ivory; carved, engraved, damascened with gold, gilded

Overall length 51⅜ in. (130.5 cm);
length of barrel 38⅜ in. (97.5 cm);
calibre 0.35 in. (9 mm)

Provenance: historic collection of the Armoury

Moscow Kremlin Museums inv. no. OR–1999

MS sources: Armoury and Royal Treasury Inventory Book 1686–7, f. 223; Armoury Inventory 1808, f. 539, no. 6061; Armoury Inventory 1835, f. 139, no. 6309

Published sources: Armoury Inventory 1884–93, part 5, book 4, no. 7474

Baskets of flowers, vases, female figures, half-figures, masks and stylized tendrils are engraved on the barrel of this hunting gun. Attached to the breech end is a projecting sight in the form of a fan with two openings of different diameter, and there is a round iron foresight on the muzzle. One third of the barrel has five facets, then a number of transverse decorative bands, after which the barrel is round, with an octagonal funnel-shaped opening to the muzzle. There is gold damascening on the muzzle between two bands of ornament.

To judge by the form of the barrel with its flaring end, typical of early English firearms, and the overall decoration and construction, the gun must have been produced in England. It can be identified with an entry in the Armoury and Royal Treasury Inventory Book of 1686–7: 'English fowling harquebus barrel gilded all chased, stock of beech with shell engraved with vegetation, ivory mount by the hinge, one piece of shell lost by the muzzle … Humbly presented to the Sovereign Tsar and Grand Duke Mikhail Fyodorovich of All Russia by the English merchant Fanbin Ulyanov'. Thus it is clear that Fabian Smith (called 'Ulyanov' in Russian documents) brought the gun to Russia and presented it to Tsar Mikhail Fyodorovich, although the date of presentation remains unknown.

The use of the term 'fowling' suggests a relatively small gun of small calibre. Today the gun in question has a new stock of birch and the whole of the surface is adorned with carved and engraved ornament; but there is not the slightest trace of gilding. An explanation for the difference is found in the Armoury Inventory for 1808, where the description of the gun is followed by a note: 'Gilding has come off in places. Beech stock very worn, adorned with insets of shell and ivory, many of which have fallen out'.

The gun's Anglo-Dutch lock has an external safety, and there are parallel lines engraved on the jaws of the cocking-piece. Traces of engraved ornament are visible on the surface of the lock-plate, and probably once matched that on the barrel. The trigger is shaped like an acorn. The stock and ramrod were produced, presumably to replace worn parts, sometime between 1808 and 1835.

E.Y.

41

Long-barrelled belt pistol

London, 1600s–10s

Steel, copper alloy, wood, ivory, mother-of-pearl;
encrustation, engraving

Overall length 31⅞ in. (81 cm);
length of barrel 24⅜ in. (61.8 cm);
calibre 0.4 in. (10 mm)

Provenance: historic collection of the Armoury

Moscow Kremlin Museums inv. no. OR–2955

MS sources: Armoury and Royal Treasury Inventory Book
1686–7, f. 422r,v

Published sources: Armoury Inventory 1884–93, part 5,
book 4, no. 8300

Literature: Russia–Britain 2003, no. 151

This is a rare example of an English long-barrelled pistol with a loop for attaching it to a belt. Such pistols were probably not worn on a belt but in holsters, since they were intended for use by cuirassiers or cavalry soldiers. A well-known engraving, published in Captain John Bingham's *The Tactiks of Aelian* (1616), shows a cuirassier in full armour with two long-barrelled pistols (Blackmore 1990, p. 5). The form of the handles with their apple pommels is identical to that of the Kremlin's pistol.

Mother-of-pearl encrustations on the handle are in the form of fruits and leaves linked by stems of brass wire, with brass leaves and stars set between them. The contours of the handle are encrusted with straight ivory bands engraved with woven ornament. One encrusted figured plaque showing a bird has survived.

The barrel has five facets along one third of its length, then a decorative band, after which it is round. There is a prominent muzzle ring as well as a projecting band by the breech end and traces of engraved ornament over the barrel surface. The safety of the Anglo-Dutch lock is fully preserved. The left end of the lock-plate is carved in the form of a dragon's head. The fence of the pan-cover is round and convex. The trigger is cone-shaped.

42–3

Pair of belt pistols

London, 1610s

Presented by Zhdan Shipov, *d'yak* (secretary) of the
Treasury Office, to Tsar Mikhail Fyodorovich in 1613 (?)

Steel, wood, copper alloy, mother-of-pearl, ivory, fabric;
carved, damascened with gold, encrusted, engraved, gilded

Overall length 22¼ in. (56.5 cm);
length of barrel 14¼ in. (36.2 cm);
calibre 0.45 in. (11 mm)

Provenance: historic collection of the Armoury

Moscow Kremlin Museums inv. nos. OR–288, OR–289

MS sources: Armoury and Royal Treasury Inventory Book
1686–7, f. 409v

Published sources: Armoury Inventory 1884–93, part 5,
book 4, no. 8297

Literature: Yablonskaya 1990, pp. 192–3; Russia–Britain 2003,
nos. 152–3

Records show that these English pistols were a gift to Tsar Mikhail
Fyodorovich from the Russian secretary of the Treasury Office. They are
described as a 'Pair of English pistols. Barrels and locks gilded and chased.
Beech stocks ending in apple pommels and with belt hooks, and with
shells, and with ivory … by the cocking-piece crimson silk braid with gold,
crimson satin pads. Presented to the Sovereign Tsar and Grand Duke
Mikhail Fyodorovich of all Russia by *d'yak* Zhdan Shipov' (Armoury and
Royal Treasury Inventory Book 1686–7).

Sadly the inventory does not indicate the date of the gift, and we can only
hypothesize that these handsome foreign weapons were presented as a
token of thanks to the Tsar in 1613, when Shipov received the prestigious
post of secretary in the most important government office.

Round barrels which flare towards the muzzle were traditional in English
guns. The surface of these barrels is adorned with stylized vegetation
and in places completely gilded. The composition includes masks and
Mannerist figures. There are Anglo-Dutch locks with external safeties
(the lock-plates ornamented to match the barrel), a sliding pan-cover and
a round fence. The handles are encrusted with mother-of-pearl plaques
engraved with flowers and leaves and thin bands of ivory. Attached to
both handles are padded cushions of red silk intended to protect the
hand when firing the trigger.

E.Y.

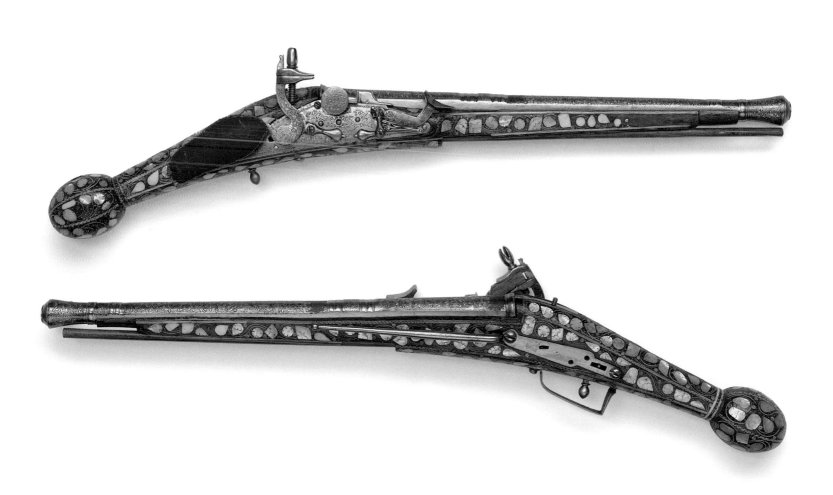

153

44–5

Pair of belt pistols

London, 1617 (?)

Steel, wood, mother-of-pearl, ivory, fabric; engraved, gilded, carved, encrusted

OR–3599: Overall length 18¼ in. (46.4 cm); length of barrel 12⅜ in. (31.4 cm); calibre 0.5 in. (12 mm)

OR–3600: Overall length 17¾ in. (45.2 cm); length of barrel 12 in. (30.5 cm); calibre 0.5 in. (12 mm)

Marks: breech of the barrel – heart beneath a crown

Provenance: historic collection of the Armoury

Moscow Kremlin Museums inv. nos. OR–3599, OR–3600

MS sources: Armoury and Royal Treasury Inventory Book 1686–7, f. 418v; Armoury Inventory 1835, f. 750, no. 7596

Published sources: Armoury Inventory 1884–93, part 5, book 4, no. 8239

Literature: Yablonskaya 1999, pp. 55–6

The barrels of these guns are inlaid with gold over pounced vegetation and incorporate medallions with gilded figures. The two medallions on OR–3599 contain full-length male figures in sixteenth-century costume (see fig. 37; p. 137). One wears knee-length stuffed trunk-hose, a doublet, a broad sash over his right shoulder and a high-crowned hat with a narrow brim and a luxuriant feather. He holds in his left hand a staff or more probably a musket stand for use during firing. The other figure differs slightly: he wears narrow hose, his doublet is fastened with a row of buttons and his hat is conical, while he holds a pistol (?) in his right hand.

One medallion on OR–3600 depicts a musketeer in sixteenth-century attire. On his shoulder he supports a musket with a long fuse – we can just pick out the powder-flask and part of his sword. The upper part of the image in the other medallion is badly worn and cannot be identified, although it clearly shows a male figure.

Both guns have a round barrel with profiled lateral facets and a projecting band by the end of the breech. There are four transverse bands on OR–3600, three on OR–3599. The barrel widens towards the muzzle, then narrows again at the end. The triangular barrel-tang bears traces of ornament. There is an Anglo-Dutch lock with a safety. On the jaws of the cocking-piece are double parallel engraved bands, the upper part of the cocking-piece and lower part of the steel or frizzle arm support have a rounded surface. The left end of the lock-plate is carved in the form of a dragon's head. The lock-plate was adorned with engraved ornament and there are remains of ornamental vegetation to match that on the barrel. The number 5792 is stamped into the round pan-cover.

The iron mount has a rectangular safety-catch, belt attachment and trigger shaped like a cone. The beech handle is encrusted with mother-of-pearl insets in the form of stylized leaves and flowers on thin ivory stems. The mother-of-pearl encrustation is intermingled with small round ivory insets with an engraved circle with a dot at the centre. The ivory plaque beneath the safety-catch is engraved with woven ornament with a round eye at the centre. The contours of the handle are outlined with thin ivory bands, the handle ending in fish-tail pommels.

E.Y.

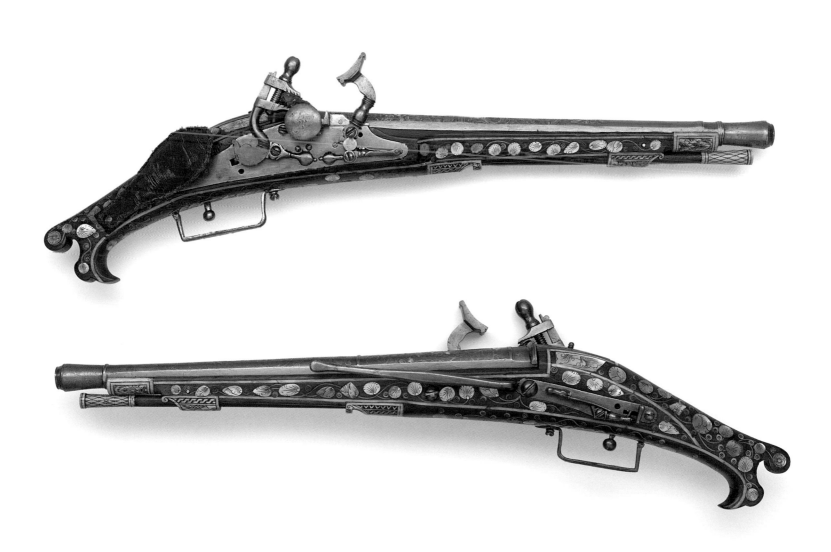

155

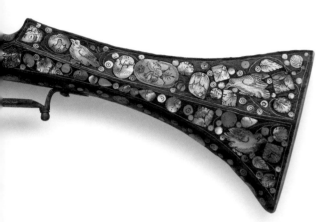

46

Carbine

London, 1618–23

Maker Henry Burrows (Burroughs, Borrowes) (?)

Steel, wood, mother-of-pearl, ivory; engraved, gilded, carved, encrusted, inlaid with gold

Overall length 48½ in. (122.6 cm);
length of barrel 34½ in. (87.7 cm);
calibre 0.45 in. (11.5 mm)

Marks: barrel (top of the breech) and lock-plate –
HB in a shield beneath a helmet (Blackmore 1986, p. 65)

Provenance: historic collection of the Armoury

Moscow Kremlin Museums inv. no. OR–4292

MS sources: Armoury and Royal Treasury Inventory Book 1686–7, f. 222; Armoury Inventory 1835, *delo* 6, no. 6307

Published sources: Armoury Inventory 1884–93, part 5, book 4, no. 7477

Literature: Eaves 1976, p. 290; Treasures 1998, no. 41; Yablonskaya 1999, p. 57; Sovereign's Armoury 2002, no. 90; Russia–Britain 2003, no. 156

This is one of an elegant pair of seventeenth-century carbines (the other Moscow Kremlin Museums inv. no. OR–2248). There can be no doubt of their English origin. They are recorded as being English works in the Armoury and Royal Treasury Inventory Book of 1686–7 and in all surviving inventories of the Armoury from the eighteenth and nineteenth centuries. It has not proved possible, however, to uncover any specific information that would throw light on who brought them to Russia and when, although they must undoubtedly have been intended as a gift for the Tsar. This is confirmed by the presence on the butt of a two-headed eagle wearing a triple crown with a unicorn on its breast, a version of the Russian state emblem well known in England. The unicorn was introduced to the state emblems by Ivan the Terrible and it appeared on the Tsar's Great State Seal around 1582. Boris Godunov also used such seals on his letters to Queen Elizabeth.

In the Musée de l'Armée in Paris a similar gun bears not only the same mark but also an engraved date, 1622. Formerly kept in the gun cabinet of Louis XIII, it was listed as an English gun in the inventory (Eaves 1976, p. 29A). The gun had been in the collection of William Renwick and was acquired at auction by the Musée de l'Armée in 1997 (Musée de l'Armée 1997, p. S-3).

The outside of the barrel has five facets along a third of its length, then gilded transverse bands after which it is round. It has the multi-faceted flaring muzzle characteristic of English firearms. A V-shaped back-sight is set into the end of the breech. The barrel is covered with inlaid gold patterns consisting mostly of elongated frames filled with tiny elegant gold curls and circles.

The Anglo-Dutch lock is fitted with a sliding safety catch attached behind the cocking-piece. Depicted on the round fence of the pan-cover is a male head in a helmet. A similar profile is engraved on the ivory tip of the fore-end of an English musket dated 1588 (Livrustkammaren / Royal Armoury, Stockholm; see Drejholt 1996, pp. 200–1). A similar image features in a medallion on another work produced in London, a silver cup of 1557–8 (cat. 1). We know that during the second half of the sixteenth century, cups decorated with miniature busts in classical armour and emblems came into fashion in England. Images of military busts and classicizing profiles in medallions occur among the sketches that Hans Holbein the Younger produced for precious vessels for the marriage of Henry VIII and Jane Seymour in 1536. Holbein produced not only portraits for Henry's court, but also designs for parade armour, jewellery and all kinds of precious vessels.

The lock-plate is ornamented with gold inlay to match the barrel. According to Blackmore, the mark on the lock-plate may be that of the London gunsmith Henry Burrows and should thus be dated 1618–23 (Blackmore 1986, p. 65). The beech stock, with its flat musket butt and finger niche, is encrusted with twirls of silver wire and engraved mother-of-pearl, including figurative insets showing a running dog, a hare and birds. On both sides of the butt are oval plaques engraved – carelessly or perhaps with a lack of skill – with two-headed eagles with a unicorn on their breast.

E.Y.

47

Snaphaunce musket

Holland, 1620s

Presented by Fabian Smith of the Muscovy Company
to Tsar Mikhail Fyodorovich in 1625

Steel, wood, ivory, mother-of-pearl; wrought, engraved,
carved, encrusted, silver-gilt

Overall length 63⅝ in. (161.7 cm);
length of barrel 49 in. (124.4 cm);
calibre 0.75 in. (19 mm)

Marks: barrel (below) – flower on a stem, repeated three
times; lock – T beneath a crown

Provenance: historic collection of the Armoury

Moscow Kremlin Museums inv. no. OR–272

MS sources: Book of Receipts and Allocations 1625, f. 34;
Armoury and Royal Treasury Inventory Book 1686–7,
f. 215

Published sources: Armoury Inventory 1884–93, part 5,
book 4, no. 6783

Literature: Sobolev and Ermolov 1954, pp. 421–4;
Blackmore 1965, p. 31; Hoff 1978, p. 67; Dutch Guns
1996, no. K.4, pp. 64–5; Treasures 1998, no. 57; Sovereign's
Armoury 2002, p. 393; Russia–Britain 2003, no. 52

Heavy large-calibre guns or muskets were used to arm the infantry in many European states, including Russia. They were usually equipped with matchlocks, or more rarely with wheel-locks or snaphaunce locks. This parade musket has a snaphaunce lock of Anglo-Dutch type. Its construction is unusual. The rectangular steel of the lock is combined with the pan-cover, but the pan also has a separate swivelling cover on a hinge, like matchlock muskets. Mounted on the lock-plate is an external safety. The lock-plate and carved details of the lock preserve traces of silvering. The lower end of the S-shaped cocking-piece is carved in the form of a dolphin's head.

One particularly expressive detail is the cast brass sight. It takes the common form of a miniature cannon ending in a relief male head in a turban. The stock of the parade musket, with its flat, almost triangular butt and deep niche cut out for the thumb, is encrusted with shaped mother-of-pearl insets.

There is some basis to suggest that the musket was a gift to Tsar Mikhail Fyodorovich. It may have been offered on the occasion of the Tsar's marriage in January 1625 by Fabian Smith, the English agent and governor of the Muscovy Company in London. In the Book of Receipts and Allocations for the Armoury Office for 1625 two *samopals* (guns) are mentioned among the gifts presented by Smith. These entered the Armoury in 1625 from the Treasury Court where precious items of the imperial treasury were kept; the pair was valued at 16 rubles.

Engraved on the barrel of each musket is a patriotic inscription referring to the Dutch battles against Spanish rule in the sixteenth century: NOCH WAERT BETER TE STRIDEN MET ORANIE INT VELT DAN GEBRACHT MET LIST ONDER HET SPAEN GHEWE<LT> ('Better to do battle in the field with [the Prince of] Orange than to fall under Spanish dominion'). This is the only musket in the Armoury collection with an inscribed device on the barrel. Both the presence of the inscription and the link with Fabian Smith were noted in the Armoury and Royal Treasury Inventory Book of 1686–7, where the musket features among the items of first consequence and highest quality. It is listed as: 'foreign harquebus musket, on the barrel carved Latin words, beech stock, set into it shells, carved English lock, the lock-plate was silvered, Fabinskaya [i.e. of Fabian] … value fifty rubles'.

E.Y.

48

Snaphaunce musket

Holland, 1620s

Presented by Fabian Smith of the Muscovy Company
to Tsar Mikhail Fyodorovich in 1625

Steel, wood, ivory, mother-of-pearl; carved, engraved,
encrusted

Overall length 69¾ in. (177 cm);
length of barrel 54¾ in. (139.2 cm);
calibre 0.8 in. (20 mm)

Marks: barrel (below) – stamped five-petalled flower
on a stem, repeated three times

Provenance: historic collection of the Armoury

Moscow Kremlin Museums inv. no. OR–273/1–2

MS sources: Book of Receipts and Allocations 1625, f. 34;
Armoury and Royal Treasury Inventory Book 1686–7,
f. 226

Published sources: Armoury Inventory 1884–93, part 5,
book 4, no. 6784

Literature: Sobolev and Ermolov 1954, pp. 421–4; Blackmore
1965, p. 31; Hoff 1978, p. 67; Dutch Guns 1996, no. K.5,
pp. 66–7; Treasures 1998, no. 58; Sovereign's Armoury 2002,
p. 394; Russia–Britain 2003, no. 53

This musket was possibly presented by Fabian Smith at the same time as
the previous one (cat. 47). It has an octagonal barrel, with a sight attached
to the breech in the form of a grooved stub. The surface of the massive
flintlock of Anglo-Dutch type is engraved. The rectangular steel is linked
with the pan-cover. Like cat. 47, the pan also has a separate hinged cover.

The beech stock – with its fore-end running the length of the barrel and
a short flat musket butt – is encrusted with fine stems and little circles of
ivory, serving as background for larger engraved mother-of-pearl insets.

E.Y.

49

Belt pistol

London, 1640s

Maker Warner Pin (Pinne, Pinn) (?)

Steel, wood, silver, ebony; wrought, carved, encrusted, engraved

Overall length 15 in. (38.1 cm);
length of barrel 8⅞ in. (22.5 cm);
calibre 0.5 in. (12 mm)

Marks: barrel (top of the breech) – WP beneath a crown in a shield (Blackmore 1986, p. 214, no. 181)

Provenance: historic collection of the Armoury

Moscow Kremlin Museums inv. no. OR–3483

MS sources: Armoury and Royal Treasury Inventory Book 1686–7, f. 409v

Published sources: Armoury Inventory 1884–93, part 5, book 4, no. 8260

Literature: Treasures 1998, no. 59; Yablonskaya 1999, p. 59; Sovereign's Armoury 2002, no. 91; Russia–Britain 2003, no. 157

The mark on the barrel of this gun may be that of the gunsmith Warner Pin. A native of Germany, Pin settled in London in 1615 and worked as a gunstock maker and encruster. In 1625 he made fusils and carbines with wheel-locks on contract for the Royal Ordnance and in 1640 he was elected an assistant of the Gunmakers Company, becoming a Master in 1641. It was at that time that he became Gunstock Maker-in-Ordinary to Charles I (Blackmore 1986, p. 59).

The pistol's barrel has five facets at the top, but is smooth below. There is a slight flaring at the muzzle with a thickening of the walls at the end. At the breech end of the barrel is a projecting band with a grooved sight. Chevron ornament has been carved by the barrel-tang.

The lock is of English type, a version of the snaphaunce lock that appeared in the early seventeenth century and quickly became widespread; it was possibly invented in England. Engraved vertical parallel bands adorn the jaws of the cocking-piece, a characteristic decorative feature on English seventeenth-century locks. The handle is of ebony and encrusted with openwork silver plaques. The pistol is one of a pair. The other was transferred to the Museum of the Imperial Tula Armoury Factory by the Ministry of the Imperial Court in 1883 (current location unknown).

E.Y.

163

50

Seven-shot magazine hunting gun

London (?), 1658

Presented by Charles II, via the embassy of Charles Howard, Earl of Carlisle, to Tsarevich Fyodor Alexeevich in 1664

Makers Caspar Kalthoff the Elder and Harman Barne

Steel, copper alloy, wood; engraved, carved, damascened with gold

Overall length 53⅞ in. (136.7 cm);
length of barrel 35⅞ in. (91.2 cm);
calibre 0.6 in. (15.5 mm)

Marks: plate over the magazine – engraved inscription: CASPAR KALTHOF ME FECIT AN 1658; lock-plate – former inscription, now erased: H BARNE (Armoury Inventory 1808)

Provenance: historic collection of the Armoury

Moscow Kremlin Museums inv. no. OR–104

MS sources: Armoury and Royal Treasury Inventory Book 1686–7, f. 224; Armoury Inventory 1808, f. 555

Published sources: Armoury Inventory 1884–93, part 5, book 4, no. 7539

Literature: Sovereign's Armoury 2002, no. 92; Russia–Britain 2003, no. 158

Repeater guns such as this one can fire consecutive shots without having to be reloaded. The gun was described as a 'fast-shooting harquebus' in seventeenth-century Russia. It was previously thought that the maker, Caspar Kalthoff, made this gun in the Kremlin workshops. But a careful comparison with a description in the Armoury archives allows us to link its appearance in the Tsar's armoury with the embassy sent from Charles II in 1664.

The gun presented to Tsarevich Fyodor Alexeevich is described in detail in the inventory of 1686–7:

> Smooth English harquebus, fast-shooting. Barrel round, is primed from a store, on the store engraving in places. Stock of walnut, on the stock an iron frame in five places; on the frame on the breech screw applied gold, along the end of the breech screw a silver plate with engraved marks. Carved flintlock. Beneath the catch and by the catch gilding in places inlaid gold. On a plate is written: To the great sovereign Tsarevich and grand duke Fyodor Alexeevich autocrat of All great and small and white Russia presented as gift from the English King Charles by the ambassador Prince Charles Howard in 172 [1664] February the 11th day…

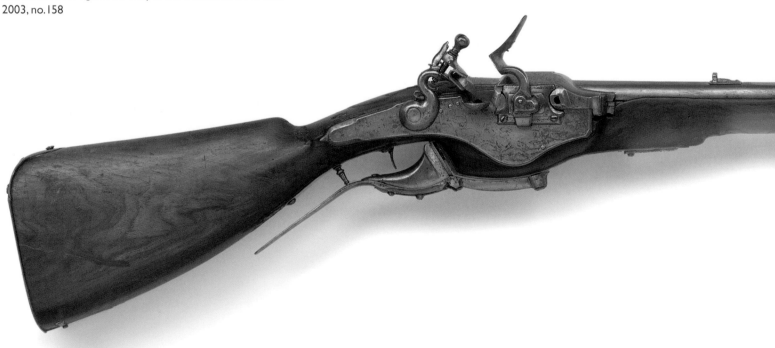

The absence of the engraved silver plate noted in the Inventory Book threw doubt on the attribution. But it is confirmed by a description in the Armoury Inventory of 1808. There the now lost plate was described thus: 'Attached to the small of the butt is an elongated round plate, on which are engraved the English arms, one with the signature: *Hony soit qui mal y pense*.' The 1808 inventory also mentions a lost image on the lock-plate: 'On the plate engraved a hunt for deer with dogs, and along the edge H. Barne', identifying another gunsmith involved in making the gun.

The gun's round barrel with a smooth bore is linked to the breech block, inside which is a horizontally sliding box with drilled magazines for bullets and gunpowder. The ball-magazine for seven bullets is in the fore-end, the powder-magazine carved into the lock part of the wooden stock. In the safety-catch is a transporter into which a little more gunpowder is placed than is necessary for firing. Reloading the gun with the muzzle upwards is done by turning the trigger-guard forwards and backwards 180 degrees. The turning brings into action the toothed mechanism which moves the sliding block horizontally, left and right. The ball and gunpowder are thus moved into the barrel, the trigger is cocked and the gunpowder remaining in the transporter is tipped out onto the pan. The sight is attached to the breech.

Engraved on the plate covering the block are the name of the master and the date. Caspar Kalthoff the Elder was a Dutch gunsmith and inventor who worked in England from 1628. In 1634 he was allocated a forge and lodgings in the Tower of London and an experimental firing range was erected for him at Vauxhall. In 1655 Kalthoff returned to Holland and was elected burgomeister of Dordrecht. He was apparently so offended by the actions of Cromwell's Parliament that he invented a catapult for the purpose of killing the Lord Protector. After the restoration of the house of Stuart, Kalthoff returned to London where in 1663 he demonstrated a seven-shot gun to the Royal Society (see Blackmore 1986, p. 125).

Beneath the three screws that fix the barrel are metal plates adorned with stylized tendrils damascened in gold. The flintlock is of French type. Engraved on the lock-plate is a hunting scene with dogs and a deer. The surface of the cocking-piece is engraved with a dragon, with a leaf projecting from the curve of the cocking-piece. The iron safety-catch has traces of engraved ornament. The fore-end of the walnut stock runs the length of the barrel. The projection on the butt signals that a plaque was formerly attached there. A similar gun with the engraved inscription C. KALTHOF, produced around 1660, is in the Royal Collection at Windsor Castle (Blackmore 1968, p. 36).

E.Y.

51

Five-shot magazine gun

London, *c.*1660

Maker Harman Barne (Haerman Barnevelt)

Steel, wood; engraved, carved, inlaid with gold

Overall length 47½ in. (120.5 cm);
length of barrel 32¾ in. (83 cm);
calibre 0.5 in. (13 mm); rifling grooves 8

Marks: breech – engraved inscription: HARMAN BARN;
lock-plate – former inscription, now erased: LONDINI
(Armoury Inventory 1835)

Provenance: historic collection of the Armoury

Moscow Kremlin Museums inv. no. OR–1181

MS sources: Armoury and Royal Treasury Inventory Book
1686–7, f. 299; Armoury Inventory 1835, no. 6311

Published sources: Armoury Inventory 1884–93, part 5,
book 4, no. 8260

Literature: Dutch Guns 1996, K.26, pp. 106–7; Yablonskaya
1999, p. 58; Russia–Britain 2003, no. 159

This repeater gun uses the Kalthoff system (cat. 50). The name of the gunsmith, repeated twice on the gun, may be an anglicized form of Haerman Barnevelt, a Dutch gunsmith born in the Hague. Barnevelt seems to have travelled to England in the suite of Prince Rupert in 1642 and during the Civil War produced arms for the Royalists. After the war he was arrested and sent to prison, but was later freed and permitted to continue working. Barnevelt may indeed have worked with Caspar Kalthoff in Vauxhall (Blackmore 1986, p. 47). In 1657 he became a member of the Company of Armourers, but in 1659 was arrested once more, and the store of weapons in his workshop confiscated. Liberated in 1660, Barnevelt was appointed handgun maker to Charles II. He died the following year, but his armoury business was continued by his widow Ursula (Blackmore 1986, p. 47).

The round barrel of the gun has a prominent muzzle ring. The bore is rifled with eight hemispherical grooves. The sight is a groove in a raised hand by the end of the breech. Set into the breech is a chamber for repeated loading. Turning the trigger-guard 180 degrees brings the breech block with two hollows into movement, and thus the necessary amount of powder and a lead bullet is inserted into the channel of the barrel from the magazine. A transporter is mounted into the trigger-guard to transfer powder from the magazine in the stock to the forward part of the lock.

The gun has a Miquelet lock. The springs of the cocking-piece and steel (frizzle-sprint) are mounted into the outer surface of the lock-plate, which is adorned with engraved vegetation. The walnut stock has a long fore-end and a flat rectangular butt adorned with carving, though the end is plain. The cap of the fore-end and the screws attaching the barrel to the stock are adorned with inlaid gold ornament in the manner characteristic of English weapons.

E.Y.

52–3

Pair of pistols

Armoury workshops, Moscow, 1600–25

Maker Pervusha Isaev

Steel, silver, wood, mother-of-pearl; engraved, encrusted, gilded, silver-gilt

Overall length 22⅞ in. (58 cm);
length of barrel 14⅛ in. (35.9 cm);
calibre 0.6 in. (16 mm)

Marks: lock-plates – swan in a shield

Provenance: historic collection of the Armoury

Moscow Kremlin Museums inv. nos. OR–156, OR–157

MS sources: Armoury and Royal Treasury Inventory Book 1686–7, f. 413r,v

Published sources: Armoury Inventory 1884–93, part 5, book 4, no. 8307

Literature: Sovereign's Armoury 2002, no. 72; Russia–Britain 2003, nos. 162–3

The name of the craftsman is Pervusha Isaev, Pervusha being the diminutive of his first name Pervoy – literally 'first', indicating that he was the first child of a marriage. Archive documents relating to the Armoury for 1613–25 describe him as the 'lockmaster Pervusha Isaev'. He not only made locks, however, but also ornamented them, and was from time to time entrusted with other decorative work on metal. The Kremlin Museums have a five-shot revolving gun and a six-shot revolver by the same master (Moscow Kremlin Museums inv. nos OR–153, OR–160). These complicated revolving weapons reveal Isaev to have been a good constructor, knowledgeable in contemporary European firing technology.

The Armoury inventory for 1686–7 notes that these pistols were produced according to an English model:

> Pair of Moscow pistols in the English manner, steel barrels, on the barrels from the breech and by the muzzle two medallions inlaid with gold, one medallion having a two-headed eagle. Locks gilded and silver-plated in places. Stocks of applewood, on the barrels silver patterns, in places set into the barrels are carved shells, mount for the barrels silver-plated in two places and no catch... and finding accordance in a comparison between the present inventory of 195 [1686–7] and the same pair in earlier inventory books, value eight rubles ...'

The lock-plates are engraved with ornamental vegetation and depict a subject popular in both Russian and European art: an eagle doing battle with a snake, a conventional allegory for the battle between good and evil.

The form and decoration of the handle, with its fanciful carved ends, find analogies in the works of European – particularly Scottish – gun-stock makers. These Mannerist forms are known as 'fish-tails', but in seventeenth-century Russia were described as 'boots'. Set into the rich encrusted decoration are mother-of-pearl plaques in the shape of birds, snake-like monsters and interwoven tendrils against a background encrusted with silver wire and stars. On the side opposite the lock-plate, a decorative grotesque composition includes a male half-figure in Russian attire and a conical hat very like a helmet. The smooth decorative bands, the thick silver-plating of the engraved ornament on the barrels, and the construction of the Anglo-Dutch locks are typical features of English guns of the age.

E.Y.

169

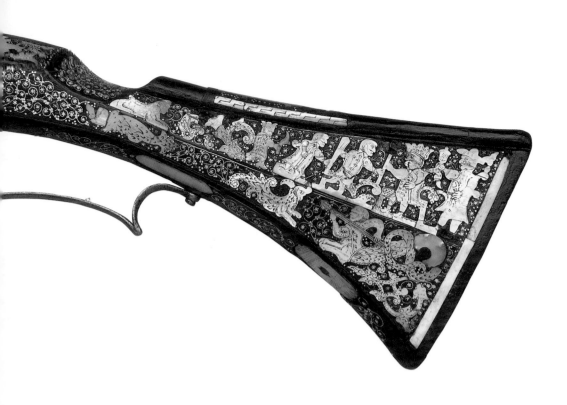

54

Hunting harquebus

Armoury workshops, Moscow, 1626–34

Maker Timofey Luchaninov

Steel, wood, silver, mother-of-pearl; wrought, engraved, carved, encrusted, gilded, silver-gilt

Overall length 49⅛ in. (124.8 cm);
length of barrel 35¼ in. (89.6 cm);
calibre 0.4 in. (10 mm)

Provenance: historic collection of the Armoury

Moscow Kremlin Museums inv. no. OR–152

MS sources: Armoury and Royal Treasury Inventory Book 1686–7, ff. 214v–215

Published sources: Armoury Inventory 1884–93, part 5, book 4, no. 7467

Literature: Sovereign's Armoury 2002, no. 73; Russia–Britain 2003, no. 166

A snake with gilt and silver-plated scales is engraved along the length of the rifled barrel of this harquebus. This type of gun, with a snake on the barrel, was known in seventeenth-century Russia as a *zmeyka*, from the Russian *zmeya* (snake). The breech is adorned with relief floral ornament and what are probably the master's initials engraved on the sight.

The hunting gun has an Anglo-Dutch lock with S-shaped hammer and steel. The pan-cover has a sliding lid and a fence attached to the side. The details of the lock are very inventive: carved floral ornament on the steel support, the jaws of the hammer in the form of a lion's head beneath a crown, the lower end of the hammer shaped like an animal's head. On the pan-cover is an engraved shell. The surface of the lock-plate is gilded and adorned with stylized floral ornament. The decoration on the wooden stock is also striking. It is entirely encrusted with mother-of-pearl insets, silver wire, pinks and stars. Clearly the work of a master gun-stock maker, the encrustation demonstrates the influence of western European firearms, notably English, which were being imitated here.

The firearm is described in the 1686–7 inventory: 'Rifled harquebus *zmeyka* made by Timofeev Luchaninov. Barrel covered with gold and silver over scales, around the snake to the breech engraved arabesque tendrils, silvered. Lock chased and gilded. Stock of applewood, set into it shells, in places silver inlay. Made in the time of boyar Vasily Ivanovich Streshnev.' The *zmeyka* must therefore have been made between 1626 and 1634, when Vasily Streshnev, a relative of Tsar Mikhail Fyodorovich's wife, was in charge of the Armoury Office.

E.Y.

55

Seven-shot magazine fowling piece

Moscow, 1665

Maker Caspar Kalthoff the Younger

Steel, wood, copper alloy; wrought, carved, engraved

Overall length 46¼ in. (117.5 cm);
length of barrel 28⅜ in. (72 cm);
calibre 0.5 in. (12.3 mm)

Marks: breech – engraved inscription: K. KALTHOF FECIT, MOSCOVA 1665

Provenance: historic collection of the Armoury

Moscow Kremlin Museums inv. no. OR–1947

Published sources: Armoury Inventory 1884–93, part 5, book 4, no. 7538

Literature: Blackmore 1986, p. 125; Russia–Britain 2003, no. 167

Caspar Kalthoff the Younger (see p. 135) used the Kalthoff system (cat. 50) pioneered by his father in the making of this gun. The barrel's smooth bore is linked to the breech. Its snaphaunce lock has a right-angled cocking-piece and external main spring, and the lock-plate is flat and smooth, with traces of worn engraving. Small stylized tendrils are engraved on parts of the lock and priming mechanism. The fore-end of the stock runs along three quarters of the barrel. The butt-end is of copper alloy, as is the powder holder on the steel release catch.

E.Y.

3

The Presentation of Gifts

So in order as we rode, we assended the staires and a stone gallery: where on each side stood many Nobles, and Courtiers, in faire coates of Persian stuffe, velvet, Damaske &c. At the entry to the great chamb. Two Councellors incountred the Ambassa[dor] to conduct him thorogh that roome, rounde about which sat many grave and richly apparrelled personages. Then we entred the Presents, whether being come, and making obeysance, we staide to hear, but not understand, a very gallant Nobleman, named Peter Basman, deliver the Emperors title: Then the particular of the Presentes, and some other ceremonies: which performed, the Ambassa[dor] having liberty, delivered so much of his Ambassage, as the time and occasion then affoorded: After which the Emperor arising from his throne, demanded of the King of Englands health, the Princes, and Queenes: then of the Ambassadours and the Kinges Gentlemen, and how they had bene used since they entred within his dominions: to al which with obeysance we answered as was meete.

—Sir Thomas Smithes Voiage and Entertainment in Rushia (London, 1605)

English Diplomats at the Court of the Tsars

Irina Zagorodnaya

The mid-sixteenth century, when the foundation of Anglo Russian relations was being laid, was an important – and stormy – period in the establishment of Russian state institutions and the development of Muscovy's external diplomacy. The unexpected arrival at the Tsar's court in 1554 of representatives of the island power came only a few years after a key event in the building of the state, the birth of the Ambassadorial Office, which would play a major role in the history of Anglo-Russian relations and the fate of many high-ranking and wealthy Englishmen. S. A. Belokurov, who has traced the history of the Ambassadorial Office, established 1549 as the date of its foundation, although evidence suggests it may have existed even earlier, albeit as a less formal structure. This becomes clear from documents recording the development of hierarchical ranks in charge of external political affairs and from the highly ordered, extensive and varied surviving records, above all the ambassadorial books.[1] These books, of which around twenty cover the links between Russia and England, are our main source for studying the history of contacts between the two countries from the mid-sixteenth to the mid-seventeenth century.[2] They contain copious information on visits to Russia by diplomats, merchants and specialists, ambassadorial ceremony, the conduct of audiences with the monarch and diplomatic gifts.

Documents relating to government administration tend to be extremely reliable in terms of the factual information they provide. Other sources are more 'literary', including the reports of envoys and the *d'yaks* or secretaries of the Ambassadorial Office, and memoirs by those in state service containing vivid sketches of ceremonial events and incidents of everyday life. There are also the magnificent works created by London silversmiths and armourers that were frequently brought to Russia as gifts and are today in the Armoury of the Moscow Kremlin Museums. These contemporary resources enable us to recreate a picture of the stay of foreign diplomats in Moscow.

Russia's international relations were conducted in the sixteenth and seventeenth centuries through shuttle diplomacy. There were no permanent foreign representations in Moscow, nor did Moscow establish its own permanent representations abroad until the last third of the seventeenth century. In their own lands these diplomats enjoyed differing status. Some came from court circles; others of more modest origin were in state service or were merchants and traders. This interweaving of international politics, trade and scholarly and cultural activity was characteristic of the medieval and early modern period. Diplomatic suites travelled thousands of miles bearing letters or secret instructions in their heads, carrying official gifts, trading documents and goods. Their paths lay across the open seas, along rivers, through crossings and portage, from town to town, from camp to camp. They travelled for months, on dangerous journeys complicated by climate, natural disasters, disease and the actions of ill-wishers. They might spend anything from several weeks to several years at their destination.

Over the course of one and a half centuries, Anglo-Russian contact brought London diplomats of various professions and status to Russia. Most were 'envoys' and only more rarely 'ambassadors', although documents also

44. The Arms of the Muscovy Company, 1596.
British Library, London

include more indeterminate terms such as *gost*, the term used to describe a wealthy or important merchant, or simply *dvoryanin* (nobleman). Whoever they were, one thing was clear: nearly all of them represented the interests of the Muscovy Company, founded in 1555, and British merchants in general (fig. 44). Presenting royal letters of introduction and royal gifts, merchants were officially transformed into representatives of the throne, essentially carrying out tasks not only for the company but also on behalf of the British government. Such a combination was facilitated by the nature of the Muscovy Company's organization and status in England, where it had close links with the aristocracy and the court, uniting not only businessmen and wealthy merchants but also members of the nobility.[3] In Moscow this was well understood, and there was thus no essential difference between the reception accorded London's trading agents and that of titled diplomats from other countries on continental Europe with which Moscow had long maintained contacts.[4]

What was an ambassador and how did he differ from diplomats of other ranks in the eyes of the Ambassadorial Office? Even by the start of the sixteenth century there was a precisely defined gradation of diplomatic representatives in Russia: 'ambassadors', 'envoys' and 'couriers'. Thereafter this was further refined to include 'great ambassadors' (*posly velikie*), 'lesser ambassadors' (*legkie posly*), 'envoys' (*poslanniki*), 'couriers' (*gontsy*) and 'messengers' (*poslantsy* or *poslannye*). Russian ambassadors were usually appointed from among the boyars, the highest ranking of the nobles around the Tsar. As the Tsar's agents, they had the right to conduct negotiations, sign agreements and draft the texts of treaties, final approval of which resting, of course, with the Tsar himself (fig. 45). Envoys were appointed from among the lesser nobles, perhaps a secretary (*d'yak*) of one of the state offices or more rarely a secretary's assistant known as a *pod'yachiy*. They were dispatched on less important matters. Couriers were obliged to deliver the letters entrusted to them or convey a message personally without engaging in diplomatic negotiations. They were appointed from among the *pod'yachiy*, interpreters and *stol'niks* (nobles of lower rank than the boyars).[5] If a representative of a foreign court was endowed with broad powers, he was, in Russia, accorded the status of ambassador.

Undoubtedly important political matters justified the arrival of English ambassadors and the negotiations they requested. But the interests of English merchants and competition with other traders on the Russian market remained a key subject. Regardless of the status they enjoyed, all the envoys and messengers from London, without exception, were seeking to establish or maintain trading monopolies in Russia.

Diplomatic ties in the sixteenth century

The most active period in trading and diplomatic relations was the second half of the sixteenth century, with numerous official visitors from London, of whom three were received in the Kremlin: Thomas Randolph, Jerome Bowes and Richard Lee.[6] In 1568 Thomas Randolph's embassy was intended to neutralize Ivan IV's inconveniently insistent desire for a military

45. *Ivan Vasil'yevich* [Ivan the Terrible], anonymous, late 17th century, State History Museum, Moscow

IOHANNES BASILIDES MAGNUS MOSCOVITARUM DUX.   G.HGD.

alliance with England and to tone down the formulation of the two parties' obligations, even if possible to get away with only high-flown but largely meaningless speeches. Randolph was closely linked with Francis Walsingham, privy counselor and principal secretary to Elizabeth I, and a supporter of broad international coalitions against the power of Spain. It would seem that he had no objection to bringing the Tsar of Muscovy into the battle against the Catholic powers. Queen Elizabeth too was concerned by sharper competition on the Russian market between the English and merchants from Lübeck and Denmark.

Jerome Bowes set off for Moscow with the Russian ambassador Fyodor Pisemsky in June 1583 and remained until 1584, when he was expelled in disgrace, mainly because of his own overweening pride and ambition. Unlike Randolph, he supported a cautious international policy, for which reason he was chosen to undertake the trip to Russia: the Queen's attitude to an alliance with Muscovy remained ambiguous. He was also entrusted with a more specific task, to offer English mediation in the Russo-Swedish war. His embassy ended in utter failure. The English trading monopoly in Russia was repealed, largely thanks to Bowes' avoidance of any serious negotiations on political subjects. Departing from Russia, he sent Tsar Fyodor Ivanovich (fig. 46) a sharp letter regarding the boyar Nikita Romanov (the future Patriarch Philaret and father of Mikhail Romanov, who was to be elected first Tsar of the Romanov dynasty in 1613) and the *d'yak* Andrey Shchelkalov, head of the Ambassadorial Office, whom he perceived as his main opponents. During his last stop at Kholmogory he left behind both the letters he had received from the Tsar and the imperial gifts. The result was a scandal. Elizabeth I eventually sent a letter of apology for the inappropriate behaviour of her representative.

Lee, last of the ambassadors of the sixteenth century, was dispatched in 1600 to congratulate Boris Godunov on his election to the throne and to remind the new Tsar of the traditional privileges enjoyed by English merchants in the Muscovite state (fig. 47).

Other English merchant-diplomats of the second half of the sixteenth century acted as messengers and envoys. Among these was Anthony Jenkinson, who arrived in Moscow in 1557 with Osip Nepeya, the first Russian diplomat to visit the English court (during the reign of Mary I). Jenkinson intended to travel on to China, but made it only as far as Bukhara. In 1561 the Muscovy Company again delegated him to the court of Ivan the Terrible, but his aim on that occasion was Persia. Once again the merchant failed to reach his final destination and he returned home three years later. He did not arrive in Moscow with empty hands, however. His arsenal included a chest filled with precious gifts for the Tsar.[7] He visited Moscow again a few years later, in connection with the threatened loss of all English trading privileges on the Russian market, and a fourth time in 1571.

Some English merchants of the Muscovy Company spent many years living in Moscow. They had their own houses, brought up their children and carried out any diplomatic tasks required by the governments of both London and Moscow. Among these was Jerome Horsey, who represented English

46. Dominicus Custos after Giacomo Franco, *Tsar Fyodor Ivanovich*, after 1598. State History Museum, Moscow

merchant circles. Between 1573 and 1591 he carried out numerous tasks for both courts, while conducting his own successful commercial activity. He would seem initially to have been merely an employee of the Muscovy Company, but by 1580 he had risen to take charge of the office in Moscow. Having successfully carried out the Tsar's request that he organize supplies of gunpowder, lead, copper and saltpetre from England (during difficulties that arose during the Livonian War) he also achieved a unique position of great trust among the Russians and had extensive connections at court. In 1585 he was accorded the honour of performing a most particular mission, carrying to England the news of Fyodor Ivanovich's accession to the throne as well as complaints about the recent conduct of Anglo-Russian relations:

> do yow send us sutch of your good people, that maie goe with speede, that maie come unto us with knowledge in messadges, as the manner and use is to sutch great princes, not in sutch sorte as your embassador Jerome Bowes did with many unseemly dealings … And our interpreter Reignold was shewed great dishonour in your kingdome; not in sutch sorte interteined as messengers are between us and such like great princes our brothers … And theis our letters we send unto yow, our most lovinge sister, by your sublecte Jerom Horsey, sonne of William. [8]

Reginald (Robert) Beckman, the Russian ambassador who had been 'shewed great dishonour', was a Livonian who carried out many tasks for the Muscovite government. In 1585 he had presented a complaint to Queen Elizabeth regarding the 'unfitting' behaviour of Jerome Bowes. He visited England again in the summer of 1588 to complain about the English merchants and to discover 'with whom the Queen now enjoys friendship and love and who is banished … and with whom she is now at war'.[9] In London, however, Beckman was perceived to be aligned with the interests of the Dutch, England's main rivals in matters of trade. He supported the Antwerp merchant Jan de Wale, who was a successful merchant in Moscow where he also represented the interests of the Spanish crown and the Habsburgs.[10] In the end, the Queen did not receive Beckman in the official reception hall, as was due to a diplomat of his rank, but 'in a cabbage patch, planted with onions and garlick'.[11] Such a reception, not surprisingly, led to indignation in Moscow and a lengthy correspondence.

Giles Fletcher had the status of envoy when he arrived in 1588. However unsuccessful it may have been, his visit was dominated once again by the interests of the Muscovy Company. Departing from Russia, Fletcher travelled with Jerome Horsey, who was being sent home and who convinced him of his utter innocence of any responsibility for the failure of his mission, even persuading Fletcher to support him in his communications with the London merchants. Another English representative closely linked with Russia was Francis Cherry, father-in-law of a key figure in later years, John Merrick. Cherry played an extremely important role in the history of Russian international affairs. Resident in Moscow from his youth, he spoke good Russian and was employed by the Ambassadorial Office as a translator, carrying letters from Moscow to London and back in 1587 and 1591, and in 1598 being dispatched as messenger to Moscow by Elizabeth I to put an end to rumours of an Anglo-Turkish alliance.

47. *Tsar Boris Godunov*, anonymous, early 18th century, from F.C. Khevenhiller, *Conterfet Kupfferstich (soviel man deren zu handeln bringen konnen) deren jenigen regierenden grossen Herren…* Leipzig, 1721. State History Museum, Moscow

48. *G. I. Mikulin*, anonymous, early 17th century.
State History Museum, Moscow

On the other hand, the directors and leading merchants of the Muscovy Company played an active part in receiving Moscow's embassies when they arrived in England. This is clear from the Russian diplomats' reports.[12] Attached to ambassador Fyodor Pisemsky in 1582 was John Barne (Barnes), governor and chief merchant of the Muscovy Company. He was accompanied by 'English merchants whose business is done in Moscow': Martin, Towerson and Pullison. All of these men enjoyed high status in the City and served as aldermen. John Barne was among those London businessmen who financed the ships travelling in search of a route to China and India which found, by accident, the northern route to Muscovy. In his report, Pisemsky also mentioned Christopher Hoddesdon, another leading merchant who was involved in Muscovy and Baltic companies such as the Company of Merchant-Adventurers. Another figure in Pisemsky's report was John Hart, also a governor of the Muscovy Company. Barne accompanied the ambassadors at negotiations and participated in the farewell dinner. After the ambassadors had been released by the Queen, Barne and Martin presented them with the royal reward or gratuity: Fyodor Pisemsky and the clerk Neudacha Khorvalev each received a gift of a silver cup. Barne, Martin and Hoddesdon entertained the ambassadors, even taking them on a deer hunt.

There were of course more high-ranking individuals involved in receiving the embassy of Fyodor Pisemsky, such as Thomas Randolph, former ambassador to Moscow. He met them before their audience with the Queen, passed on speeches from her, acted as the official 'greeter' when the ambassadorial train moved towards the palace and was then presented in the audience hall, officially inviting the ambassadors to the celebrations for St George's day. Moreover, he took part in the 'inspection' of Mary Hastings – a proposed bride for Ivan the Terrible – and presented the ambassador with her portrait to be delivered to the Tsar.

In 1600 the embassy led by Grigory Mikulin was received in similar fashion (fig. 48). English merchants greeted the Russian diplomats at Archangel, according them a respectful welcome and accompanying them on their journey. Among these were John Merrick, son and heir of one of the founders of the Muscovy Company, and Francis Cherry who acted as couriers until the Russians reached English soil and a courtier took over. On this occasion the man chosen for the latter task was another former ambassador to Russia, Jerome Bowes. Together with merchants engaged in trading in Muscovy he accompanied the ambassadors to their audience and to look upon the Queen and her courtiers on St George's Day. Cherry and Merrick were present at the negotiations 'for translation and information'. They explained events in London to Mikulin after Essex's attempted palace coup in the winter of 1600–1.[13]

Ranks of visitors in the seventeenth century

In the following century neither the situation nor indeed the overall theme of the negotiations changed, although there was greater clarification in the order and description of the different ranks. Thomas Smith (see cat. 78) served as ambassador to Boris Godunov, and on numerous occasions John Merrick was the official British representative to the court of Mikhail Romanov. One of the English representatives sent to Mikhail's successor, Alexey Mikhaylovich, was John Culpepper who in May 1650 brought news of events in England (including the execution of Charles I) from the heir to the throne, then living in France. The last, highest ranking and most controversial ambassador to Moscow in this period was Charles Howard, 1st Earl of Carlisle, who left England in 1663, arriving in Moscow in the spring of 1664 (see pp.116–17 and cat.80).[14]

Thomas Smith, governor of the East India Company, visited Russia in 1604–5.[15] He received an audience with Tsar Boris Godunov, who was seeking to create an alliance against the Turks. In the context of this complex international situation, the question of privileges for English merchants was resolved positively and indeed overall the ambassador was notably successfully in carrying out the King's requests at the court of the anglomaniac Tsar. Smith was referred to with emphatic respect in the Ambassadorial Book for that year as 'ambassador and knight'.[16] In 1613 that same Thomas Smith, we read in the documents of the Ambassadorial Office, came to Moscow once more, this time with the rank of envoy.[17] It is interesting to note that another document, the Book of Receipts for 1613, describes him simply as a high-ranking English merchant.[18]

The new head of the Muscovy Company and Resident (a title acknowledging the trust of the English government), Sir John Merrick, spent long periods in Moscow on a number of occasions. One of his letters of passage, drawn up in the Ambassadorial Office, dates from 1600, and of course mentions the right to customs-free trading:

> and when he, Ivan [John] and his people come into this our town you shall let him and his people with goods, under this our letter of passage, through all our towns without restraint, and not take our duties of passage from him, Ivan, and from his goods, and from those people who shall be with him, in those our towns, under this letter granted by the Tsar.[19]

He visited the court of Muscovy as emissary from the Crown on several occasions: for example, in 1607 as envoy with congratulations to Tsar Vasily Shuysky on his accession to the throne, in 1613–14, and in 1620–1 again as plenipotentiary ambassador to Tsar Mikhail Fyodorovich.[20] Merrick's diplomatic success was essential. The future of the English in the Russian market depended on him and so did the continuation of the privileged conditions achieved half a century before and reaffirmed by Tsar Boris.

The first time Merrick acted as ambassador to Mikhail Fyodorovich, he served as intermediary in negotiations between Moscow and Stockholm, negotiations that concluded with the Peace of Stolbovo in 1617. His appearance in Moscow was a result of semi-official and personal contacts with the head of the Ambassadorial Office, Ivan Gramotin.[21] Through their contribution to the regulation of Russo-Swedish relations the English hoped not only to have a hand in directing those relations – since trade in the Baltic was vital for England – but also in establishing their own right to transit trade with Iran via Russia. The second time Merrick worked with Mikhail Fyodorovich, they discussed not only commerce but also official English

congratulations to Patriarch Philaret on his return from captivity in Poland in 1619 (see cat. 58) and of course the 'eternal agreement' – an alliance between Russia and Britain – which was never to come about.

Charles II's representative, Charles Howard, 1st Earl of Carlisle (fig.34), was titled by the Russians 'great and plenipotentiary ambassador'.[22] A member of the nobility from Charles' own circle, he had no direct relation to Anglo-Russian trade. As emissary from the Crown, however, he was obliged to protect the interests of English merchants in Muscovy.

The remaining visitors generally had the status of 'messengers'; they were described variously as 'nobles', 'merchants', 'visiting English merchants' or 'agents'.[23] Yet into the 1660s they brought royal gifts to Moscow, as did the fully-fledged ambassadors. Contemporary practice in Russia's diplomatic relations with continental powers was that gifts from foreign rulers and governments were brought by high-ranking ambassadors, within which context England formed a notable exception. Thus, for instance, the 'noble' Simon Digby – who replaced the 'merchant' Thomas Vench as representative of the Muscovy Company in 1635, and who is named several times in the relevant Ambassadorial Books as 'envoy'[24] – informed the Russian officials sent to greet him at the border and the local military commander that he was travelling 'from the English Carlus with a letter and with gifts', as well as with his family and a suite of some twenty persons.[25] In this case his letter was a letter of credence, affirming his plenipotentiary powers and the range of his duties in the name of the English monarch.

Despite formal changes in status, the role of the English at the Tsar's court remained as noticeable as before in the seventeenth century. This is certainly true of the two John Hebdons, father and son, who visited Moscow as envoys, the elder several times in the 1660s, the younger in 1668 and 1676, and to the envoy and resident Spenser Britton, who arrived in 1646. The latter found himself one of those respected professionals to whom the government of Moscow turned for consultation on numerous occasions. He worked alongside some of the most authoritative members of foreign merchant circles: Peter de la Dalle, Dutch representative of a wealthy merchant family present on the Russian market since the 1620s; Peter Marselis, a Dane who arranged a Russo-Danish dynastic marriage in the 1640s; and Andrew Kellerman, representative of the corporation of foreigners trading in Moscow. Together with the staff of the Ambassadorial Office they discussed legal practice in resolving civil and criminal matters.[26]

The procession to the Kremlin

What exactly happened when a foreign diplomat crossed the Russian border? How did his life in Russia unfold? Help in answering these questions comes from the memoirs of foreign observers and administrative documents from the offices of the Muscovite state.[27] To judge by these sources, the overall scheme of ambassadorial ceremony, perhaps not surprisingly, differed little from those accepted in European states. Ambassadorial ceremony is one of the self-portraits that a state offers to the eyes of the visitor and thus to the eyes of the visitor's own sovereign. Financial and human

and flasks and a lavabo set or basin and ewer. In addition to the traditional silver and textiles, the Tsar received two parrots and an antelope for his menagerie. Cups and livery pots were given not only to the Tsar but also to his father the Patriarch, and featured in the presentation from the ambassador and nobles. Items for the Patriarch included two further objects not at all typical of English gifts: an armchair upholstered in deep burgundy velvet and embroidered with gold thread, and a clock, the body of which was made of some green semi-precious stone.[89] We know that the ambassador and all participants in his mission received the gift of furs valued at double what they had brought. They took back furs not only for themselves, but also for King James: the list of gifts sent to him includes pairs and 'forties' of sables, fox and ermine, as well as Persian velvet and a bow and arrows. So interested was the Patriarch in concluding an anti-Polish alliance with the English that he personally added gifts from himself: textiles, a Persian carpet and a gold *bratina* or loving cup with precious stones.[90]

A frequent visitor to the court of Moscow was the agent Fabian Smith. In 1625 he informed the Tsar's government of alterations to the status of the Muscovy Company back in Britain. Smith and his cohorts were permitted to trade without payment of customs duties, but the remaining British merchants were to pay duties at a rate of half that paid by other European merchants.[91] Smith's visit to the court marked the appearance in the sovereign's armoury of two decorated muskets of Dutch make (cats. 47–8).[92]

Gifts sent by Charles I via the agent Simon Digby, presented on 3 January 1636 in the Gold Chamber, included not only cloth but satin and velvet, a pair of gourd cups (in Russian described as 'to the gourd fashion'), pairs of livery pots with flat-chased bodies showing 'people of the sea riding sea-fish and masks and shells', flasks 'chased in the manner of shells' and single-branch candlesticks. The value put on all this in the Treasury Office came, according to surviving documents, to some 470 rubles. Among the royal gifts was also a ewer and basin designed on a sea theme. The basin was square and decorated in four places with 'beasts of the sea in the sea waters, between them four whales with two tails …along the edge is chased the sea, in which are beasts of the sea and shells', while the ewer 'to the gourd fashion' had 'on the handle a woman's head, over the ewer beasts of the sea, on the belly a winged mask' (this basin is now in the Trinity Monastery of St Sergius). A month later the merchant and other English traders visited the Tsar's sister, Tatyana Mikhaylovna, and presented her with cups, a basin and ewer and precious textiles.[93] All these gifts were accepted into the treasury 'with respect'. Digby was a notable figure on the Russian market in the early 1640s, one of the few to be given the right to produce potash. The Russians rarely and only most unwillingly allowed foreigners to set up any kind of production in the country, fearing colonization.

Of particular significance for the imperial treasury were the gifts made after the Restoration, brought from Charles II by Carlisle's embassy of 1664.[94] Carlisle's official purpose was to declare the King's return to the throne and re-establish English merchants' privileges. Through his insistence, he not only received an official audience, but was also permitted to visit the Tsar in his private chambers and conduct secret talks with him.

Careful thought went into the composition of the royal gifts Carlisle brought: they had specific – and important – ideological and emotional meaning, possibly influenced by memories of the Muscovite government's assistance to Charles II during his time in exile. The inclusion of silver objects and gifts from the royal collection (the Jewel House) was deeply symbolic. Heading the list was a commemorative item: a gun that had belonged to Charles I. Then came the silver, headed by a ewer and basin that once belonged to Charles II's mother, Henrietta Maria, daughter of Henri IV of France; this commemorative piece would have recalled the now re-established magnificence of the ruling dynasty in the kingdom of England and Scotland, and made clear the regime's desire to re-establish former relations. The remaining works repeat the silver forms sent in 1636 – pairs of cups, livery pots, flasks and candlesticks. In addition came newly fashionable fruit dishes (used for salted vegetables and pickles in Russia) and a perfuming pot.[95] Once it had passed into the treasury, the English silver was not forgotten and the documents of the Treasury Office record that in March 1664 'the sovereign came into the treasury to look over the English gifts'.[96]

In addition to traditional items of silver and textiles – all kinds of 'good solid cloth of different colours', both English and 'Shkotskikh' (Scottish) – Charles II sent six copper cannon to Russia. The early 1660s was a difficult time for the Russian army, at war with the Polish state in Ukraine and Belorussia, and these cannon were intended as a hint that the English were ready to provide concrete aid, in exchange, of course, for the right to trade duty-free on the Russian market. Mikhail Fyodorovich also received artillery among gifts from Holland: in 1630–1 the embassy of Conrad Burch brought all kinds of defensive weapons for pike-men, cuirassiers and harquebusiers, two pairs of pistols, carbine barrels and eight cannon of varied calibre with gun-carriages in the Netherlandish manner, and a hundred balls for each cannon.[97] The gift was followed by large orders of ordnance by the Russian government.

Charles sent gifts not only for the Tsar but also for his sons Alexey and Fyodor. They received similar sets of firearms, clocks and textiles, but only Alexey, the heir to the throne, received a pair of pistols.[98]

There were in effect no royal gifts from London to Moscow from the 1670s to 1690s, the sole exception being the frigate sent for Peter the Great, but even that did not make it to the capital. Envoys and trading agents presented only personal tokens of respect. Despite the lack of royal gifts, however, all diplomats received honours in accordance with their status and the personal gifts were willingly accepted into the treasury. The role played in the formation of the Kremlin's treasury by English gold- and silversmiths and armourers, as well as the English textile industry, was considerable.

Today, international diplomatic norms are standardized, varying only very slightly to reflect national differences and traditions and of course the balance of political forces at the very time of the visit by a monarch, head of government or official delegation. Today, ambassadors spend long years in the country to which they are appointed, in a tradition that started in

Europe, notably in Italy, back in the late fifteenth and early sixteenth centuries. That tradition reached Russia in the seventeenth century; it was then that resident ambassadors first appeared, accompanied by their servants and a veritable suite, representing at court the states necessary for political and commercial reasons. But even then, the shuttle diplomacy that had been regular practice since ancient times did not come to an end.

Notes

1 Rogozhin 2002, pp. 16–17. The history of the Ambassadorial Office has been the subject of a number of studies, including the publication of documents and biographies of the most celebrated Russian diplomats. The history of the question is set out in detail in a monograph by N. M. Rogozhin: see Rogozhin 2003, pp. 13–17.

2 See Rogozhin 2003, p. 334.

3 For the history of the Muscovy Company, see subject bibliography.

4 There was a similar practice in Russo-Dutch diplomatic relations from the time they were officially established under Tsar Mikhail Fyodorovich: Dutch merchants represented both their own interests and those of the government without having the rank of ambassador.

5 Rogozhin 2002, pp. 36, 40.

6 Bantysh-Kamensky 1894, pp. 92, 94.

7 Gamel 1865–9, issue 2, p. 124.

8 Fyodor to Elizabeth I, September 1585 in Tolstoy 1875, p. 259; original translation, 'The perfite copy of Jerom Horsseyes translacion of the king of Russyas letter brought by him who cam with the same to London at Christmas 1585' in Tolstoy 1875, p. 260.

9 Many of the documents relating to Beckman's journey and his complaints are published in Tolstoy 1875.

10 Y. S. Lure, 'Angliyskaya politika na Rusi kontsa XVI veka' ['English Politics in Rus at the End of the Sixteenth Century'], *Uchyonnye zapiski Leningradskogo gosudarstvennogo pedagogicheskogo instituta A. I. Gertsena* ['Scientific Notes of Leningrad A. I. Herzen State Pedagogical Institute'] 61 (1947), pp. 130–4.

11 Ambassadors' reports published in *Sbornik Russkogo Istoricheskogo Obshchestva* ['Anthology of the Russian Historical Society'], vol. 38 (St Petersburg, 1883), pp. 167–8, 181.

12 Ambassadors' Travels 1954, pp. 111–20, 126–7, 130, 136, 139, 144, 152–5.

13 Ambassadors' Travels 1954, pp. 156–7, 162, 164, 168, 171, 179–83.

14 Bantysh-Kamensky 1894, pp. 100–1, 104, 116–17.

15 For more information on Thomas Smith, see subject bibliography.

16 With this title he was announced at the audience when he presented his personal gifts to Tsar Boris Godunov and his son Fyodor: see Arel and Bogatyrov 1997, p. 453.

17 Bantysh-Kamensky 1894, p. 101.

18 Book of Receipts 1613–14, f. 36.

19 *Sbornik Russkogo Istoricheskogo Obshchestva* ['Anthology of the Russian Historical Society'], vol. 38 (St Petersburg, 1883), p. 301.

20 Like Thomas Smith earlier, John Merrick was described as an ambassador during the first audience and negotiations (see Bantysh-Kamensky 1894, pp. 100–1, 104).

21 G. M. Phipps, *Sir John Merrick: English Merchant-Diplomat in Seventeenth-Century Russia* (Newtonville, MA, 1983).

22 Bantysh-Kamensky 1894, p. 118.

23 Bantysh-Kamensky 1894, pp. 106–18.

24 Simon Digby was described in the heading in the Ambassadorial Book as a nobleman, and during audiences and negotiations as an envoy or messenger (*poslannik*) (Bantysh-Kamensky 1894, p. 110).

25 Ambassadorial Book 1635–6, f. 1.

26 S. P. Orlenko, *Vykhodtsy iz Zapadnoy Evropy v Rossii XVII veka: Pravovoy status i real'noe polozhenie* ['Natives of Western Europe in Seventeenth-Century Russia: Legal Status and True Status'] (Moscow, 2004), p. 137.

27 On the early period and origins of Moscow ambassadorial ceremonial, see L. A. Yuzefovich, *Kak v posol'skikh obychayakh vedyotsya …* ['As 'tis According to Ambassadorial Custom …'] (Moscow, 1988).

28 Ambassadorial Book 1635–6, ff. 27, 34, 39; see also Bantysh-Kamensky 1894, pp. 106, 120–1.

29 Ambassadorial Book 1635–6, f. 19; Ambassadorial Book 1620–1, f. 154.

30 See *Pamyatniki arkhitektury Moskvy: Kreml', Kitay-gorod, Tsentral'nye ploshchadi* ['Moscow's Architectural Monuments: Kremlin, Kitay gorod, Central Squares'] (Moscow, 1982), pp. 51, 53, 56–7.

31 Ambassadorial Book 1663–4, f. 154v; Ambassadorial Book 1676, ff. 45, 59v. This luxurious mansion not far from the Kremlin was often used to house not only English but also Polish, Swedish and Dutch diplomats.

32 Ambassadorial Book 1663–4, f. 196v. By comparison, the embassy from Poland in 1686 involved more than 150 people being present at the audience.

33 Purchas 1626, p. 983.

34 Meierberg 1997, p. 85. Similar information is recorded in other memoirs, such as those of Andrey Rode, secretary of the Danish embassy of 1659, 'Opisanie vtorogo posol'stva v Rossiyu datskogo poslannika Gansa Ol'delanda v 1659, sostavlennoe posol'skim sekretarem Andreem Rode' ['Description of the Second Embassy to Russia by the Danish Envoy Hans Oldeland in 1659, Compiled by the Ambassadorial Secretary Andrey Rode'] in History of Russia 1997, p. 141. A compatriot J. Ulfeldt, who headed the embassy to Ivan IV in 1578, also mentioned the presence of two thousand fully equipped archers flanking the ambassadorial train (Ulfeldt 2002, p. 318).

35 Ambassadorial Book 1614–17, f. 52; Ambassadorial Book 1620–1, f. 153v.

36 Russian State Archive of Ancient Acts, Moscow, fund 35, *opis'* 1, *delo* 18, ff. 57v, 60v, 108v.

37 Ambassadorial Book 1663–4, f. 196v. In describing the greeting accorded Bowes in 1583, Jerome Horsey noted that three hundred riders took part in the procession. This is clearly an exaggeration – there are indeed a number of such errors in the description of the audience.

38 Ambassadorial Book 1667, f. 278v; Ambassadorial Book 1641, f. 241; Ambassadorial Affairs 1644, no. 1, f. 58.

39 Ambassadorial Book 1614–17, f. 52; Ambassadorial Book 1620–1, f. 154.

40 Ambassadorial Book 1663–4, f. 197. The English description of this, by Guy de Miège, notes the same details: 'The Eleventh day being come, there were a hundred and thirty persons of the Tzars Guards, and threescore sledges sent to carry the Presents from the King, the greatest part of which was designed for the Tzar, the rest for the two young Princes Knetz, Alexey, Alexevitz, and Pheodor Alexevitz his Sons,' (Carlisle 1669, p. 142).

41 Purchas 1626, p. 983.

42 Purchas 1626, p. 988.

43 N. Witsen [Vitsen], *Puteshestvie v Moskoviyu 1664–1665: Dnevnik* ['Journey to Muscovy, 1664–5: Diary'], tr. into Russian by V. G. Trisman (St Petersburg, 1996), pp. 93–4.

44 Ambassadorial Book 1663–4, f. 148: 'Pure' bridles indicate a harness unadorned with precious stones.

45 Certainly this was where ambassador John Merrick (Ambassadorial Book 1614–17, f. 52; Ambassadorial Book 1620–1, f. 153v), the Earl of Carlisle (Ambassadorial Book 1663–4, f. 196v) and the envoy John Hebdon (Ambassadorial Book 1676, ff. 60v, 109) all dismounted.

46 Like the uniforms of other participants in the audience, these robes were handed out from the treasury, the inventories of the treasury containing descriptions of just such robes (Treasury Inventory 1690, ff. 312v–18v).

47 Ambassadorial Book 1663–4, f. 715v.

48 Ambassadorial Book 1663–4, ff. 197–8.

49 Ambassadorial Book 1614–17, f. 53; Ambassadorial Book 1620–1, f. 154v.

50 Ambassadorial Book 1635–6, ff. 48, 110.

51 Ambassadorial Book 1614–17, ff. 53, 455; Ambassadorial Book 1620–1, ff. 151v, 481v–483v; Ambassadorial Book 1635–6, f. 16.

52 Ambassadorial Book 1663–4, ff. 198, 714v.

53 Russian State Archive of Ancient Acts, Moscow, fund 35, *opis'* 1, *delo* 18, ff. 58, 61, 109, 329v–33.

54 A. Olearius, *The Voyages & Travels of the Ambassadors Sent by Frederick Duke of Holstein, to the Great Duke of Muscovy, and the King of Persia,* tr. John Davies (London, 1662), p. 17.

55 Hakluyt 1598, p. 459. Numerous details regarding the decoration of the hall and the sovereign's throne, attire and jewellery are provided by other visitors (Ulfeldt 2002, pp. 320–2; Meierberg 1997, pp. 85–6).

56 Ambassadorial Book 1663–4, f. 198v.

57 Russian State Archive of Ancient Acts, Moscow, fund 35, *opis'* 1, *delo* 18, ff. 18, 109.

58 Ambassadorial Book 1620–1, ff. 155v–6v; Ambassadorial Book 1635–6, f. 12.

59 Arel and Bogatyryov 1997, p. 422; Ambassadorial Book 1614–17, ff. 455–67; Ambassadorial Book 1620–1, ff. 491–3v; Ambassadorial Book 1663–4, ff. 275–80.

60 Ambassadorial Book 1614–17, f. 466f; Ambassadorial Book 1620–1, f. 492.

61 Ambassadorial Book 1663–4, f. 275.

62 Ambassadorial Book 1663–4, f. 279.

63 Smith 1605, f. F1r,v.

64 For example, Treasury Inventory 1663, ff. 27–8v.

65 Ambassadorial Book 1614–17, f. 465v; Ambassadorial Book 1620–1, f. 491r,v.

66 For more information on the Treasury Office, see A. K. Leontev, *Obrazovanie prikaznoy sistemy upravleniya v Russkom gosudarstve: Iz istorii sozdaniya tsentral'nogo gosudarstvennogo apparata v kontse XV–nachale XVI veka* ['The Formation of the Office System of Government in the Russian State: From the History of the Creation of a Centralized State Apparatus in the late Fifteenth–early Sixteenth Centuries'] (Moscow, 1961), pp. 43–59.

67 Goldberg 1954, p. 438.

68 Jones 1909, p. xix.

69 Purchas 1626, pp. 988–9.

70 'The Ambassage of the right worshipfull Master Thomas Randolfe, Esquire, to the Emperour of Russia, in the yeere 1568, briefly written by himselfe' in Hakluyt 1598, p. 377.

71 Purchas 1626, p. 983.

72 'Stateynyy spisok priezda i prebyvaniya v Rossii angliyskogo posla Elizara Fletchera' ['Report on the Arrival and Stay in Russia of the English Ambassador Elizar [Giles] Fletcher'], *Vremennik Obshchestva istorii i drevnostey rossiyskikh* ['Annals of the Society for Russian History and Antiquities'] 8 (Moscow, 1850), p. 5.

73 I. G. Spassky, '"Zolotye" – voinskie nagrady do-petrovskoy Rusi' ['"Gold" – Military Awards in pre-Petrine Rus'], *Trudy Gosudarstvennogo Ermitazha: Numizmatika* ['Papers of the State Hermitage Museum: Numismatics'] 4 (Leningrad, 1961).

74 I. Massa, 'Kratkoe izvestie o nachale i proiskhozhdenii sovremennykh voyn i smut v Moskovii, sluchivshikhsya do 1610 goda za korotkoe vremya pravleniya gosudarey' ['Brief Information on the Commencement and Origins of the Contemporary Wars and Upheaval in Muscovy that Occurred before 1610 during the Short Reigns of Several Sovereigns'] in History of Russia 1997, p. 51.

75 Goldberg 1954, p. 442. Cited also in Oman 1961, p. 27.

76 'Travels of Sir Jerome Horsey, 1572–89', British Library, Harl. MS 1813.

77 Ambassadorial Book 1676, ff. 361v–4.

78 Ambassadorial Book 1614–17, ff. 469–70; Ambassadorial Book 1620–1, f. 565; see S. M. Solovyov, *Sochineniya* ['Writings'] (Moscow, 1990) book 5, vols 9–10, p. 90. Merrick later mentioned this *kovsh* separately in his will, bequeathing it to his brother-in-law: see Phillippa Glanville, p. 49.

79 Ambassadorial Book 1662–3, ff. 94–6. These are mentioned also by John Evelyn in his diary for 9 February 1664/5.

80 Ambassadorial Book 1620–1, ff. 564–5.

81 Ambassadorial Book 1676, ff. 105, 113v, 295, 316, 370r,v.

82 Treasury Inventory 1690, f. 97.

83 Goldberg 1954, p. 448.

84 Treasury Inventory 1663, ff. 182v–183; Veltman 1844, p. 115.

85 The museum was founded in 1806. The first publications appeared in the 1840s. See Veltman 1844, pp. 115, 136; Antiquities 1849–53, p. 57.

86 Goldberg 1954, p. 444; Oman 1961, pp. 29–30.

87 Russian State Archive of Ancient Acts, Moscow, fund 35, *opis'* 1, 1697, no. 265.

88 Ambassadorial Book 1614–17, ff 57–58v: see Kologrivov 1911, pp. 20–1, although the ambassador's name is given incorrectly; Goldberg 1954, p. 446.

89 Ambassadorial Book 1620–1, ff. 168–74v, 567–71v, 573–5; Kologrivov 1911, pp. 48–57; Goldberg 1954, pp. 448–51. The inclusion of exotic beasts in gifts was characteristic of an earlier age, but in the seventeenth century we do know of cases when birds and beasts were brought to Russia as gifts. Among the Polish ambassadorial gifts of 1686 we find mention of a *gamayun* or Sirin bird, which was unknown to the Moscow merchants and remained thus without a value: see Ambassadorial Book 1686, ff. 480, 844v.

90 Ambassadorial Book 1620–1, ff. 572, 574r,v, 578–80.

91 See Dyomkin 1994, issue 1, p. 47.

92 The story of the arrival of two Dutch muskets in the Armoury was traced by L. L. Yakovlev (Armoury Inventory 1884–93, part 5, book 4, no. 6783).

93 Ambassadorial Book 1635–6, f. 56; Book of Receipts 1636–7, ff. 32v–7, 44r,v; Goldberg 1954, pp. 451–2.

94 Ambassadorial Book 1663–4, ff. 201v–203v, 283v–286v; see also Goldberg 1954, pp. 455–6.

95 Ambassadorial Book 1663–64, ff. 201v–202v, 274v–278, 283v–286v, 445–56; Antiquities 1849–53, section 5, p. 136; Goldberg 1954, pp. 455–6; UK National Archives, Public Record Office, LC5/107, p. 100, and LC5/137, p. 144.

96 Treasury Inventory 1663–6, ff. 186, 192.

97 See V. A. Kordt, 'Ocherk snosheniy Moskovskogo gosudarstva s Respublikoyu Soedinyonnykh Niderlandov do 1631 g.' ['Essay on the Relations between the Muscovite State and the Republic of the United Netherlands before 1631'] in *Sbornik Russkogo Istoricheskogo Obshchestva* ['Anthology of the Russian Historical Society'], vol. 116 (St Petersburg, 1902), p. 35.

98 For more detail see Sovereign's Armoury 2002, pp. 390–2.

57. Detail of the English 'Charyott' for Tsar Boris Godunov

An English 'Charyott' for Tsar Boris Godunov

Lyubov Kirillova

Among the Armoury's celebrated collection is an outstanding English late sixteenth-century carriage. Few European royal houses owned a carriage of this scale and complexity. Such are its links to historical events and individuals that the carriage has an almost mythical aura.

Despite its large size, the carriage was intended to seat only two people. Its handsome body is suspended on straps, the roof supported on eight pillars. The open upper part of the body is hung with curtains: carriages did not have glass windows at this time. On both sides the walls double as fold-down steps. Despite its luxury, the carriage was not the most convenient form of conveyance. With no turntable or springs, such a heavy vehicle could be turned only with great difficulty, and often the rear wheels had to be physically lifted off the ground and moved. Nor is there a coachman's box or footboards, and the coachman had either to walk alongside the horses or guide them from a position seated on one of the leaders.

58. The English 'Charyott'

In design, the carriage has all the marks of the late Renaissance: a clearly expressed overall design, precise construction and coordinated decorative forms and images. Multi-figure compositions carved in high relief, painted predominantly in red and green, fill the lower part of the carriage. They share a common theme, reflecting the complex relations between the European states and Turkey: on the back wall is a battle between Christians and Muslims, on the front a procession of Christians accompanying the victors' chariot. Rising above local patriotism, the artist depicts the warriors not as coarsely triumphant but marching in an orderly manner, filled with quiet pride. On the side walls are scenes of boar, tiger and lion hunts. Detailed attention is paid to the riders' costumes and elements of the horses' caparison.

Harmoniously combined with the carving is the painting that covers the upper side walls. In the top row are idealized landscapes with parks and buildings, while skillfully drawn hunting scenes occupy the second row, the whole employing an elegant colour scheme. On the front and back are gilded bas-reliefs with Russian arms and sculptures in which folds of drapery alternately conceal and highlight the bodies' mass and form, creating a fascinating play of light and shade across the surface. The figures' heads are somewhat over-large for the bodies, a feature which made them more easily read from a distance. The gilded relief carving of vegetation on the wheels differs from the rest of the decoration.

196

For more than eighty years the carriage was used by Russian monarchs for their ceremonial 'exits' through the city. These parades carried great political significance and occupied an important place in the strictly regimented life of the court and diplomatic etiquette. They embodied the whole idea of the majesty of the state and the royal throne, and their organization was determined by questions of statesmanship, ideology and diplomacy. Moreover, they reflected contemporary customs and manners, as well as the intellectual and aesthetic ideals of the age. When the carriage became too fragile for use, its history and importance were such that in 1834 it was transferred to the Armoury.[1]

Study of the Armoury collections began in the 19th century. The museum was to be one of the great Russian research centres, and leading scholars were drawn to this magnificent carriage. In 1844 A. Veltman dated it to the late sixteenth century, arguing that it featured among gifts brought from England for Boris Godunov.[2] Alfred Jones and Charles Oman emphasized that the carriage had been a royal gift, suggesting it had been brought to Russia with the embassy of Sir Thomas Smith in 1604[3] or that of Richard Lee in 1600.[4] More recent literature has been less united in its identification, some authors even suggesting that it may be of Russian work.[5]

Comparative analysis of the available sources – archive materials, miniatures, prints and easel paintings showing sixteenth-century carriages – enable us to establish more clearly the date and place of production and the carriage's origins.[6] A study of documents relating to the Armoury and the Ambassadorial Office confirms that the carriage was indeed the work of sixteenth-century English craftsmen and that it was brought to Russia as a gift from James I to Boris Godunov.[7] It should perhaps be identified with the 'charyott' that heads the list of gifts brought by Sir Thomas Smith in 1604: 'A preasent to the greate Emperor and greate Duke Borris Pheodorow^ch of all Russia and to the Empriss Marya Gryoryevna from James the Great, Kinge of all England'.[8]

The two gilded bas-reliefs on the rear of the body show the arms of the Russian state during the reign of Boris Godunov (1598–1605) – and not of Mikhail Fyodorovich (1613–45), as some have suggested. The expressive figures on those arms are depicted in the European manner, according to the rules of western European heraldry: they face right not left, as would only be the case if they were produced in a European, i.e. English, workshop.[9] This suggests that the carriage was made especially for export to Russia, or rather as an official gift to the monarch of a land that was an important trading partner.

As a number of scholars have pointed out, one of the aims of Sir Thomas Smith's embassy in 1604 was to discuss the Anglo-Russian alliance against the Turks that Boris Godunov wished to conclude. Although the British monarch had no desire to enter into such a firm alliance, the imagery on the carriage – a Christian victory over the Turks – would have been easily read as a suggestion that all Christians – Protestant and Orthodox – were united against non-Christians.

The composition of the engraved decoration on the front and back walls may relate to engravings by Jost Amman (c. 1539–91).[10] N. A. Kuznetsova of the Pushkin Museum of Fine Arts in Moscow has suggested that the paintings were by a Netherlandish artist.[11] Certainly Netherlandish works were known across continental Europe and in England, and there were artists from Holland and Flanders working in London. The paintings on the carriage reflect a typical northern interest in the loving depiction of small details. The painting on the pillars, however, is the work of the Russian painter Ivan Bezmin and dates from the second half of the seventeenth century when the carriage underwent renewal.[12]

Despite that renewal, there is good reason to suggest that the carriage was never subject to serious reworking. Archive documents record that the Tsar's chair was replaced in the first half of the seventeenth century, the new chair being taken from the 'ceremonial sledge' of Tsar Mikhail Fyodorovich. It was then 'freshened up' in 1677–8 to be used in greeting a Polish embassy and during Easter celebrations.[13] New wheels were made and these were covered with gilded carving and bound with iron, 'the work to be undertaken by painter Ivan Bezmin with fellows and master blacksmith Pavkov with his pupils'. The carriage was again restored in 1816 when the order was given for all carriages to be put in suitable order after victory in the war with Napoleon following his unsuccessful occupation of Moscow in 1812.[14] Thus the carriage that we see today survives almost as it was when it first arrived in Russia four hundred years ago.

1   Russian State Archive of Ancient Acts, Moscow, fund 1239, *opis'* 3, part 15, *delo* 16008, ff. 3, 4; Department of Manuscripts, Printed and Graphic Reserves of the Moscow Kremlin Museums, fund 1, *delo* 34, f. 77.
2   Veltman 1844, p. 170, pl. 32.
3   Oman 1961, pp. 29–30, pls. 6–7.
4   Jones 1909, p. xxi.
5   H. Kreisel, *Prunkwagen und Schlitten* ['Stately Carriages and Sledges'] (Leipzig, 1927).
6   Russian State Archive of Ancient Acts, Moscow, fund 396, *opis'* 2, part 2, *delo* 1022, ff. 325, 396, 397; *delo* 1023, f. 471.
7   Russian State Archive of Ancient Acts, Moscow, fund 396, *opis'* 2, part 2, *delo* 1022, ff. 395–7; *delo* 1023, f. 471; *delo* 1264, f. 760; Department of Manuscripts, Printed and Graphic Reserves of the Moscow Kremlin Museums, fund 1, *delo* 34, f. 77.
8   The list of gifts carried by Smith in 1604 is cited in A. Maskell, *Russian Art and Art Objects in Russia: A Handbook to the Reproductions of Goldsmiths' Work and Other Art Treasures from that Country in the South Kensington Museum* (London, 1884), pp. 231–2.
9   V. K. Lukomsky, *Russkaya geral'dika: Rukovodstvo, sostavlenie i opisanie gerbov* ['Russian Heraldry: Handbook for the Compilation and Description of Coats-of-arms'] (St Petersburg, 1915); A. V. Lakier, *Russkaya geral'dika* ['Russian Heraldry'] (St Petersburg, 1854), p. 20.
10 See A. Bartsch et al., *The Illustrated Bartsch*, vol. 20: Jost Amman (New York, 1985); L. I. Tananaeva, *Rudol'fintsy* ['The Rudolphines'] (Moscow, 1996), p. 216.
11 Personal communication to the author, 1985.
12 A. Uspensky, 'Ivan Artemevich Bezmin i ego proizvedeniya' ['Ivan Artemevich Bezmin and his Works'], *Starye gody* ['Days of Yore'], April 1908, p. 208.
13 Russian State Archive of Ancient Acts, Moscow, fund 396, *delo* 1022, ff. 395–6.
14 Russian State Archive of Ancient Acts, Moscow, fund 396, *opis'* 1, part 11, *delo* 16433, f. 4.

Ambassadorial Gifts

Maija Jansson

59. Szymon Boguszowicz (attrib.), *A Tsar Receiving a Delegation in the Reception Hall of the Faceted Chamber in the Moscow Kremlin*, early 17th century. Hungarian National Museum, Budapest

Giving gifts is a practice as old as mankind itself.[1] While it has no traceable beginning, we can see it reshaped in endless patterns over the course of human history. The Trojan horse famously reminds us of the darker side of giving and provides a lasting currency to Virgil's phrase, 'Beware of Greeks bearing gifts'. Other Classical authors wrote of the 'triple rhythm of generosity' consisting of 'giving, accepting, and returning'.[2] Religions of the world in different places and at different times cast the practice in more expansive terms, preaching of God's infinite gifts to mankind – charity, grace and mercy – words that also occupy a place in the vocabulary of worldly kingdoms.

In early modern Europe the presentation of royal gifts from one ruler to another was part of a highly ritualized ceremony that preceded every ambassadorial audience with a head of state. Why was the presentation important and why were the gifts given? The significance of the ceremony is marked by its order within the diplomatic mission: it came first and preceded the negotiations, with the gift as its centrepiece, marking the beginning and not the end of an embassy. At each embassy the gifts were presented as a tangible, expression of goodwill from the ruler of the visiting ambassador to his host. The gift represented the majesty of the giver and assured that the embassy began graciously, bestowing respect and friendship on the host ruler. It signalled a desire to work together rather than exist in a state of isolation as potential enemies.

In a sense the gift that preceded diplomatic negotiation was the catalyst for peace. Patricia Fumerton concludes that the possibility of peace and stability among states rested to a certain extent on a system of gift exchange. Speaking of the gift in society at large, she writes that 'human society arises as the alternative to the submerged genesis of gift: the state of war'. In other words, in a state of war every man is a potential enemy but through gifts those enemies can be converted into friends.[3] Gift exchange, she continues, 'transmits the trust and generosity of friendship'.[4]

We see the 'generosity of friendship', the tangible expression of goodwill, in the silver presented to the Tsar. For the most part war was not an issue here, but economic expansion and the English need for naval stores were. Under Queen Elizabeth, England sought stable and peaceful relations with Russia that would promote the commercial interests of the Muscovy Company in their economic competition with the Dutch. Later, under her successor James I, an alliance with the Protestant and Orthodox north became essential as Catholic Poland expanded under Sigismund III and Europe edged toward the Thirty Years War. Although geographically separated, Russia provided a strategic alliance of great importance to England that made possible an English and Protestant presence in the north.[5]

The value that England placed on friendship with Russia was reflected in the value of the gifts made on behalf of both the English Crown and the Muscovy Company. Generally speaking, the ambassadorial gifts exchanged in early modern Europe represented a country's resources and the skills of her artisans. The French were famous for their tapestries and embroidered cloths and fabric; the Italians, at least in the north, for their firearms. The Russians were known throughout Europe and the East for their sable and black fox pelts, furs much sought after in London. In 1617 they brought live sables to King James, playing to his interest in animal husbandry and breeding.[6] The Russians also brought presents from Persia and the East – silks, carpets, tooled swords, and daggers encrusted with precious stones and pearls.[7]

Paradoxically, much of the 'English silver' that was well known in court and diplomatic circles abroad, since it was a permanent feature of diplomatic gifts during the late sixteenth and early seventeenth centuries, was not in fact English in origin. Firstly, the metal itself may have been mined elsewhere. Native mining of English silver produced only relatively small quantities;[8] for a long time it was thought that raw silver in this period came to England from Spanish treasure ships, but the theory no longer holds.[9] Moreover, the metal was frequently worked in England not by English craftsmen but by silversmiths of foreign birth and, often, foreign training.[10]

How do we speak about these anticipated gifts and the expectations they in turn engendered? While it is true that the ambassadorial ceremonies are well described in contemporary literature, little is said there about the nature of the gifts themselves and nothing about who chose them and why. It was not until the twentieth century that a vocabulary and forms for studying ritualized giving – as in the case of ambassadorial gifts – came with the groundbreaking work of three anthropologists: Marcel Mauss, Marshall Sahlins and Bronislaw Malinowski. Historians and scholars of the Renaissance have used their works as a basis for examining social concepts of giving during an earlier period. Natalie Zemon Davis, writing about the French in the sixteenth century, provides some insight into the English experience of the same time. With the advent of a market society, she comments, the nature of the relationship between the gift and the organization and function of the society in question is changed. Money comes to play a part and value is measured in monetary terms.[11]

Much of what Davis, relying on Mauss, describes for society at large is apparent in the principles of ambassadorial gift exchange. Lisa Klein, writing about England, concludes that gifts given to Queen Elizabeth that were 'in theory voluntary, disinterested and spontaneous' were, in fact, 'obligatory and interested'.[12] She suggests that these gifts are 'closely bound up with expenditure' and that the money spent on gifts created an obligation in the receiver to reciprocate. Moreover, as Klein points out, 'until the recipient returns the favour, the giver retains an edge'.[13] This point was critical to the success of early modern England's patronage-structured society, and to the principles and rhythm of ambassadorial exchange described below.

Another aspect of ambassadorial giving that was shaped by the idea of reciprocation is that of hospitality or diet. Historian Felicity Heal finds the idea of hospitality as gift intrinsically part of the English religious and educational experience. She writes of 'the duty of generosity' that was proclaimed from the pulpit as one of the 'foundations of moral economy'.[14]

The notion of hospitality in early modern England was bound to the idea of reciprocity: 'the exchange of gifts and rewards to which value not simply

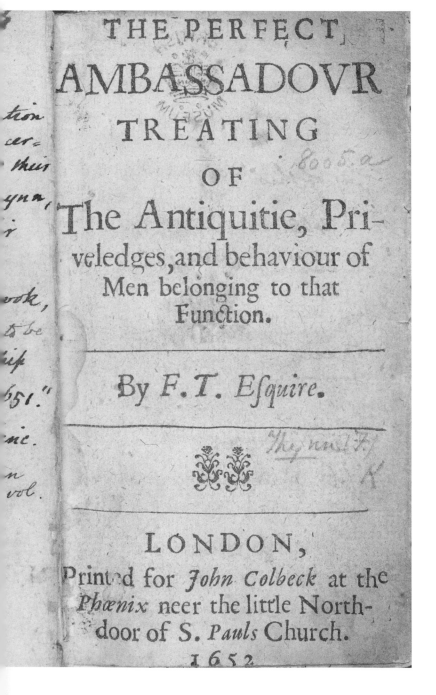

60. Title page from Francis Thynne, *The Perfect Ambassadour: Treating of The Antiquitie, Priveledges, and behaviour of Men belonging to that function*, London, 1652. British Library, London

articulated in money terms attaches'.[15] 'Constant rituals of exchange,' Heal says, were a natural and integral part of elite behaviour from the medieval period on, citing the example of the heads of monastic houses travelling from monastery to monastery being cared for one by the other. Even in a burgeoning market economy, the historic experience of generous hospitality prevailed.

By the sixteenth century, with the expansion of the grammar school curriculum, Classical authors were read in every schoolroom in England. Cicero's writings had an overwhelming influence on the ethics of Tudor society. His reflections on gift-giving in *De Officiis* in particular emphasize a kind of moderation and an expectation of reciprocity. He states that while honouring strangers is noble and a credit to one's country, there should be an 'expectation' of return on this investment, as it would gain loyal adherents.[16] As we have seen, the motive of the ambassadorial gift was not only to show courtesy and extend friendship from one ruler to another but also to pave the way for positive negotiations. There was an expectation of return.

Role of the ambassador

The role of ambassador was well defined in numerous treatises (fig. 60) and courtesy books written from the fifteenth century through the seventeenth.[17] In the manner of Castiglione's manual *The Courtier* (1528), these books are filled with every detail regarding the diplomat's deportment, his social rank and educational background and, most importantly, his responsibility as a servant of the ruler. He was to be the eyes, ears and voice of the King. It is from these early descriptive handbooks, coupled with the instructions to and reports from the ambassadors themselves, that we learn the details of the profession.

By definition, ambassadors were sent from a sovereign prince 'to his equal form'. Other kinds of emissaries carried out diplomatic missions at various levels: envoys, messengers, agents, commissioners and members of trading companies (in the case of England, those of the Muscovy Company). These lesser emissaries, however, were not bound by the protocols of exchange demanded by the formal relations between ruler and ruler; nor were they protected by the usual immunities granted to full ambassadors. Although sometimes sent in the name of the ruler, their gifts rarely carried the weight of a royal gift presented in the course of an ambassadorial audience. Nor did the arrival of these lesser emissaries signal to the ruler a need to cover the expenses of diet and lodging before an audience, which was an integral part of ambassadorial exchange.

The exception to these rules regarding the use of emissaries other than ambassadors was that of the Russia or Muscovy Company of London. The lines of protocol seem to have been blurred on both sides in the diplomatic exchanges between the British monarchy and the Tsars by the merchants of the company. Irina Zagorodnaya has noted that 'the main feature of Russian diplomatic etiquette in relation to the British throne was that no essential difference existed between the receiving of diplomats and trading agents'.[18] On the English side, the Crown and the Muscovy Company enjoyed a symbiotic relationship that served them well. In order to have a presence in the north, the Crown depended on the linguistic skills and transport of the company which, in turn, benefitted from the occasional customs relief and authority in commercial transactions that only the Crown could provide.[19] English diplomats were trained in Latin, French, Italian, Spanish and sometimes German, but rarely Arabic, Russian or Portuguese. In 1624 the Secretary of State, George Calvert, informed Sir Richard Weston that he had sent a letter for Muscovy to Sir John Merrick 'to be translated with all speed', an example of the government's reliance on the skills of the Company.[20] During the early Stuart period a number of members of the Muscovy Company spoke Russian and, of course, as regards negotiations dealing with trade, they knew their commercial interests better than anyone else. The Company also saved the Crown from having to invest in its own fleet of ships for the northern run. Moreover, the Company often shared with the Crown the cost of paying for hospitality or diet and lodging that a formal ambassadorial mission to England would have required the Crown alone to pay for.

On several occasions prominent members of the Muscovy Company were granted full ambassadorial status from the Crown. Sir Thomas Smith, for example, in 1604, and Sir John Merrick, who went as special ambassador to Russia in 1613, 1614 and 1620.[21]

Ambassadors extraordinary, those appointed for particular and special missions, and resident ambassadors, those in residence in a particular place for a period of time, both negotiated state business. Such business might have a personal as well as a public side as, for example, in the matter of marriage treaties. The instruction books for ambassadors also speak of two kinds of embassies: one of ceremony and one of negotiation. By ceremony was meant an embassy of goodwill and greeting where no business was to be transacted, and hence no gift given. Three years after Charles I acceded to the throne, Vasily Demetrovich Esipov arrived in London in the autumn of 1628. He brought no gifts because, as the Master of Ceremonies noted: 'his message was only congratulatory for the King's assumption of the Crown, and in that regard might be thought to bring honour and respect enough with it without other present'.[22] In other words, honour and respect were the greatest gifts that could be given. Clearly, however, it was the gifts that appealed to the readers of the popular press. In the absence of furs and silks, no reports of this embassy appeared in the *corantos* and newsletters. Even the Venetians were not enchanted. Alvise Contarini, the Venetian ambassador in London, wrote to the Doge and Senate: 'There is a Muscovite ambassador here, who has come to compliment the King on his accession; so it must be supposed that news arrives very late in those cold regions.'[23]

61. Wenceslaus Hollar, *Whitehall Palace, Eastern Front*, c.1647. The British Museum, London

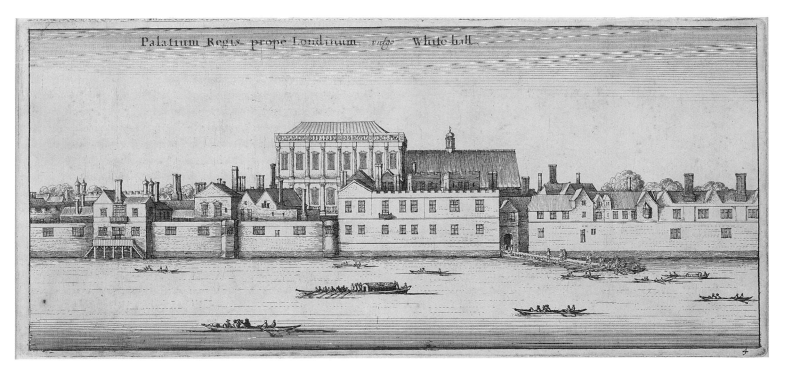

Letters from English Monarchs to Russian Tsars

From the Russian State Archive of Ancient Acts, Moscow

56

Letter from Elizabeth I to Tsar Ivan IV

18 May 1570

Parchment manuscript, bearing Elizabeth's signature

12⅛ x 17⅞ in. (30.8 x 45.5 cm)

Provenance: papers of the Ambassadorial Office; transferred as part of the Moscow State Archive of the Ministry of Foreign Affairs in 1925

Russian State Archive of Ancient Acts, Moscow, fund 35, *opis'* 2, no. 3, Relations Between Russia and England

Literature: Tolstoy 1875, nos. 25–6, pp. 90–101; Bantysh-Kamensky 1894, p. 92

In 1569 Ivan IV found himself in a difficult situation, with rising opposition to the *oprichnina* (the lands and bodies under his personal control) among the higher clergy, civil servants and boyars. He ordered his Russian ambassador to England, Andrey Grigorievich Sovin, to ask at an audience with Queen Elizabeth whether in the event that some adversity befall him through his enemies, he would be permitted to come to England. Sovin was entitled to promise that if the same should threaten the Queen, she would be allowed to travel freely to Russia. On 18 May 1570 Elizabeth replied, promising Ivan IV and his family that they would be welcomed in England in the event that they were forced to flee.

> this our secrit lettre
>
> When wee have by other our lettres delivered to your highnes ambassadour the noble person Andrew Gregriwiche Saviena made aunswere to the greatest part of such messages and lettres as the said ambassador declared and brought to us, wee have thought good in some secreite manner to send your highnes for a manifest and certaine token of our good will to your highnes estate and suertye: this our secrit lettre whereunto none are privie besides our selfe, but our most secreite councell, wee doe so regard the suertie of you the Emperour and great Duke, as we offer that yf at anie time it so mishappe that you L. our brother Emperour and great Duke, bee by anie casuall chaunce either of secrite conspiracie or outward hostillitie driven to change your countries and shall like to repaire into our kingdome and dominions, with the noble empresse your wife and youre deare children the princes, we shall with such honors and curtesies receive and intreate your highnes then, as shall become so great a prince and shall earnestlie endeavour to make all thinges fall out accordinge to your ma[jes]ties desire, to the free and quiett breedinge of your highnes life, with all those whom you shall bringe with you: and that it maie be lawfull for you the Emperour and great Duke to use your Christian religeon in such sorte, as it shall like you: for nether meane wee to atempt anie thinge to offend either your ma[jes]tie or anie of your people nor intermeddle anie waies with your highnes faith and religion, nor yet to severre your highnes household from you or to suffer anie of yours to be taken from you by violence.
>
> Besides wee shall appointe you the Emperour and great Duke a place in our kingdom fitt upon your owne charge, as longe as ye shall like to remaine with us.
>
> And yf it shall seeme good unto you the Emperour and great Duke, to depart from our countries, wee shall suffer you with all yours quietlie to depart either into your empire of Muscovia or else whither it shall best like you to passe through our dominions and countries. Neither shall wee anie waie lett or staie you, but with all offices and curtisies let you our deare brother Emperour and great Duke passe into your countrie or els where at your pleasure.
>
> This wee promise by virtue of these our lettres and by the word of a Christian Prince, in witness whereof and for the further fortificacon of this our lettre. Wee Q. Elizabethe doe subscribe this with our owne hand in the presence of these our nobles and councellors ...
>
> C.P.

58

Letter from James I to Patriarch Philaret

24 June 1620

Parchment manuscript, bearing James's signature, gold, coloured inks

22¾ x 24⅞ in. (58 x 63.3 cm)

Provenance: papers of the Ambassadorial Office; transferred as part of the Moscow State Archive of the Ministry of Foreign Affairs in 1925.

Russian State Archive of Ancient Acts, Moscow, fund 35, *opis'* 2, No. 28, Relations Between Russia and England

Literature: Bantysh-Kamensky 1894, p. 104

John Merrick arrived in Moscow on 4 December 1620 as ambassador from James I. He presented Patriarch Philaret – father of the reigning Tsar Mikhail Fyodorovich – with James's letter in which the King congratulated the Patriarch on his return from captivity (he had been taken prisoner by the Poles) and his elevation to the post of Patriarch in 1619. He also took the opportunity to request protection for the English merchant Fabian Smith and other British subjects.

The margins are filled with characteristic English Renaissance ornament composed of daisies and pinks, stylized harebells and pomegranates on a dark blue ground. At the centre of the upper margin is the initial 'J' in a shield with a lion and a unicorn. On the reverse are seven heraldic images against a dark blue ground, among them the arms of France, Ireland and Scotland.

C.P.

AMES BY THE

grace of God King of great Brittany, France, and Ireland, defendor of the faith &c. To the most reuerend great Lord, and holy Patriach Feloret N. Arfeth of Mosco & of all Russia our moste deere and louinge Cozen, Greeting. Moste reuerend Lord, Hauinge resolued for diuers important causes. And specially for the better strengtheninge & confirmaton of the Amitie and corespondence betwene vs, and our most deere and louinge brother, the great Lord, Emperor & great Duke Michaell Feodorowich of Russia sole comaunder, y most worthie & renowned Son, to send ouer thither this o Ambassador, o trustie & welbeloued Seruante S John Merick Knight a gentleman nighe vnto vs, of o priuie Chamber. And heretofore imployed by vs in y same place, to mediate and conclude y happie peace agreed vpon, betwene our said good brother, y great Lord, Emperor, & great Duke, & y King of Sweden. We haue giuen him speciall Comission & charge, to attend you y great Lord, & holy Patriarch of all Russia, in this o princely addresse of congratulacon as well for y peaceable & successfull raigne of our said good brother, the great Lord Emperor & great Duke, yo most famous & euer beloued Son, as alsoe yo safe & happie retorne into yo owne Country, after soe longe a tyme of captiuitie, together likewise in y high & reuerend dignity, to yo haue by providence most deseruedly attayned vnto, as a due rewarde of your worth and high merite, to your great honor, and the generall good of that greate Empire, of which happines, as wee shall euer wishe all prosperous continuance & increase, soe wee doe hereby acknowledge the many and great fauors you haue shewed to our Marchants, not only heretofore, but especially now, since your wished retorne, and particulerly to our Agent Fabyan Smith, and others of our subiects residing there. And doe withall pray you, to holde them still vnder the protecon of your grace and fauour, as wee for our parte, shall euer be redy to afforde the like princely request, vpon all occasions, wherein wee may any way gratifie you, to whome wee wishe all health and eternall happines. And soe wee leaue yo to the protecon of Almighty God, from our Mannor of Greenwich the foure & twentith day of June 1620. And our raigne of great Brittaine, France & Ireland, the eighteenth.

James R

213

59

Letter from Charles I to Tsar Mikhail Fyodorovich

23 April 1629

Parchment manuscript, bearing Charles's signature, gold, paint

23 x 27¼ in. (58.5 x 69.4 cm)

Provenance: papers of the Ambassadorial Office; transferred as part of the Moscow State Archive of the Ministry of Foreign Affairs in 1925.

Russian State Archive of Ancient Acts, Moscow, fund 35, *opis'* 2, no. 42, Relations Between Russia and England

Literature: Bantysh-Kamensky 1894, p. 107

In 1628, Tsar Mikhail Fyodorovich dispatched the messenger Vasily Demetrovich Esipov and the translator A. Angler to England. On their return in 1629 they presented two royal letters to the Tsar. That dated 23 April requests that the Tsar permit the English merchants to employ Russian servants and sail large ships into the River Dvina via the Berezov Estuary, and allow the English messenger Dormer Cobbon to pass through Russia on his way to Persia. The letter also notes that the son of the translator Johann Elmson, sent from Moscow to study at Cambridge University, was in France and on his return would study medicine.

The margins are richly adorned with colourful Renaissance ornament composed of vegetation and flowers, cornucopias, bunches of fruit, winged cupids and grotesques, as well as heraldic images.

C.P.

4

The Russian Context

The Tzar like a sparkling Sun (to speak in the Russian dialect) darted
forth most sumptuous rays, being most magnificently placed upon his
Throne with his Scepter in his hand, and having his Crown on his Head.
His Throne was of massy Silver gilt, wrought curiously on the top with
several works and Pyramids; and being seven or eight steps higher than
the floor, it rendered the person of this Prince transcendently Majestick.
His Crown (which he wore upon a Cap lined with black Sables) was
covered quite over with precious stones, it terminated towards the top
in the form of a Pyramid with a golden cross at the spire. The Scepter
glittered also all over with jewels, his vest was sett with the like from
the top to the bottom down the opening before, and his collar was
answerable to the same.

—A Relation of the Three Embassies from his Sacred Majestie Charles II
to the Great Duke of Muscovie ... Performed by the Right Honorable
the Earle of Carlisle in the Years 1663 & 1664 (London, 1669)

The Moscow Kremlin and its History

Paul Bushkovitch

The Kremlin did not impress Richard Chancellor, the first Englishman to visit Moscow. In 1554 the Kremlin seemed to him a good fortress from a military point of view, 'a very fair castle, strong and furnished with artillery . . . This castle hath on one side a dry ditch, and on the other side the river … whereby it is made almost inexpugnable.' He was lukewarm about the churches, 'not altogether unhandsome', but he did not like the palace at all: 'As for the king's court and palace, it is not of the neatest, only in form it is foursquare and of low building, much surpassed and excelled by the beauty and elegancy of the houses of the kings of England.' He thought the windows too narrow, not letting in enough light, and bemoaned the absence of the cloth of gold that covered the walls of English palaces.[1]

Unlike later tourists, Chancellor did not dwell on the truly Russian spirit that the buildings seem to convey. Indeed for most people, Russians and others, the Moscow Kremlin is the quintessentially Russian space, the incarnation of Russian cultural traditions, of the artistic styles of the old Russia before Peter the Great brought Western culture and architecture to the country. The paradox is that virtually nothing of the Kremlin that Chancellor saw in 1554 was the work of Russians. The walls, all the main churches save two (the lost Saviour in the Pine Grove and the main palace Church of the Annunciation) and the Tsar's palace were and remain the work of Italians. Ironically it is the Neo-classical and eclectic buildings of the eighteenth and nineteenth centuries that were built by Russians, Matvey Kazakov (1738–1812) and later Konstantin Ton (1794–1881).

Italian and Russian styles

For two hundred years the Moscow Kremlin that we see today, the fortress walls, the churches and monasteries, and the palace of the Tsars, formed the centre of Russian politics, the Russian state and the Orthodox Church (fig. 63). The Kremlin of today includes many buildings of the eighteenth and nineteenth centuries. Some of the ancient buildings have been lost: the south wing of the old palace disappeared in the eighteenth century. The 1930s swept away the 1330 Church of the Saviour in the Pine Grove, the Chudovo Monastery and the Convent of the Ascension, with its church in which Russian princesses and Tsarinas from before 1700 lay buried. For the modern observer the most important change, however, is the Great Kremlin Palace, which Ton built in classical style in 1838–49, with many interventions by Tsar Nicholas I, who wanted it bigger than the architect projected.[2] It in turn replaced a small Baroque palace of the 1740s, a building by Bartolomeo Rastrelli (1700–71) which Empress Elizabeth ordered erected on the site of the south wing of the old palace. Ton's huge (for the time) construction, especially seen from the opposite bank of the Moscow River, did more to change the fundamental look and message of the Kremlin than the anti-religious depredations of the 1930s.[3]

The Kremlin was not the first fortress and complex of buildings to stand on this site. Moscow as a place first features in a chronicle reference from 1147, but only in 1156 did Prince Yury Dolgoruky ('The Long-Armed'), Grand Duke of neighbouring Vladimir, build a small wooden fort on the high point

63. View of the Moscow Kremlin

of land where the river Neglinnaya (now channelled underground) falls into the River Moscow. A tiny provincial town, Moscow became the capital of a small principality of its own in 1272. It grew rapidly. By the early fourteenth century its princes were among the most powerful in the lands of what is now Russia; in 1328 Moscow's Prince Ivan Danilovich (1304?–40), known as Kalita ('The Moneybag'), convinced Russia's overlord, the Khan of the Golden Horde on the lower River Volga, to let him succeed to the title and lands of the Grand Princes of Vladimir. From then on, Moscow was the centre of Russian politics and in keeping with his new status Ivan Kalita built the first Kremlin of oak walls in 1339–40, just before his death. Throughout the fourteenth and fifteenth centuries the Moscow princes managed to incorporate, peacefully or by conquest, all the principalities that made up the lands populated by Russians (fig. 64).[4]

64. 'Moskuae Urbis', from Joan Blaeu, *Geographie Blavianae*, Amsterdam, 1662. Yale Center for British Art, Paul Mellon Collection

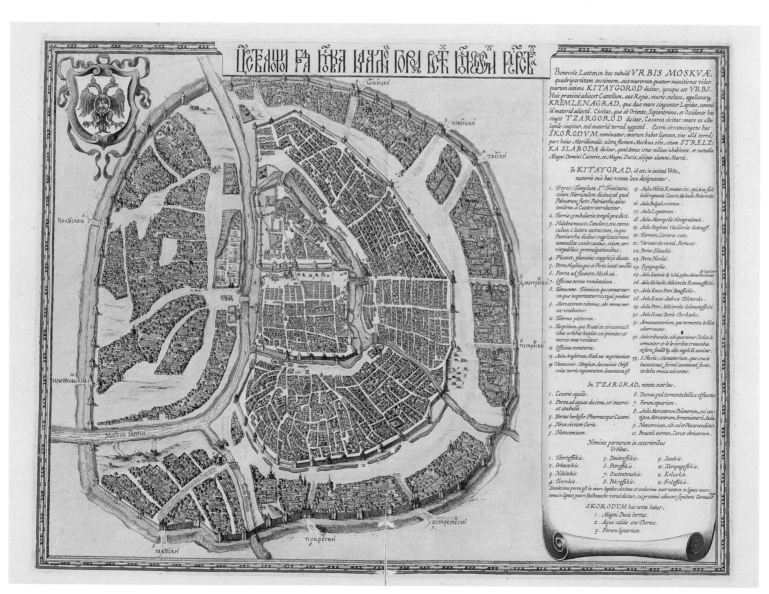

The centre of all these intrigues and wars, marriages and treaties was the Kremlin. In 1367 Prince Dmitry Ivanovich (known as Dmitry Donskoy because of his 1380 victory over the Horde at Kulikovo in the upper reaches of the River Don) replaced the oak walls of the Kremlin with white stone, a structure that lasted another hundred years. The Kremlin of Dmitry Donskoy was not merely a fortress. It included the prince's residence, about which we know very little, the wooden houses of the boyar aristocracy and the prince's servants, but also many houses of humbler folk. At this stage the Kremlin was simply the inner fortification of the town of Moscow, which already stretched some distance beyond the open market to the east of the Kremlin that came to be known as Red Square. The Kremlin already included several stone churches, only one of which (the Saviour in the Pine Grove) survived into the twentieth century. The concentration of churches was partly to serve the palace and the town. But the Kremlin also became the seat of the Orthodox Church, the other major institution of late medieval Russia. Russia had adopted Christianity in 988 and the head of the Church, the Metropolitan, had resided in the then political capital, Kiev, in the south. With the fragmentation of the country and the Mongol invasion (1237–40), Kiev ceased to be a major centre and in 1325 Metropolitan Peter, still calling himself Metropolitan of Kiev and all Rus, took up residence in Moscow. Thus the Moscow Kremlin took on a sacred as well as political significance. The main cathedral in the Kremlin, the Cathedral of the Dormition, was the Metropolitan's church, not the palace church, of which there were several.

The form of the Kremlin walls and towers that survives today, as well as that of most of the churches and the older part of the palace, took shape over little more than a generation, from the 1480s to the 1520s (fig. 65). It came about at the command of Ivan III (1462–1505) and marked a new departure in Russian architecture. Earlier Russians had followed Byzantine models for their churches, and both Greek and occasionally European artists participated in the work. Ivan turned to Italy, more specifically to Milan and then Venice. His intermediaries were again Greeks, this time subjects of the Ottomans who came to Russia or Greek refugees in Italy who made the same journey. Some came in the entourage of Sophia (Zoe) Paleologue, daughter of the last Greek despot of Morea, whom Ivan married in December 1472.[5] There are many mysteries about Sophia. As a descendant of Byzantine emperors, she might be thought to have brought some sort of imperial claim to Russia, but in fact the Russians never mentioned any such thing and the Moscow princes took the imperial title of Tsar only much later, in 1549. Sophia was also a ward of the Pope, and the Russian ambassador who brought her to Moscow first married her as proxy for his sovereign in St Peter's Cathedral in Rome. The event prompted the poet Luigi Pulci to write to Lorenzo de' Medici that the new wife of the Moscow Grand Prince was enormously fat, 'a dome of Norcia pork, a mountain of lard', as he ungraciously put it.[6] In any case, the marriage cemented Moscow's ties with Italy for a generation and Greek emissaries soon arrived at the Sforza court and elsewhere looking for architects and builders.

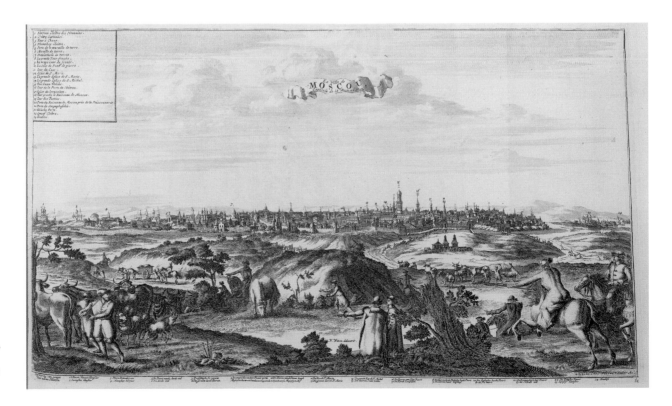

65. 'La Ville de Moscou,' by N. Witsen, from Pieter van der Aa, *La Galerie Agréable du Monde*, plate 31, Leiden, 1729. Yale Center for British Art, Paul Mellon Collection

The Italians came at first only to rebuild the cathedral. In the spring after the wedding one of many great fires struck the Kremlin which was packed with wooden buildings. The Cathedral Church of the Dormition of the Mother of God was seriously damaged and was rebuilt on a larger scale and in more magnificent style. Russia's best builders came from Pskov in the north-west, but they were experienced only in fairly small buildings. Ivan found other builders and work started quickly, but on 20 May 1474, around sunset, the new cathedral collapsed. The Metropolitan had entrusted care of the cathedral to a Greek who had been in Moscow for decades and had reached the pinnacle of power as the city's treasurer, holding boyar rank. Presumably it was he who suggested the mission to Italy. The Russian emissary returned in spring 1475. With him came the Bolognese architect Aristotele Fioravanti (c.1415–86), the first of the Italians, best known in Italy as an engineer who had succeeded in moving church towers intact and working on fortifications and canals in Milan. He had also been recently accused of making or passing false coins in Rome and may have needed to leave Italy for a while. Using all sorts of devices unknown to the Russians, and building with stronger cement and better walls, Fioravanti completed the church in four years.[7]

From this moment on Ivan III employed almost exclusively Italian architects for the Kremlin. In 1485–9 Pskov builders constructed the main palace church, the Annunciation Cathedral, and a few smaller churches, but the larger work was Italian. In 1485, about the time that Fioravanti disappears from the sources, two more Italians, Pietro Antonio Solari (1450–93) from Milan and one 'Marco the Italian', arrived in Russia to take over even more grandiose projects. Over the next ten years Solari and Marco built most of the walls and towers extant today, and they built them to a particular model. As another Italian builder wrote home to Milan in 1496, 'the duke of this country wants a castle like that in Milan'. The prototype of the Kremlin was to be Milan's Sforza Castle, a resemblance that is strikingly visible even today.[8] At the same time Solari and Marco went to work on the prince's palace. Of their work the most important part remains, the Faceted Chamber (fig. 66) facing the cathedral square, one of the palace's two main audience rooms. Starting in 1499 another Milanese, Aloisio da Caresano, began on the living quarters of the palace. By completion in 1508 the result was in the shape of a flat-bottomed 'U', with the lower part containing the two audience rooms by Solari and Marco Ruffo which faced the square. It was this part that visitors and ambassadors first saw when they came to the palace, entering by the Red Staircase to the left of the Faceted Chamber. The two arms of the 'U', an addition by the Venetian Alevise Novi, stretched back on either side toward the west, the more southerly wing being the men's side and the northerly the women's side of the palace. Both wings of the 'U' were built on top of a Renaissance arcaded gallery and were stone buildings with a tiled roof. The galleries surrounded an internal courtyard like that of the Sforza Castle and many other northern Italian palaces and other buildings of the early Renaissance.[9]

The last part of the ensemble came in the reign of Ivan III's son, Vasily III (1503–30): Novi's Cathedral of the Archangel Michael (1505–9), the necropolis of the Moscow princes and Tsars until Peter I, and the bell tower known as Ivan the Great. The bell tower was actually several churches crowned by a tower, including one of St John Climacus, and it followed Italian designs in its original form. The Kremlin was now more or less complete. What came after was rebuilding and modest expansion of some of the palace buildings.

For the modern observer the most interesting question is the fate of the Italian architecture. Why does a complex of buildings built by Italians of the Renaissance look so 'Russian'? One reason is that the Italians stopped coming, apparently no longer invited. The last Italian work was the (now lost) earlier version of the Ivan the Great Bell Tower, built in 1543. The other reason is that later additions were the work of Russian builders who adopted little besides some decorative motifs from the Italians. Boris Godunov (1598–1605) had grand plans, only some of which he was able to realize, and the style of his time continued Russian models, not Italian ones. The Ivan the Great Bell Tower we see today was erected in 1600 in clearly Russian style. Boris also enlarged the palace with a row of rooms and gardens paralleling the south wing along the bluff over the river. Over the years numerous fires – and particularly destruction wrought during the Time of Troubles – damaged both palace and churches. As the Archangel Cathedral was repeatedly rebuilt, each time the Renaissance elements faded.[10] The palace suffered an even more drastic fate. The galleries were built over and above them appeared the seventeenth-century palace with its *terem*, the small and dark (but warm) living quarters of the women and children. It was refurbished in the highly decorated Russian style of the seventeenth century. Narrow windows of mica instead of glass let in a half-light but preserved the heat put out by the massive Russian stoves in the winter. Bright red woollen cloth (mostly imported from England) lined the walls, and the dark, gilded wood reflected candle-light as did the silver and gold of the ewers and plates on the tables.

Even the Kremlin walls changed (fig. 64). The original Solari walls had mimicked the Sforza Castle, though without the Milanese prototype's rectangular plan. The Kremlin followed the terrain, making a rough triangle with the palace at the apex. The crenellations of the walls had, and still have, the characteristic shape of Italian cities loyal to the Ghibelline or imperial faction, the *merle* or blackbirds named from the resemblance of their curves to the outlines of the wings of a bird in flight. (Guelph towns had flat-topped crenellations.) The towers were made to be practical, with flattish roofs and room for archers and other soldiers. Some of the secondary Kremlin towers are today not so far from this version, though early drawings show towers with even flatter roofs like those of the secondary towers in the castello of Milan. It is the half dozen towers with long pointed spires ending in red stars (which used to be double eagles) that give the modern incarnation of the Kremlin its uniquely 'Russian' look. Those too are additions of the seventeenth century and it seems to have been an Englishman who started the rebuilding. The first to be so rebuilt was the Saviour Tower, the main gate on the side of Red Square. Solari's tower had a bell to ring the hours, but some time in the succeeding century a clock was put in its place.

66. Ivan Alekseevich Sokolov, 'Interior Perspective of the Reception Hall, Palace of Facets,' from *Obstoiatel'noe opisan‾ie torzhestvennykh poriadkov*, plate 31, St Petersburg, 1744. Slavic and Baltic Division, The New York Public Library, Astor, Lenox and Tilden Foundations

67. Pieter Picaert and Jean Blicklandt, *Panorama of Moscow from Kamenny Bridge*, 1707–8. The State Hermitage Museum, St Petersburg

This clock was ruined in the Time of Troubles and in the 1620s Tsar Michael hired an Englishman, Christopher Halloway (Galloway), to replace it. Halloway made a mechanical clock of some complexity which required a higher tower around it. Statues graced the result, a problem for Orthodox traditionalists, but above the clock Russian builders added the high pointed spire that has survived today. The other towers acquired high pointed roofs after 1680, when the Tsar ordered long-needed repairs. It was thus only a few years before Peter the Great abandoned Russian architectural tradition for good that the Kremlin received its very 'Russian' appearance.[11]

Private and public spaces

The Kremlin was not primarily a monument to anyone's architecture. It was the residence of the Tsar, the head of the Orthodox Church in Russia (titled Patriarch after 1589) and many of the boyars, the elite of Russian society and the state. Virtually everything important in Russian politics, other than warfare, took place in and around the Kremlin palace. In the sixteenth and seventeenth centuries the boyars who were in Moscow and not with the army or ruling the provinces came to the palace almost every day. There they met with the Tsar in his council, the Duma, in one of the two large halls that Solari and Ruffo had built, during the sixteenth century usually in the Gold Chamber immediately adjacent to the Faceted Chamber to the south. These meetings took place several times a week and by the 1650s had become so numerous that Tsar Alexey tried to regulate them by days of the week, but apparently did not get very far. Larger or more formal gatherings, and from the time of Boris Godunov the meetings of the Duma, took place in the Faceted Chamber. Here it was that foreign ambassadors had audiences with the Tsar to present their messages and gifts.

Business of state that involved routine administration rather than the making of decisions also took place in the Kremlin. Next to the palace, running east along the high bluff along the river, were some dozen – later twenty or thirty – offices, wooden buildings with deep cellars for storage and offices on the upper floors. Here perhaps a hundred men, each with a staff of about ten clerks, copyists and messengers under him, administered a country stretching from the border with Finland to the Pacific Ocean and numbering, by the later seventeenth century, about eleven million people. Among these offices was the Ambassadorial Office, built by Ivan the Terrible in 1565 to house the newly founded institution (before 1554 a division of the treasury took care of foreign affairs). It is the Ambassadorial Office whose archive preserves today immense detail relating to both the negotiations and ceremony of foreign policy and of the embassies to and from Russia, including the gifts sent and received.

Besides politics and administration the Kremlin was also the centre of the Church. While the Patriarch, who resided there, did not have an army of clerks – indeed the Russian Church operated with scarcely any administrative staff at all – what Church offices did exist found their homes in the Kremlin. As a spiritual centre, its success depended on the charisma of the Patriarchs, some of them men of great fame and authority, others scarcely

noticed in the stream of time. The presence of the Patriarch did ensure a great library and the production of books, including printed books after the end of the sixteenth century. From earliest Byzantine times it was monks who usually had the greatest spiritual authority in the Orthodox Church and Russia was no different. In this sense the Kremlin was not the unique centre for religion that it was in politics, for most of the great monasteries lay elsewhere. Two of the greatest, the Kirillov and Solovetsky Monasteries, were far to the north, but the Trinity Monastery, founded in the fourteenth century by St Sergius of Radonezh, was only a day's journey north of Moscow. Every year in September the entire court went there on foot to mark the saint's festival and the monastery maintained a substantial yard and church in the Kremlin. The Trinity and Kirillov monasteries also kept their representatives, so to speak, in the Kremlin, for both had a house and church within its walls. Besides that, the Kremlin housed its own Monastery of the Miracle (Chudovo) of St Michael and the Convent of the Ascension, and in the sixteenth century both still had churches built by Italians. The Tsars usually had their children baptized in the Church of the Monastery of the Miracle, where the relics of its founder, the fourteenth-century Metropolitan St Alexey rested. The Ascension Convent was the place of retirement and burial for the women of the dynasty.[12]

The court and the Church were not separate entities. The Tsar was usually baptized, as were his children, in the Monastery of the Miracle. He was married in the Annunciation or Dormition Cathedral and buried in the Archangel Cathedral; his wife would be buried in the Ascension Convent, all located within the Kremlin. The grandest ceremony uniting Church and monarch was the coronation, celebrated by the Patriarch in the Dormition Cathedral, the largest of the Kremlin churches and the Patriarch's principal church. The huge ceremony lasted several days and involved the whole boyar elite, the palace servants and many lesser nobles who served in the army or in the palace, as well as the main bishops and the hegumens and archimandrites of the chief Russian monasteries. In addition to these extraordinary ceremonies, the Tsar went to one or another church for the liturgy at least once a day, normally in one of the churches inside the palace, for the whole of his life. Moreover, nearly every week the court celebrated at least one other Church festival, a saint's day, the commemoration of a miracle-working icon, or one of the days of the great cycle of Lent and Easter (see fig. 5). These important holidays were most often celebrated in one of the larger Kremlin churches and the Tsar went in procession accompanied by the boyars and dozens of palace servants. Among the chief Christian holidays marked especially in the Kremlin were Epiphany and Palm Sunday. At Epiphany the Tsar and Patriarch went down to the frozen River Moskva, where they stood by a hole cut in the ice with a tent over it; it was called the Jordan in memory of Christ's baptism in the River Jordan. There the Patriarch plunged a cross into the water, blessed the water, gave some to the Tsar and then sprinkled it on the surrounding multitude, repeating the baptism of the Russian land. Palm Sunday was even more solemn. The Patriarch mounted a donkey and the Tsar walked by his side holding the bridle (fig. 68). Replicating the entry of Christ into Jerusalem, they went in procession from the Dormition Cathedral through the main street of the Kremlin out the Saviour Gate to the Church of St Basil, where the procession ended at a side altar devoted to the entrance into Jerusalem. Moscow was the New Jerusalem, the Holy City, the Patriarch the image of Christ, and the Tsar the servant of Christ.[13]

Religious Orthodoxy and Russian spirit

The centrality of religion to court life up to the end of the seventeenth century gives a clue to the fate of the Italian buildings and their architectural form. The 'russification' of the Kremlin was not immediate, for as late as the 1630s the Holstein ambassador Adam Olearius noted that the Kremlin palace was Italian in form.[14] Even Olearius, however, found the complex as a whole to be alien and only moderately attractive, and this is not surprising. In spite of its Italian foundation, the Moscow Kremlin did not convey a message that Europeans of the sixteenth and seventeenth centuries could read. European palaces and their environs from the Renaissance onwards conveyed the glory and power of the monarch. Their symmetrical façades and designs conveyed a certain sense of the order of the world, at the centre of which stood the monarch in all his or her earthly glory. Power, magnificence and wealth comprised the message, sometimes accompanied by allegories of justice or mercy. This was what Europeans expected, but in the Kremlin they did not find it.

68. 'Kremelin, Das Schloss in Muscau', [Kremlin, the Palace in Moscow], from Adam Olearius, *Vermehrte newe Beschreibung der muscowitischen und persischen Reyse*, Schlesswig, 1656. Rare Books Division, Department of Rare Books and Special Collections, Princeton University Library

Russian Ecclesiastical Objects

60

Altar cross

Cross: Russia, sixteenth century

Handle: Russia, eighteenth century

Gold, silver, sapphires, pearls; chased, filigree, carved

Height 9 in. (23 cm); width 3¾ in. (9.4 cm)

Provenance: transferred from the Solovetsky Monastery

Moscow Kremlin Museums inv. no. MR–1197

MS sources: Solovetsky Inventory 1824, f. 4r,v; Solovetsky Collection 1928, part 1, f. 30

Literature: Dosifey 1836, part 1, p. 290; Solovetsky Monastery 2001, p. 156

The carved inscription informs us that this marvelous gold cross adorned with filigree and precious stones was presented to the Solovetsky Monastery by Tsar Ivan IV. Over the whole surface runs a favorite traditional Russian metalworking technique, fine openwork filigree; the form here – heart-shaped tendrils – indicates that the cross was produced by craftsmen from Novgorod. Large precious stones and pearls complete the ornamentation.

Originally the cross would have been worn around the neck, but it was converted in the eighteenth century for use as an altar cross. The altar cross plays an important role in Orthodox rites, symbolizing Christ's death for the salvation of mankind; it stands on the altar during the liturgy, is present at all rituals and is used by the priest to bless believers at the end of the service.

Beneath Christ's feet we see Golgotha or Calvary, the hill upon which the cross was raised, and the skull of Adam, since the Church teaches that Christ was crucified on the very spot where Adam was buried. Orthodox Church altar crosses generally differ from those of western Christianity in having eight tips, i.e. two additional cross bars, one at the top and a diagonal one below. The most common theological explanation for the diagonal lower bar is that the raised end symbolizes the road to heaven, while the lower indicates the path to hell.

V.F.

61

Icon: The Virgin of Vladimir

Painting: Russia, late sixteenth or early seventeenth century

Silver cover: Russia, early seventeenth century

Silver, sapphires, emeralds, turquoises, coloured stones, pearls, wood, mica, brocade, enamel, gesso, egg tempera; chased, carved, filigree, enamelled, flat-chased, gilded

Height 15 in. (38 cm); width 11¾ in. (28.7 cm)

Provenance: via Gokhran [State Valuables Administration] in 1924; formerly collection Count Alexey Musin-Pushkin, Moscow

Moscow Kremlin Museums inv. no. Zh–1764/1–2

MS sources: Armoury Inventory 1914–30, no. 18005

Literature: Prakhov 1907, pp. 170–4; Russian Enamel 1974, pp. 46, 48; Martynova 2002, p. 53

Since the early Byzantine era the adoration of miraculous icons of the Virgin has played a central part in Orthodox religious practice. Most surviving images of the Virgin are in fact copies made of earlier celebrated and revered works; while retaining many of their characteristic iconographical features, the copies can vary significantly in size from the original.

The original Virgin of Vladimir was one of the most revered icons in Russia. It was brought from Constantinople to ancient Rus in the early twelfth century as a gift from the Patriarch of Constantinople, Lucas Chrysoberges. The icon was a symbol of the profound link between Byzantine and Russian culture, and the spiritual ties that bound the Greek and Slavic worlds. Originally kept in Kiev, then capital of Rus, the icon was transferred by Prince Andrey Bogolubov in 1155 to the new capital, Vladimir, whence it takes its name. As Muscovy grew to be the most important principality in Rus, in the late fourteenth century the holy icon was transferred to its capital, the new spiritual and political center, and placed in the Dormition Cathedral of the Kremlin (it is today held in the Tretyakov Gallery, Moscow). Chronicles describe the rich ceremonies that accompanied the icon's arrival and the event led to the establishment of the festival of the Greeting (*Sretenie*) of the Vladimir Icon of Holy Mary. A monastery was established – the Sretensky Monastery (Monastery of the Greeting) – on the spot where Muscovites, headed by Metropolitan Kiprian, came out to greet the miraculous icon.

Numerous copies of the original Greek icon were hung in churches and private houses around Russia. This late sixteenth- or early seventeenth-century example is set in a precious case that concentrates the viewer's attention on the faces of the Virgin and Child. Running along the inner edge of the frame is a prayer to the Virgin, 'In thee, thou full of grace, all creation rejoices', while the plaques in the margins depict some of the most important festivals in the gospels: the Presentation of the Virgin in the Temple, the Nativity, Crucifixion, Resurrection, Transformation and Assumption of Christ, and the Dormition of the Virgin.

One rare detail for sixteenth-century Russian jewellery is the use of several unusually large turquoises arranged to emphasize the structure of the icon case. These rich pale blue accents, the intensely coloured sapphires and almandine, are finely balanced by the elegant soft enamelled blue and green leaves against the filigree covering the surface.

V.F.

62

Icon: The Virgin of Kazan

Moscow, early seventeenth century

Silver, sapphires, emeralds, tourmalines, pearls, tempera; chased, carved, nielloed, flat-chased, gilded

Height 12⅝ in. (32); width 11 in. (28 cm)

Provenance: transferred from the Archangel Cathedral of the Moscow Kremlin

Moscow Kremlin Museums inv. no. Zh–537/1–2

The English envoy Anthony Jenkinson describes seeing an icon such as this when he visited Muscovy in the mid-sixteenth century:

> They shewed me the church, wherein were as many images as could hang about, or upon the wals of the Church round about, and even the roofe of the church was painted ful of images. The chiefe image was of our Ladie, which was garnished with gold, rubies, saphirs and other rich stones abundantly … All their churches are full of images, unto the which the people when they assemble, doe bowe and knocke their heads, as I have before said, that some will have knobbes upon their foreheads with knocking, as great as egges … (Hakluyt 1598, pp. 320–1).

Like the Virgin of Vladimir (cat. 61), this icon is a copy of a celebrated original, in this case the Virgin of Kazan. It had been acquired in Kazan in 1579 and placed by order of Ivan IV ('The Terrible') in a monastery he founded specially. The Virgin of Kazan is based on the Byzantine iconographical type known as the Virgin Hodegetria ('showing the way', that is, pointing at Christ who is the 'true way'). It is one of the oldest and most widespread images in the Eastern Christian world, and the most adored in Russian Orthodoxy. Here the case is adorned with precious stones and a striking network of pearls covering the Virgin's head.

V.F.

63

Pectoral cross

Russia, early seventeenth century

Gold, silver, emeralds, sapphires, pearls; cast, chased,
carved, nielloed, flat-chased

Height 7⅝ in. (19.4 cm);
width 4⅞ in. (12.5 cm);
depth ½ in. (1.2 cm)

Provenance: transferred from the Chudovo Monastery
(Monastery of the Miracle) in 1918

Moscow Kremlin Museums inv. no. MR–5767/1–2

MS sources: Armoury Inventory 1914–30, no. 13679

The cross is a superb example of Russian jewellery of the early
seventeenth century. Made of gold and covered with elegant niello
ornament, its design looks back to the sixteenth century, when the art
of niello (a dense black inlay) flourished among Moscow's court jewellers.
At the tips of the cross are four large intensely coloured sapphires; the
whole is finished with a row of pearls running around the edge.

Although the cross bears no inscription, the unusually precious materials
and skilful execution suggest that it was produced for a very high-ranking
member of the clergy.

V.F.

64

Altar Gospels

Manuscript; Russia, sixteenth century

Cover: Moscow (?), 1613

Donated by Prince Dmitry Mikhaylovich Pozharsky to the Solovetsky Monastery, probably in 1613

Wood, paper, textiles, silver, sapphires, glass, pearls; chased, nielloed, carved, gilded

Height 17¾ in. (45 cm); width 11¼ in. (28.5 cm)

Provenance: transferred from the Solovetsky Monastery, northern Russia

Moscow Kremlin Museums inv. no. KN–198

MS sources: Book of Deposits 1539–1776, f. 38v; Church Inventory Nineteenth Century, f. 88; Solovetsky Collection 1928, part 3, ff. 31–2

Literature: Dosifey 1836, vol. 1, p. 292; Solovetsky Monastery 2001, p. 168

The book of Gospels that stands on the altar is one of the central items in Orthodox rite. In liturgy, the holy book symbolizes Jesus Christ himself. The decoration of altar Gospels was therefore given particular attention. According to centuries-old tradition, the front of Russian bindings bore images of entreaty or *deesis* (Christ with the Virgin and St John acting as intercessors on behalf of mankind), the Crucifixion or the Harrowing of Hell at the centre, with the corners occupied by the four Evangelists, Matthew, Mark, Luke and John.

Here the chased central scene is of the Crucifixion, amid a cover decorated with freely curling niello tendrils and leaves, with sapphires, turquoises, red glass and threads of pearls. On the first page of the book is a donor's inscription, evidence that the Gospels were given to the Solovetsky Monastery, one of the most revered holy sites in all Russia. The donor was Prince Dmitry Mikhaylovich Pozharsky (1578–1642), a leading figure during the political upheavals of the first decade of the seventeenth century.

V.F.

65

Altar Gospels

Printed book, Moscow, 1606

Cover. Novgorod, sixteenth century; corners and central plaque Novgorod, 1600–50

Donated by the Patriarch of Moscow and All Russia, Ioasaf I (1634–40) to the Solovetsky Monastery in 1638

Silver, almandine, turquoise, glass, pearls, brocade, satin, wood, paper; chased, filigree, carved, flat-chased, gilded, engraved, printed

Height 14⅛ in. (36 cm); width 9 in. (23 cm)

Provenance: transferred from Solovetsky Monastery in northern Russia in 1922 via Gokhran [State Valuables Administration]

Moscow Kremlin Museums inv. no. KN–44/1–2

MS sources: Solovetsky Inventory 1824, f. 8r,v; Solovetsky Inventory 19th Century, vol. 3, f. 69; Solovetsky Collection 1928, part 1, ff. 25–6

Literature: Dosifey 1836, part 1, p. 227; Solovetsky Monastery 1899, p. 84

On the front of the silver-gilt case are chased medallions with high-relief images of the crucifixion and the four evangelists against an architectural and landscape background. The rest of the surface is covered with tendrils forming a heart-shaped pattern, the whole complemented by almandines, turquoises, pearls and other semi-precious stones.

According to the inscription on the first pages, the book of gospels was given to the Solovetsky Monastery in 1638 by Patriarch Ioasaf, who had been chosen as successor to Patriarch Philaret (father of the Tsar, Mikhail Fyodorovich) by Philaret himself in 1633. Ioasaf was described by a contemporary as 'virtuous in mind and in his life, and not audacious towards the Tsar' (Makarius, p. 314).

V.F.

66

Icon: John the Baptist

Painting: Moscow Kremlin workshops, seventeenth
century

Case: Russia, seventeenth century

Gold, rubies, emeralds, pearls, wood, brocade, gesso,
enamel, tempera, damask; carved, enamelled, filigree

Height 11¼ in. (28.7 cm); width 9¼ in. (23.5 cm)

Provenance: transferred from the Novodevichy Monastery
(New Monastery of the Virgin), Moscow

Moscow Kremlin Museums inv. no. Zh–1758/1–2

MS sources: Armoury Inventory 1914–30, no. 20458

When Richard Chancellor arrived in Moscow in 1553, he was struck
by the painted icons:

> their pictures painted in tables they have in great abundance, which they
> do adore and offer unto, and burne waxe candles before them, and cast
> holy water upon them … In their private houses they have images for their
> household saints, and for the most part, they are put in the darkest place
> of the house; hee that comes into his neighbours house doth first salute his
> saints, although he see them not. If any foorme or stoole stand in his way,
> hee often times beateth his browe upon the same, and often ducking downe
> with his head, and body, worshipeth the chiefe Image.'
> (Hakluyt, 1598 p. 253)

In the Orthodox Church John the Baptist (usually called John the
Forerunner) is the most revered saint after the Virgin Mary. Born into
a pious family, John lived in the desert, preparing himself to serve God
through a strict life of fasting and prayer. He remained a hermit until
the Lord called him to preach at the age of thirty. He is described in
theological texts as an 'angel', since he was sent to inform the people
of the coming of the Saviour.

Several iconographical types developed for the depiction of John, one
of the most widespread being 'John the Forerunner as an angel of the
desert'. In this role John has the wings of an angel and holds a chalice
on which we see not the usual sacrificial lamb but the head of Christ
himself, with a tree and hatchet – symbol of retribution for sins – at
his feet. This iconographical composition, filled with motifs intended
to remind the viewer of the terrible payment to be exacted at the
Last Judgment, became particularly widespread in Russian art in the
sixteenth century. Towards the last quarter of the seventeenth century
the drama of the composition was replaced in Russian icon painting
by a more pious narrative, as here, where the tree and hatchet are
surrounded by a marvelous garden recalling paradise where miraculous
plants grow and lions and deer walk in harmony.

V.F.

67

Sakkos of Patriarch Philaret

Brocaded velvet, Italy, 1600–50

Decorative embroidery: Moscow Kremlin workshops,
1600–50

Brocade, velvet, taffeta, satin, gold thread, gold, silver,
pearls; woven, embroidered

Length 52¾ in. (134 cm); shoulder width with sleeves
55½ in. (141 cm)

Provenance: transferred from the Patriarch's vestry in 1920

Moscow Kremlin Museums inv. no. TK–18

MS sources: Armoury Inventory 1922–4, no. 12024

Published sources: Viktorov 1875, p. 11, no. 51; Savva 1896,
p. 20, no. 14; Popov 1910, p. 20, no. 44

Literature: Kleyn 1925, ill. p. 19, p. 21; Treasures 1995, p. 40;
Vishnevskaya 2002, p. 78, ill. 41; Italy and the Court of
Moscow 2004, p. 73, no. 97

When Anthony Jenkinson witnessed the Palm Sunday
celebrations in Russia in the sixteenth century, he
remarked upon:

> 'then followed 6 carying painted images upon their shoulders,
> after the images followed certaine priests to the number
> of 100 or more, with goodly vestures, wherof 10 or 12 are of
> white damaske set and imbrodered round about with faire
> and orient pearles, as great as pease, and among them certaine
> Saphires and other stones … in [the Metropolitan's] lappe lieth
> a faire booke, with a crucifix of Goldsmiths worke upon the
> cover, which he holdeth fast with his left hand, and in his right
> hand he hath a crosse of gold, with which crosse he ceaseth
> not to blesse the people as he rideth'.
> (Hakluyt 1598, p. 318).

Most important of all Orthodox vestments is the *sakkos*. It derives its
theological significance from the purple robe of Christ's Passion: 'And the
soldiers platted a crown of thorns, and put it on his head, and they put on
him a purple robe, And said, Hail, King of the Jews! And they smote him
with their hands' (John 19: 2–3). This *sakkos* is a long robe, unstitched
along the sides, with short broad sleeves and round shoulders; it has
separate panels along the shoulders, hem and sides, and a narrow vertical
band running up the middle of the front, a feature typical of the middle of
the seventeenth century.

The making of each *sakkos* was always an important event. Until the 1660s
the right to conduct a service wearing a *sakkos* was enjoyed only by the
two highest figures of the Russian Orthodox Church: the Metropolitan of
Moscow and the Patriarch of all Russia. All of their robes were notable for
the richness of their fabrics and skill of execution, but a *sakkos* was 'built' –
in the term used in ancient documents – from precious and important
fabrics from the Church or royal treasury. Certain parts of the *sakkos* had
specific meaning and were picked out with different fabric or through the
addition of embroidery (ornamental or figurative) using silver and gold
sequins, pearls and precious stones.

After the death of a *sakkos*' owner his robes were transferred to the
Patriarch's vestry for storage and became the property of the Church.
Few of the older robes retain their original appearance. Most have been
subject to some degree of alteration, with individual parts being attached
to new fabric, pearl embroidery restored, sequins added or replaced. Such
unavoidable renovations did nothing to reduce the reverence accorded
to such robes, their commemorative significance or sacred essence.

This *sakkos* was made for Patriarch Philaret (1619–33) by order of
his son, Tsar Mikhail Fyodorovich, first Tsar of the Romanov dynasty.
The inscription embroidered in tiny pearls along the upper edge of the
shoulder in dark red velvet reads: 'By command of the Sovereign Tsar
and Grand Duke Mikhail Fyodorovich of All Russia this *sakkos* was made'.
Under Patriarch Nikon (1652–8) the *sakkos* was restored and gained an
'apron' marked out by a band of pearl embroidery and a new body of rich
Italian brocade known as *aksamit petelchatyy* ('velvet embroidered with
loops'). In the dense pattern of stylized acanthus leaves and stems with
flowers, gold loops are used to pick out the multi-petalled flowers.

Philaret occupies a special place in the Russian Church hierarchy. After he
was elected Patriarch in 1619, he became joint ruler on behalf of his young
son, Tsar Mikhail Fyodorovich, and even bore the title 'Great Sovereign'.
Holding the reigns of both spiritual and secular power, Philaret, with his
vast political experience, played a key role in the Russian state.

I.V.

68

Altar Cross

Moscow Kremlin workshops, 1653–4

Donated by Tsar Alexey Mikhaylovich and Tsaritsa Maria Ilinichna to the Chapel of the Entry to Jerusalem of the Annunciation Cathedral in 1653–4

Silver, pearls; chased, carved, flat-chased, gilded

Height 15¼ (38.8 cm); width 6¾ in. (17 cm)

Provenance: transferred from the Annunciation Cathedral

Moscow Kremlin Museums inv. no. MR–4982

MS sources: Annunciation Cathedral Inventory 1701, f. 210r,v; Annunction Cathedral Inventory 1745, f. 116r,v; Annunciation Cathedral Inventory 1771–2, f. 71r,v

Published sources: Annunciation Cathedral Inventory Seventeenth Century, pp. 35–6

Literature: Annunciation Cathedral 1990, pp. 86–7

The Crucifixion on the front of this eight-armed cross shows Adam at the foot, with applied figures of the Virgin, Mary (Magdalene), John the Evangelist and Longinus the centurion to the sides; two angels descend from above. The ground is filled with carved flowers and vegetation. A thread of pearls runs round the front edge, while the sides have woven ornament. On the handle is the inscription recording that the cross was a gift from Tsar Alexey Mikhaylovich and his wife to the Chapel of the Entry into Jerusalem in the Kremlin's Annunciation Cathedral in 1653–4.

According to the inventory for 1680, the cross once had a case adorned with crimson velvet and silver plaques (Annunciation Cathedral Inventory Seventeenth Century). Later inventories make clear that the cross was subsequently moved and placed in a wooden *kiot* or frame (Annunciation Cathedral Inventory 1771–2).

S.Z.

69

Panagia on a chain

Russia, late seventeenth or early eighteenth century

Silver, diamonds, rubies, emeralds, pearls, crystal, coloured stones; cast, carved, chased, flat-chased, enamelled, gilded

Height 6¼ in. (15.8 cm); width 3⅞ in. (9.8 cm)

Provenance: via Gokhran [State Valuables Administration] from Vitebsk Province in 1924

Moscow Kremlin Museums inv. no. MR–5771/1–2

MS sources: Armoury Inventory 1914–30, no. 17758

Literature: Russian Gold 1984, p. 50

Panagia is Greek for 'most holy'. It is one of the names used for the Virgin in the Orthodox Church. It can also describe communion in honour of the Virgin (the second most holy after that in honour of Jesus Christ) and the small 'ark' in which the Communion bread is contained. A *panagia* worn on the breast served as a talisman, since the Virgin's communion bread was attributed with the power of protection against all ills, particularly on long journeys. With time the *panagia*, usually without the communion bread, came to be a symbol of the highest Russian clergy, clearly marking the Church's attitude to the Virgin's role as intercessor, praying to Jesus for forgiveness for mankind's sins.

On the front of a *panagia* there is usually a small icon of the Virgin, the saviour or a saint. This rare example shows the cross on which Christ was crucified, with the instruments of Christ's Passion. The unusual choice of subject may have resulted from a growing emphasis on Christ's sacrifice to atone for mankind's sins that was manifested in Russian Orthodox art during the last quarter of the seventeenth century. The cross itself is composed of faceted pieces of crystal. To either side are the stick and spear with which Christ was tortured, with pearls encircling the whole to create a striking effect.

V.F.

Russian Secular Silver

70

Kovsh

Moscow Kremlin workshops, 1624

Belonged to Tsar Mikhail Fyodorovich

Makers Tretyak Pyostrikov and son

Gold, rubies, sapphires, pearls; chased, carved, wrought, nielloed

Height 5¾ in. (14.5 cm);
length 11⅝ in. (29.5 cm);
width 8 in. (20.5 cm)

Provenance: historic collection of the Armoury

Moscow Kremlin Museums inv. no. MR–4126

Published sources: Armoury Inventory 1884–93, part 2,
book 1, no. 529

Literature: Postnikova-Loseva 1954, p. 170

The *kovsh* is one of the most characteristic vessels of Old Russia. Archaeological excavations have brought to light wooden *kovsh* from as far back as the tenth and eleventh centuries. Later the vessel was produced in metal. Wills and bequests of princes of Muscovy from the fourteenth century repeatedly mention golden *kovsh* which were passed on to their children.

At feasts, the *kovsh* was used to serve a favourite Russian drink, 'honey' or mead. Foreigners who came to Russia in the sixteenth and seventeenth centuries called the drink 'most wonderful', comparing it with the celebrated Cretan wine. The envoy Anthony Jenkinson described being given some in 1557:

We came into the midst of the chamber, where we did reverence unto the Emperours maiestie, and then he delivered unto every one of us with his owne handes a cup of mead, which when every man had received and drunke a quantitie thereof, we were licenced to depart, and so ended that dinner. And because the Emperour would have us to be mery, hee sent to our lodging the same Evening, 3. barrels of mead of sundry sortes, of the quantitie in all of one hogshead.

The Emperour and great Duke giveth thee to drinke. All the tables aforesaid were served in vessels of pure and fine golde, as well basons and ewers, platters, dishes and sawcers, as also of great pots, with an innumerable sort of small drinking pottes of divers fashions, whereof a great number were set with stone. —Hakluyt, 1598, p. 339

Various kinds of mead were brewed according to different recipes. They were then steeped with fruits and berries to vary the taste and colour. Red mead was drunk from a golden *kovsh*, white mead from a silver *kovsh*.

In the seventeenth century a particular kind of *kovsh* developed in Moscow that was low and broad with a flat bottom. The *kovsh* of Tsar Mikhail Fyodorovich is striking for its noble severity of form and elegant decoration, the smooth polished metal set with fiery precious stones in high-chased settings. The pointed end and handle have nielloed plates framed with threads of pearls, and around the rim runs a nielloed inscription in a complex Slavonic script (*vyaz*): 'By God's grace great Sovereign Tsar and Grand Duke Mikhail Fyodorovich of all Russia, autocrat of Vladimir, Moscow and Novgorod and many other states, sovereign and owner'.

During the first half of the seventeenth century such a *kovsh* might be kept with regalia and other elements of court ceremony in the Great Treasury. It would have been used only for ceremonial receptions in the Faceted Chamber, where rich plate was set out on stepped sideboards or buffets to demonstrate to foreign guests the wealth of the Muscovite state and the elegant skill of Russian goldsmiths. Sometimes such a *kovsh* might be used to serve mead to the most honoured guests. A description of a dinner in the Patriarch's Cross Chambers records that the Patriarch was served red mead in three 'richly adorned *kovsh* with pearls and stones' (Postnikova-Loseva 1954). Philippa Glanville notes that John Merrick, whose connection with Russia lasted some forty years, bequeathed to his brother-in-law William Russell (who had also served as an envoy to Russia) a 'Kovsh of silver double gilt sett with stones given me by the Emperor of Russia, also his picture of gold with his title about it' (see p. 49).

M.M.

71

Cup

Moscow Kremlin workshops, 1620

Made for Tsar Mikhail Fyodorovich

Maker Yakov Frik

Gold, sapphires, emeralds, rubies, spinel, enamel; chased, enamelled, carved, flat-chased

Height 6¾ in. (17 cm); diameter of bowl 4½ in. (11.5 cm)

Provenance: historic collection of the Armoury

Moscow Kremlin Museums inv. no. MR–1046

Published sources: Armoury Inventory 1884–93, part 2, book 1, no. 535

Literature: Antiquities 1849–53, section 5, p. 32; Postnikova-Loseva 1954, p. 177; Russian Enamel 1974, pp. 78–9; Martynova 2002, p. 67

This luxurious flat gold cup is adorned with large precious stones and enamel. It was produced for the first Romanov Tsar, Mikhail Fyodorovich, as we learn from an inscription along the rim in gold letters against a black ground: 'By the Grace of God Great Sovereign Tsar and Grand Duke Mikhail Fyodorovich Autocrat of All Russia'. The cup is a rare example of a non-liturgical vessel from the hand of Yakov Frik, a foreigner of uncertain nationality who worked in Russia and participated in the creation of one of the most important monuments of seventeenth-century Russia, Mikhail Fyodorovich's royal crown (Moscow Kremlin Museums; Martynova 2002).

The bowl is octagonal and separated from the lobed base by a slightly flattened baluster or knop. The form recalls a chalice – Frik was probably provided with a chalice to imitate, his secular piece thus recalling a church vessel. With its rich alternation of smooth gold facets and applied gold openwork, adorned with enamel and precious stones, the gold cup is an object of truly imperial luxury.

V.F.

72

Bratina (loving cup)

Moscow Kremlin workshops, 1600–35

Belonged to Ivan Tarasievich Gramotin, *d'yak* (secretary) of the boyars' council

Silver; chased, carved, gilded

Height 4⅜ in. (11 cm); max. diameter 5½ in. (13.9 cm)

Provenance: History collection of the Armoury

Moscow Kremlin Museums inv. no. MR–4173

Literature: Troytsky 1861, p. 47; Postnikova-Loseva 1954, p. 172, ill. 19; Rogozhin 2002, pp. 120–8

The rim of this decorative *bratina* (loving cup) is engraved with lions, griffons and unicorns rampant (standing on their war paws or hooves). They support oval cartouches which bear the inscription: BRATINA IVANA TARASIEVICHA GRAMOTINA ['Bratina of Ivan Tarasievich Gramotin'].

The interest in family arms – so developed in Europe at this time – was only in its initial phase in Russia during the early part of the seventeenth century. Thus the inclusion of heraldic elements in the decoration is a most unusual feature, and surely a deliberate choice on the part of the client. Ivan Tarasievich Gramotin (d. 1638) worked in the Ambassadorial Office and his commission likely followed from the close contact he had with European diplomats and officials.

An intelligent and learned man, Gramotin played a notable role in Russian government in the early seventeenth century. His professional skills and authority in international affairs, together with his keen political intuition, enabled him to serve as head of the Ambassadorial Office on four occasions between 1606 and 1635.

M.M.

73

Beaker

Moscow Kremlin workshops, 1600–45

Belonged to Tsar Mikhail Fyodorovich

Silver; chased, carved, gilded

Height 7 in. (17.8 cm); diameter 5¼ in. (12.7 cm)

Provenance: historic collection of the Armoury

Moscow Kremlin Museums inv. no. MR–4169

Literature: Czars 2002, p. 117

'Certaine sortes of drinkes used in Russia, and commonly drunke in the Emperours court'

The first and principall meade is made of the juice or licour taken from a berrie callied in Russia, Malieno, which is of a marveilous sweete taste, and of a carmosant colour, which berry I have seene in Paris.

The second meade is called Visnova, because it is made of a berry so called, and is like a black gooseberrie: but it is like in colour and taste to the red wine of France.

The third meade is called Amarodina or Smorodina, short, of a small berry much like to the small rezin, and growth in great plenty in Russia.

The fourth meade is called Chereunikyna, which is made of the wilde blacke cherry.

The fift meade is made of hony and water, with other mixtures.

There is also a delicate drinke drawn from the root of the birch tree, called in the Russe tongue Berozevites, which drinke the noble men and others use in Aprill, May and June, which are the three moneths of the spring time: for after those moneths, the sappe of the tree dryeth, and then they cannot have it.
—Hakluyt 1589, p. 323

Broadening towards the top, this silver beaker is attached to a low stepped base adorned with a band of geometrical ornament. It has cast feet in the form of lions. The rim, base and three round medallions on the body are gilded. Engraved inscriptions run around the rim and occupy the medallions.

The selection of texts is extremely unusual for a secular object, consisting of holy songs for the Feast of the Raising of the Cross and prayers that Tsar Mikhail Fyodorovich be granted victory over his enemies. It is possible that the beaker was presented to the monarch on the eve of a military campaign which fell on the Feast of the Raising of the Cross on 14 September (27 September new style).

S.O.

74

Bowl

Moscow Kremlin workshops 1600–50

Belonged to Tsar Mikhail Fyodorovich

Gold, rubies, emeralds; chased, enamelled, carved

Height 1⅛ in. (2.9 cm); diameter 2⅝ in. (6.7 cm)

Provenance: historic collection of the Armoury

Moscow Kremlin Museums inv. no. MR–1047

Published sources: Armoury Inventory 1884–93, book 2, part 1, no. 576

Literature: Martynova 2002, p. 91

This golden bowl is adorned with enamel and precious stones. An inscription along the rim records that it belonged to Tsar Mikhail Fyodorovich: 'By the Grace of God Great Sovereign Tsar and Grand Duke Mikhail Fyodorovich Autocrat of All Russia'. Inside the bowl, on the bottom, is a two-headed eagle of transparent green and golden enamel. The body of the bowl is ornamented with tiny flowers and vegetation filled with dark green, greenish-blue and bright blue transparent enamel. Since light penetrates the enamel and illuminates the gold ground, it creates an effect of a gold surface encrusted with precious stones.

V.F.

257

75

Plate

Moscow Kremlin workshops, 1675–1700

Belonged to Prince Vasily Vasilevich Golitsyn

Silver; chased, nielloed, carved, gilded

Diameter 11⅛ in. (28.3 cm)

Provenance: historic collection of the Armoury

Moscow Kremlin Museums inv. no. MR–4206

Published sources: Armoury Inventory 1884–93, no. 1791, pl. 183

Oriental motifs and devices were used by the Russian silversmith who decorated this plate. The entire surface is covered with ornament in a manner typical of works by Persian and Turkic masters. The sense of fullness is enhanced by the larger elements (such as the pomegranate and fans) being filled with smaller patterns.

In the centre of the plate is a coat-of-arms with the letters BKVVG, standing for 'Boyar Prince Vasily Vasilevich Golitsyn' (1643–1714). Personal arms appeared in Russia later than in Western Europe and occur regularly on precious metal objects only in the second quarter of the seventeenth century. The interest in coats-of-arms – which were adopted by the boyars – surged towards the end of the century. This was facilitated in part by the unification in the mid-seventeenth century of the Muscovite state and the Ukraine, where family arms were known from the sixteenth century. Among those Muscovite nobles using a coat-of-arms to mark his possessions was Prince Vasily Golitsyn, a key figure at the Moscow court in the regency of Tsarevna Sophia (1682–9) during the minority of her brothers Ivan and Peter. Golitsyn was head of the Ambassadorial Office and Keeper of the Royal Seal.

M.M.

The Imagery of Early Anglo-Russian Relations

Edward Kasinec and Robert H. Davis, Jr

69. Matthiae Beckeri (?), 'Reception of the Dutch Ambassador by Tsar Ivan IV (the Terrible) on August 21, 1578', from Jacob Ulfeldt, *Hodoeporicon Ruthenicum*, plate 2, Frankfurt, 1608. Rare Books Division, The New York Public Library, Astor, Lenox and Tilden Foundations

Anglo-Russian diplomatic and cultural relations in the late sixteenth and seventeenth centuries have provided scholarship with a large corpus of archival, manuscript and printed documentation for study, interpretation and publication.[1] Until recently, the visual legacy of this relationship has received far less attention. This brief overview addresses in part this lacuna by noting a selection of rare illustrated works on paper at the New York Public Library and Yale University.

Maps and atlases

Atlases that brought together nautical and terrestrial maps of the known world are among the earliest and richest visual sources on Anglo-Russian relations. Commercial and diplomatic relations between England and Russia developed during the golden age of atlas and map-making (Cats. 87–90). Early topographical and nautical maps and *vedute* of Muscovy drawn by English mariners and tradesmen of the Muscovy Company were widely distributed in the great compendia of the early seventeenth century issued by Gerhard Mercator (1512–94), Abraham Ortelius (1527–98), Willem Janszoon Blaeu (1571–1638), Hessel Gerritsz (1581?–1682),[2] Nicolaes Visscher (1618–79), Frederik de Wit (1630–1706) and Pieter van der Aa (1659–1733). Atlases were a critical vehicle for conveying practical and – via the cartouches and fanciful decorative elements – cultural information to English and continental commercial and political elites.

In 1562 schoolmaster and engraver Clement Adams (*c.*1519–87) produced the earliest English cartographic representation of Muscovy on the basis of information from the 1558 voyage of Anthony Jenkinson.[3] Agent of the newly formed Muscovy Company, Jenkinson had multiple audiences with Ivan IV; his third expedition in 1566 is considered the first formal English diplomatic embassy to Russia. The map's cartouches depict the peoples and customs of the empire, while the map's many blank spaces reflect the *terra incognita* of Muscovy's interior. Compilations such as Ortelius' *Theatrum Orbis Terrarum* ['Theatre of the World'] of 1570 (cat. 87) and later editions of largely narrative compendia such as Samuel Purchas' *Hakluytus Posthumus, or Purchas his Pilgrimes* of 1625 (cat. 77) subsequently reproduced this and other early maps. Particularly noteworthy is the rare first edition of *An Account of a Voyage from Archangel in Russia in the year 1697* (London, 1699) by Thomas Allison which depicts the gateway to Muscovy, the White Sea port of Arkhangel'sk, known to the English as Archangel.

Sketches of Muscovy

The hazardous sea crossing completed, diplomatic and commercial representatives continued to Moscow, often in the company of a draughtsman to render images of the Tsardom and the rituals of diplomatic exchange. This was particularly true of continental European delegations. Among the more important travelogues is that of Augustin von Meierberg (1612–88), ambassador of the Holy Roman Emperor Leopold I to Tsar Alexey in 1662. The bibliographer Friedrich von Adelung published *Augustin Freiherr von Meyerberg und seine Reise nach Russland* ['Augustin Freiherr von Meierberg and his Journey to Russia'] (St Petersburg, 1827), a rare printed edition based on original sketches (now in Moscow, having been removed from Dresden by Soviet troops after the Second World War). Accounts of the embassies of Sigmund von Herberstein (1486–1566) in the service of the Holy Roman Empire, and of the Danish diplomat Jacob Ulfeldt (d. 1593) were important contemporary sources of textual and visual information about Muscovy. Although Ulfeldt did not visit the Gold Chamber of the Kremlin, he was eventually received at Ivan IV's refuge in Alexandrovskaya Sloboda outside Moscow. One of the images in his *Hodoeporicon Ruthenicum* ['Ruthenian Journey'] (Frankfurt, 1608; fig. 3) depicts a table in the throne room or banqueting hall, laden with what appear to be silver goblets and ornaments – some likely to have been of English provenance – set out to impress guests and petitioners. Similar rituals later appear in the accounts of the Holstein diplomat Adam Olearius (1603–71) (cat. 86). An etching by Romein de Hooghe (1645–1708) of the Dutch emissary Koenraad van Klenk in 1676, published in Balthazar Coyet's *Historisch Verhael of Beschryving Van de Voyagie: Gedaen onder de Suite van den Heere Koenraad van Klenk* ['History or Description of the Voyage undertaken under the Leadership of Koenraad van Klenk'] (Amsterdam, 1677) (cat. 84), shows packed crates of diplomatic gifts, as well as tankards, chandeliers and a stallion with fine livery.[4]

The earliest Russian glimpses into Kremlin ceremony emerged only in the nineteenth century from contemporary manuscripts and sketches in the archives. The documentary work of the anonymous court illustrators of seventeenth-century illuminated manuscripts appeared in print for the first time in rare limited editions intended for the elites of the Russian Empire. For example, *Opisanie v litsakh torzhestva ... brakosochetanii ... Mikhaila ...* ['Illustrated Description of the Solemnities Connected with the Marriage of Mikhail'] was printed in Moscow from originals in the archives only in 1810 (fig. 70). A reconstruction of events surrounding the coronation of Mikhail Romanov in 1613, sponsored by Artamon Matveev (1625–82), was published as a chromolithographic elephant folio in Moscow in 1856 entitled *Knigu ob izbranii na tsarstvo Velikago Gosudarya, Tsarya i Velikago knyaz'ya Mikhaila Fyodorovicha* ['The Book Concerning the Election as Autocrat of the Great Sovereign, Tsar, and Grand Prince Mikhail Fyodorovich']. Additional images from this archival collection were later published as *Moskva: snimki s vidov mestnostey, khramov, zdaniy i drugikh sooruzheniy* ['Moscow: Photographs and Views of Localities, Churches, Buildings and other Structures'] ([Moscow], 1886).

70. *Opisanie v litsakh torzhestva ... brakosochetanii ... Mikhaila ...* Moscow, 1810. Beinecke Rare Book and Manuscript Library, Yale University

Printing and 'secular' portraiture in Muscovy developed more than a century later than in England and on the Continent. Muscovite books of the sixteenth and seventeenth centuries were essentially scriptural or religious in nature, containing few woodcuts or (later) engravings. The personal iconography for English principals in Anglo-Russian relations is thus far more extensive than that of their Muscovite counterparts during the early modern period. A case in point are the many engraved images (and oil paintings) of English monarchs, found both as individual engravings and in larger compendia such as Henry Holland's *Basiliologia. A booke of kings beeing the true and lively effigies of all our English kings from the Conquest untill this present* ([London], 1618) or Francis Sandford's *A Genealogical History of the Kings and Queens of England* (London, [1707]), prepared in part by the noted engraver Wenceslaus Hollar (d. 1677). Of the emissaries representing English interests in Russia, images exist of Sir Thomas Smith by the Dutch engraver and draughtsman Crispijn van de Passe (c.1597–1670; cat. 78), and of the Earl of Carlisle, in Guy de Miège's *A Relation of the Three Embassies* of 1669 (cat. 80).

Portraits of contemporary Muscovite personalities, on the other hand, are few and often fanciful. Paul Oderborn's *Ioannis Basilidis, Magni Moscouiae Ducis, vita* ['The Life of Ivan Vasilevich, Ruler of Moscow'] (Wittenberg, 1585) includes a woodcut image identified as Ivan IV that possesses a complex iconographical genealogy. The original image was executed by Hans Weigel (1549–78?) on the basis of blocks depicting Vasily III, attributed to Erhardt Shen and dated to around 1520. Franz Christoph Khevenhuller includes an image by Tobias Stimmer (1539–84) purporting to be Ivan IV in *Conterfet Kupfferstich* ['Portrait Engraving'] (Leipzig, 1721–2), but in fact also a reworked image of Vasily III. The basis for the Stimmer image was an oil painting of Vasily brought to Rome in 1525 and itself based on a woodcut in *Pauli Iovii Novocomensis Libellus de legatione Basilii magni principis Moschoviae ad Clementem VII. Pontificem max.* ['Paolo Giovio of Como's Little Book on the Embassy of Vasily, Great Prince of Muscovy, to Pope Clement VII'] (Basel, 1527).

From the Russian side, the seventeenth-century manuscript *Bolshoy Titulyarnik* ['The Grand Book of Titles'], of which there are several manuscript versions, one of them in the Russian State Archive of Ancient Acts in Moscow, is a contemporary source reflecting Russia's self-perceptions and world view. In addition to leading Muscovite political and religious figures, it includes portraits by Russian artists of other world leaders, including Charles II. Originally produced and hand-copied in the atelier of the Ambassadorial Office of the Muscovite court, a limited edition was printed in St Petersburg only in 1903 as *Portrety, gerby i pechati Bolshoy gosudarstvennoy knigi 1672 g.* ['Portraits, Coats-of-Arms, and Seals of the Great State Book of 1672' fig. 71]. The standard collection of individual woodcuts and engravings of Russian rulers of the sixteenth and seventeenth centuries is contained in *Materialy dlya russkoy ikonografiy* ['Materials Towards a Russian Iconography'] (St Petersburg, 1884–90) assembled by Dmitry Rovinsky. This is based largely on contemporary western, not Russian, sources.

71. 'Mikhail Fyodorovich Romanov', no. 31, in *Portrety, gerby i pechati Bolshoy gosudarstvennoy knigi 1672 g*, Moscow, 1672, reprinted St Petersburg, 1903. Slavic and Baltic Division, The New York Public Library, Astor, Lenox and Tilden Foundations

Treasures of the Armoury

Beginning in the early nineteenth century, a wave of historicist, national and religious sentiment during the reigns of Alexander I and his brother Nicholas I fostered interest in recapturing and occasionally reinventing the Muscovite past. Medieval structures were restored, and historic manuscripts published for the first time. Diplomatic gifts symbolized the majesty, antiquity and legitimacy of the Russian state. Institutions such as the Moscow Armoury (opened as a museum in 1806) were established to house treasures that embodied Russian national importance and identity.

A. F. Malinovsky published the earliest description of the Moscow Kremlin Armoury's collections as *Istoricheskoe opisanie Drevnyago rossiyskago muzeya* ['Historical Description of the Museum of Russian Antiquity'] (Moscow, 1807). Its engravings, however, depict the Russian state regalia, not diplomatic gifts. Fyodor Solntsev's *Drevnosti Rossiyskago Gosudarstva* ['Antiquities of the Russian State'] (Moscow, 1849–53) was the first to depict foreign gifts in the Armoury (fig. 72). The six sumptuous and costly volumes contain over 600 plates, of which more than twenty are of silver objects. Solntsev was a restorer, designer and historical painter who enjoyed the patronage of the family of Nicholas I. Virtually all of his sketches were approved for circulation by the Emperor himself. An English provenance is clearly ascribed to five flagons (*suleya*) sent by Charles I in 1634. In reality, there are several more English pieces in the *Drevnosti* volume, but these are unattributed. Subsequent Armoury administrations followed Solntsev's lead. The Armoury directors A. F. Veltman and G. D. Filimonov highlighted silver treasures on display in the Faceted Chamber of the Kremlin[5] and illustrated publications with English examples.[6] From these early engravings and lithographs (and later photogravures), images of the English silver in the Armoury found their way into other major compilations on 'treasure collections' of the Russian Empire and the decorative arts of the Moscow Kremlin.[7]

Souvenirs of Russia

Many English emissaries to Muscovy returned home with mementoes and gifts. The legacy of early Anglo-Muscovite relations is particularly in evidence in British libraries. When Richard Lee returned to England in 1602, he attended the opening of the Bodleian Library, presenting copies of the 1581 Ostrog Bible (the first Slavonic Bible), the 1582 Vilna *Octoechos* ['Book of Eight Tones'], the 1598 Ostrog Primer and the 1592–1601 Vilna *Horologion* ['Book of Hours'], as well as a Tatar lamb coat presented to him by the Tsar. Emissaries Jerome Horsey and John Merrick [8] both donated printed and manuscript codices to the Bodleian, while the lexicographer Richard James gave several early seventeenth-century works to Corpus Christi College, Oxford.[9] Contemporary seventeenth-century inscriptions found in printed books and manuscripts acquired by Cambridge, Oxford, and later by the British Library frequently bear the inscriptions of physicians such as Launcelot Browne (d. 1605) and Mark Ridley (d. 1624);[10] of 'marchaunts of muskouie' such as Christopher Burrough (Borough) (fl. 1579–87) and his

father William (1536–99), Thomas Hawtrey (d. 1591) and Thomas Smith; and of others whose connections to, or interests in, Muscovy are more obscure.[11]

Museum curators and historians of the decorative arts are quite rightly concerned in the first instance with the study and display of objects. Increasingly they have turned also to the material available in archives and manuscript collections. It is only relatively recently, however, that scholars have become aware of the broad spectrum of rare printed sources such as those included here that give life, context and a more nuanced understanding of one of Old Russia's principal cultural and diplomatic engagements.

72. Fyodor Grigorevich Solntsev, 'The Goblet of Tsar Mikhail Feodorovich,' in Solntsev, *Drevnosti Rossiyskago gosudarstva*, plate 21, vol. 5, Moscow, 1849–53. Slavic and Baltic Division, The New York Public Library, Astor, Lenox and Tilden Foundations

КУБОКЪ ЦАРЯ МИХАИЛА ѲЕОДОРОВИЧА.

Notes

The authors are grateful for the assistance of Joanne Bornstein (New York Public Library), Barry Shifman (Indianapolis Museum of Art), Ann Odom (Hillwood Museum) Christine Thomas (British Library) and Irina Bogatskaia, Elena Isaeva and Svetlana Kustanyan (Library of the Moscow Kremlin Museums). The views expressed are those of the authors.

1   See, for example, Russia–Britain 2003, particularly pp. 35–6, 41, 44, 50, 53, 61, 78–9, 89–92 and 95–6.

2   In 1613, Amsterdam cartographer Gerritsz published a plan of Muscovy based on an early seventeenth-century Russian map made during the reign of Tsar Fyodor Godunov. The rights were subsequently purchased by the Blaeu family of map publishers.

3   In 1553–4 Adams had recorded the observations of Richard Chancellor (d. 1556), England's first visitor to Muscovy, upon the latter's return to England. The Muscovy Company suppressed his manuscript until 1589, when it was published in the original Latin and in an English translation by Richard Hakluyt in his widely read *The Principall Navigations, Voiages and Discoveries of the English Nation* (London, 1589), pp. 270–92 (cat. 76).

4   See also *Russen en Nederlanders: Uit de Geschiedenis van de Betrekkingen tussen Nederland en Rusland 1600–1917* ['Russians and the Dutch: History of the Relations between the Netherlands and Russia 1600–1917'], Rijksmuseum Amsterdam exh. cat. (The Hague, 1989), pp. 60–1.

5   *Opisanie novago imperatorskago dvortsa v Kremle Moskovskom* ['A Description of the New Imperial Palace in the Moscow Kremlin'] (Moscow, 1851).

6   Examples include the remarkable leopard by an English craftsman (cat. 7) and a silver-gilt ewer depicting Charles I on horseback. This latter piece, by Schwestermüller of Augsburg, was given by Charles XII of Sweden to Peter I in 1699 (illustrated in *Moskovskaya Oruzheynaya palata* ['Moscow Armoury'], Moscow, 1860).

7   The Kremlin Armoury Museum holds M. M. Panov's *Al'bom Risunok Moskovskoy oruzheynoy palaty* ['Album of Drawings of the Moscow Armoury'] (Moscow, 1884–93), a 500-photo inventory.

8   At various times Horsey represented both English and Russian interests. Although accused of fraud by the Muscovy Company, his powerful patron Sir Francis Walsingham had him appointed ambassador to Moscow in 1590–1. The account of his experiences was a source for Giles Fletcher's *Of the Russe Commonwealth* of 1591. Merrick (Meyrick), son of an original member of the Muscovy Company, served as its chief agent in Russia from 1575. Dispatched with English financial support for Tsar Mikhail, he returned to England in November 1617 with 'lavish' gifts from the Tsar to the King.

9   Bodleian Library, Oxford, MS James 43, contains a Russian-English vocabulary prepared by James, as well as transcriptions of Russian folksongs.

10 Ridley compiled 'A Dictionarie of the vulgar Russe tongue': see Bodleian Library, Oxford, MS Laud Misc 47a; repr. *A Dictionarie of the vulgar Russe Tongue, attributed to Mark Ridley*, ed. G. Stone (Cologne, 1996). Sent by Elizabeth I as physician to the Tsar, Ridley was subsequently commended by Boris Godunov in a letter to the Queen (British Library, MS Cotton Nero B. XI). Physician to Elizabeth I and James I, Browne evidently served in the Willoughby expedition to Muscovy in 1557.

11 The New York Public Library holds a printed book unknown in bibliography, a *Chasovnik* ['Book of Hours'] printed at the *Pechatnyy dvor* in Moscow in 1630. It contains English marginalia and ownership marks of, among others, one Thomas Stratford, dated 1691.

73. Cat. 87, detail

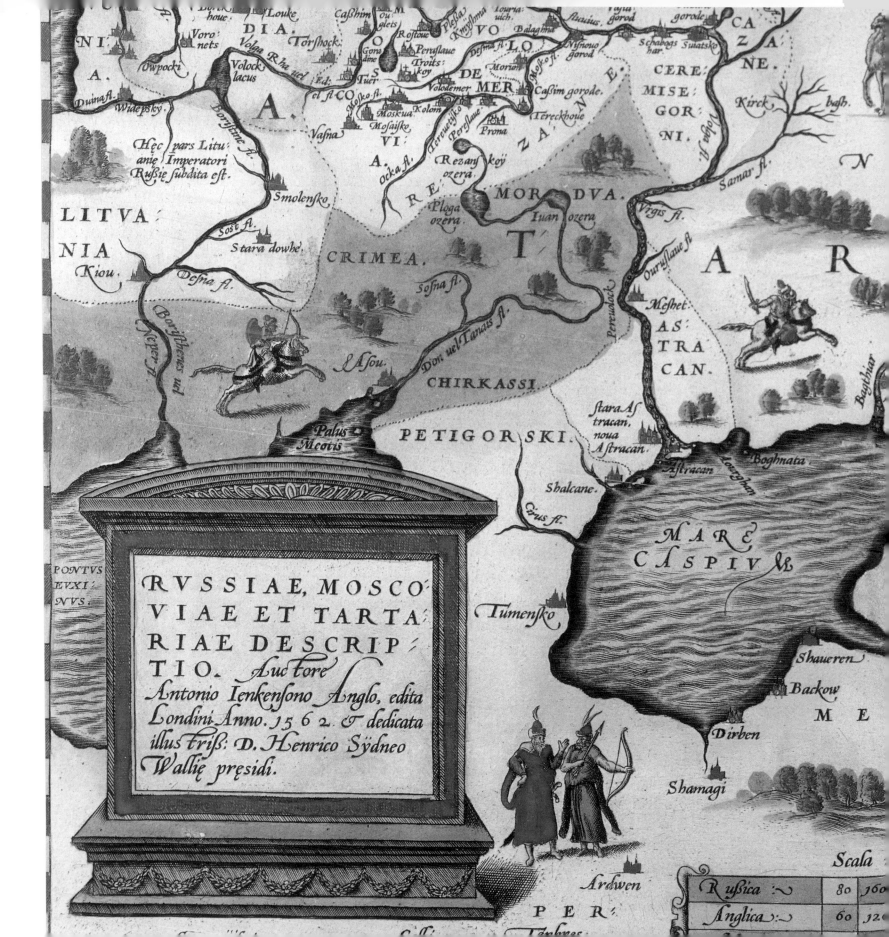

Hakluytus Posthumus, or Purchas His Pilgrimes: Contayning a History of the World, in Sea Voyages & Lande-trauells, by Englishmen and Others

Samuel Purchas (1577–1626)

Vol. 3, London, Printed by William Stansby for Henry Fetherstone, 1625

Yale Center for British Art, Paul Mellon Collection, G159 +P98 1625 v.3

Samuel Purchas was curate of Purleigh in Essex and then vicar of Eastwood, before being appointed rector of St Martin's, Ludgate, in 1613. His compilation of travel texts, *Hakluytus Posthumus*, contains a section on 'English Northerne Navigations, and Discoveries' which includes journeys to Russia. The work contains the memoirs of Jerome Horsey, who worked for the Muscovy Company in Russia from 1572–85 and frequently travelled between the two countries:

'The most solemne and magnificent coronation of PHEODOR IVANOVICH, Emperour of Russia', 1584

> After all this, the Emperour came into the Parliament house, which was richly decked: there he was placed in his royall seat adorned as before: his six crownes were set before him upon a Table: the Bason and Ewre royall of gold held by his knight of gard, with his men standing two on each side in white apparell of cloth of silver, called Kindry with scepters and battle-axes of gold in their hands, the Princes and nobility were all placed according to their degrees in all their rich roabes.

> The Emperour after a short Oration, permitted every man in order to kisse his hand: which being done, he removed to a princely seate prepared for him at the table: where he was served by his Nobles in very princely order. The three out roomes being very great and large were beset with plate of gold and silver round, from the ground up to the vauts one upon the other: among which plate were many barrels of silver and gold …

Jerome Horsey, proud Elizabethan

> The same time also Master Ierom Horsey aforesaid, remaining as servant in Russia for the Queens most excellent Maiestie, was called for to the Emperour, as he sate in his Imperiall seat, and the also famous Merchant of Netherland being newly come to Moscow (who gave him selfe out to be the King of Spaines subiect) called Iohn de Wale, was in like sort called for. Some of the Nobilitie would have preferred this subject of the Spaniard before Master Horsey servant to the Queen of England, whereunto Master Horsey would in no case agree, saying, hee would have his legges cut off by the knees, before hee would yeelde to such an indignitie offered to his Soveraigne the Queenes Maiestie of England, to bring the Emperour a present, in course after the King of Spaines subject, or any other whatsoever. The Emperour, and the Prince Boris Pheodorowich perceving the controversie, sent the Lord Treasurer Peter Ivanowich Galavyn, and Vasili Shalkan, both of the Counsell, to them, who delivered the Emperour backe Master Horseys speech: whereupon he was first in order (as good reason) admitted and presented the Emperour in the behalfe of the English Merchants trading thither, a present, wishing him joy, and long to raigne in tranquilitie, and so kissed the Emperours hand, he accepting the present with good liking, and avouching, that for his Sisters sake, Queene Elizabeth of England, he would be a gracious Lord to her Merchants, in as ample manner as ever his Father had beene: and being dismissed, he had the same day sent him, seaventie dishes of sundry kinds of meats, with three carts laden with al sorts of drinks very bountifully …

'A Royall present of Sables … and other rich things'

> It fell out not long after, that the Emperour was desirous to send a message to the most excellent Queene of England, for which service he thought no mann fitter than Master Ioerome Horsey, supposing that one of the Queenes owne men and subjects would bee the more acceptable to her. The summe of which messagge was, That the Emperor desired a continuance of that league, friendship, amitie and intercourse of traffique which was betweene his Father and the Queenes Maiestie and her Subjects, with other private affaires besides, which are not to bee made common.

In 1580 and 1585 Horsey acted as Russian emissary to England, then again in 1587, serving as English ambassador to Moscow in 1590–1.

C.P.

sinkes against him, and would speake in his defence, if I found not an vniuersall conspiracie of all Historie and Reports against him. I honour his other good parts , his wit , his learning , better then almost any other *Russe* in his time) his exemplarie seueri ty on vniust Magistrates, his Martiall skill, industrie, fortune, wherby he subdued the Kingdoms of *Casan* and *Astracan* (withall also the *Turke* sending from *Constantinople* an Armie of three hundred thousand to dispossesse him of, *A.*1569. besides his hopes and helpes from the *Tartars,* few returned to tell their disaster, and the destructions of their fellowes) besides what hee got in *Siberia* and from the *Pole, Sweden, Prussian,* extending his Conquests East, West, North, and South : yea , his memorie is fauoured still to the *Russians,* which (either of their seruile disposition needing such a bridle and whips , or for his long and prosperous reigne, or out of distaste of later tragedies) hold him in little lesse re-putation (as some haue out of their experience instructed me) then a Saint.

His loue to our Nation is magnified by our Countrimen with all thankfulnesse, whose gaine there begun by him, haue made them also in some sort seeme to turne *Russe*(in I know what loue, or feares, as if they were still shut vp in *Russia,* & to conceale whatsoeuer they know of *Russian* occurrents) that I haue sustayned no small torture with great paines of body, vexation of minde, and triall of potent interceding friends to get but neglect and silence from some, yea almost con-tempt and scorne. They alledge their thankfulnesse for benefits receiued from that Nation, and their feare of the *Dutch,* readie to take aduantage thereof , and by calumniations from hence to interuert their Trade. This for loue to my Nation I haue inserted against any Cauillers of our *Russe* Merchants : though I must needs professe that I distaste, and almost detest that (call it what you will) of Merchants to neglect Gods glorie in his prouidence , and the Worlds instru-ction from their knowledge ; who while they will conceale the *Russians* Faults, will tell no-thing of their Facts; and whiles they will be silent in mysteries of State, will reueale nothing of the histories of Fact, and that in so perplexed , diuersified chances and changes as seldome the World hath in so short a space seene on one Scene.While therefore they which seeme to know most, will in these *Russian* Relations helpe me little or nothing (except to labour and frustrated hopes) I haue(besides much conference with eye witnesses)made bold with others in such bookes as in diuers languages I haue read,and in such Letters and written Tractates as I could procure of my friends, or found with Master *Hakluyt* (as in other parts of our storie) not seeking any what to disgrace that Nation or their Princes , but onely desiring that truth of things done may bee knowne , and such memorable alterations may not passe as a dreame , or bee buried with the Doers. Sir *Ierome Horsey* shall leade you from *Iuans* Graue to *Pheodores* Coronation.

---

* Or *Theodor*

Sir *Ierom Hor-sey.*

The most solemne and magnificent coronation of PHEODOR IVANOVVICH, *Emperour of* Russia, &c. *the tenth of* Iune, *in the yeare* 1584. *seene and obserued by Master* IEROM HORSEY *Gen-tleman, and seruant to her Maiestie.*

The death of *Iuan Vasiliwich* 1584. April 18.

Lord *Boris* a-dopted as the Emperors third sonne.

WHen the old Emperor *Iuan Vasilowich* died(being about the eighteeenth of April,1584. after our computation) in the Citie of *Mosco,* hauing raigned fiftie foure yeares, there was some tumult & vprore among some of the Nobilitie and Comminaltie, which notwithstan-ding was quickly pacified. Immediately the same night, the Prince *Boris Pheodorowich Godonoua, Knez Iuon Pheodorowich, Mestbis Slasiky, Knez Iuan Petrowich Susky, Mekita Romanowich* and *Bo-dan Iacoulewich Belskoy,* being all noble men, and chiefest in the Emperours Will, especially the Lord *Boris,* whom he adopted as his third son,and was brother to the Empresse, who was a man very well liked of all estates, as no lesse worthy for his valour and wisedome : all these were ap-pointed to dispose, and settle his Sonne *Pheodor Iuanowich,* hauing one sworne another, and all the Nobilitie and Officers whosoeuer. In the morning the dead Emperour was laid into the Church of *Michael* the *Archangell,* into a hewen Sepulchre, very richly decked with Vestures fit for such a purpose : and present Proclamation was made(Emperour *Pheodor Iuanowich* of all *Rus-sia,*&c.) Throughout all the Citie of *Mosco* was great watch and ward, with Souldiors,and Gun-ners, good orders established, and Officers placed to subdue the tumulters, and maintaine quiet-nesse : to see what speede and policie was in this case vsed , was a thing worth the beholding. This being done in *Mosco,* great men of birth and accompt were also presently sent to the bor-dering Townes, as *Smolensko, Vobsko, Kasan, Nouogorod,* &c. with fresh garrison, and the old sent vp. As vpon the fourth of May a Parliament was held , wherein were assembled the Metropoli-tane, Archbishops, Bishops, Priors, and chiefe Clergie men , and all the Nobility whatsoeuer : where many matters were determined not pertinent to my purpose, yet all tended to a new re-formation in the gouernement: but especially the terme, and time was agreed vpon for the solemnizing of the new Emperours coronation. In the meane time the Empresse, wife to the old Emperour, was with her childe the Emperours son, *Charlewich Demetrie Iuanowich,* of one yeares age or there abouts, sent with her Father *Pheodor Pheodorowich Nagay,* and that kindred, being

A Relation of the Three Embassies from his Sacred Majestie Charles II to the Great Duke of Muscovie … Performed by the Right Honorable the Earle of Carlisle in the Years 1663 & 1664

Compiled by Guy de Miège (1644?–1718?)

London, John Starkey, 1669

Beinecke Rare Book and Manuscript Library,
Yale University, Bw–14 274

Guy de Miège – a young writer who declared that he had 'a constant inclination to travel' – was employed as under-secretary to the Earl of Carlisle during his 'great embassy' to Russia in 1663 (the poet Andrew Marvell was chief secretary). His book relates in detail the events of the embassy. He seeks to present Carlisle's actions in the best possible light and to deflect criticism, as his early description of the man himself reveals:

> The Earle of Carlisle, to whom the King encharged these Embassies, was without contradiction, in all respects proper for the employment. For, besides that he was of a comely and advantageous statue, a majestick mine, and not above four and thirty years of age, he had a particular grace and vivacity in his discourse, and in his actions a great promptitude and diligence. In a word, he was adorned with all perfections that could render a man acceptable, and especially with those that were requisite for the discharge of so important an affair …

In truth, Carlisle's embassy was notoriously unsuccessful. He failed to achieve the restoration of trading privileges for British merchants and ended up doing much to compromise Anglo-Russian relations. Both English and Russian scholars agree in laying a large part of the blame for this on Carlisle himself and his insistence on his own status and magnificence. He antagonized both the Tsar and the Ambassadorial Office with his behaviour.

C.P.

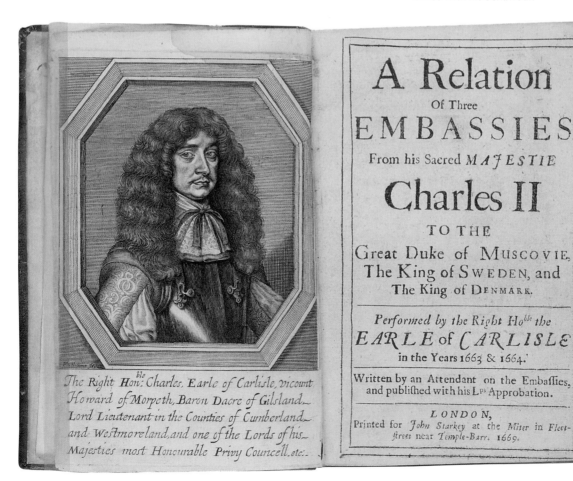

81

The Present State of Russia, In a Letter to a Friend at London; written by an eminent person residing at the great Tzars Court at Mosco for the space of nine years.

Samuel Collins (1619–70)

London, Printed by John Winter for Dorman Newman at the Kings Arms in the Poultry, 1671

Beinecke Rare Book and Manuscript Library, Yale University, 1997 882

Samuel Collins (1619–70) was invited to Russia by John Hebdon to be physician to Tsar Alexey Mikhaylovich. He arrived in 1660 but just two years later, on the death of his brother, requested permission to return to his homeland. His homeward journey was made in the suite of the Russian ambassador Prince Prozorovsky.

Collins returned to Russia in 1663 and remained until 1667. His only book, *The Present State of Russia*, first appeared in 1671 and was translated into French in 1679. The more colourful anecdotes in the book may have been written not by Collins himself but by the editors, seeking to enliven the otherwise useful picture of life in Russia.

C.P.

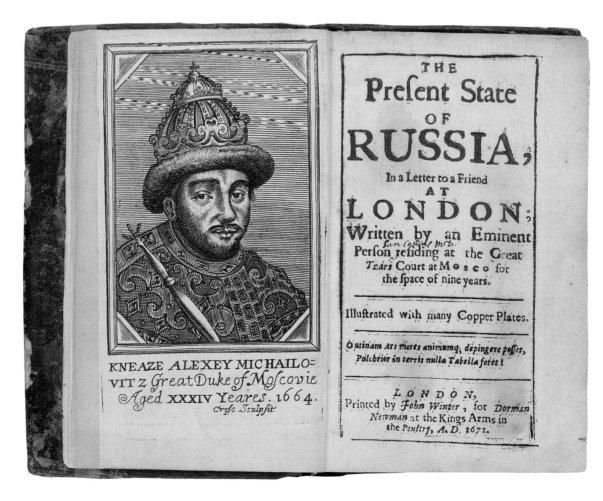

Depicting Russia

Balthasar Coyet (fl. 1670s)

Amsterdam, Jan Claesz. ten Hoorn, 1677

Beinecke Rare Book and Manuscript Library,
Yale University, 1998 1757

81

Historisch Verhael of Beschryving Van de Voyagie: Gedaen onder de Suite van den Heere Koenraad van Klenk, Extraordinaris Ambassadeur van haer Ho: Mog: de Heeren Aen Zyne Zaarsche Majesteyt van Moscovien

['History or Description of the Voyage Undertaken under the Leadership of Koenraad Van Klenk, Extraordinary Ambassador of the Dutch State to His Tsar's Majesty of Muscovy']

276

85

The Antient and Present State of Muscovy: containing a geographical, historical and political account of all those nations and territories under the jurisdiction of the present czar

Jodocus Crull (d.1713/14)

London, A. Roper and A. Bosvile, 1698

Beinecke Rare Book and Manuscript Library, Yale University, Bw5 35d

A Bojar or Muscovian Lord giving his attendance at Court or at any extraordinary Solemnity

Pag. 177

The Voyages & Travels of the Ambassadors Sent by Frederick Duke of Holstein, to the Great Duke of Muscovy, and the King of Persia

Adam Olearius (1603–71); translated by John Davies

London, Printed for Thomas Dring and John Starkey, 1662

Beinecke Rare Book and Manuscript Library,
Yale University, Ee +633g

87

Russiae, Moscoviae et Tartariae Descriptio ['A Description of Russia, Muscovy and Tatary']

Anthony Jenkinson (1529–1611)

Engraving

From Abraham Ortelius (1527–98), *Theatrum Orbis Terrarum* ['Theatre of the World']

Antwerp, A.C. Diesth, 1570

Yale Center for British Art, Paul Mellon Collection, PM Bequest / M&A / Ortelius 1570

Theatrum Orbis Terrarum, containing seventy maps, was the first modern atlas. Its Flemish publisher, the map-maker Abraham Ortelius, went on to become geographer to King Philip II of Spain.

C.P.

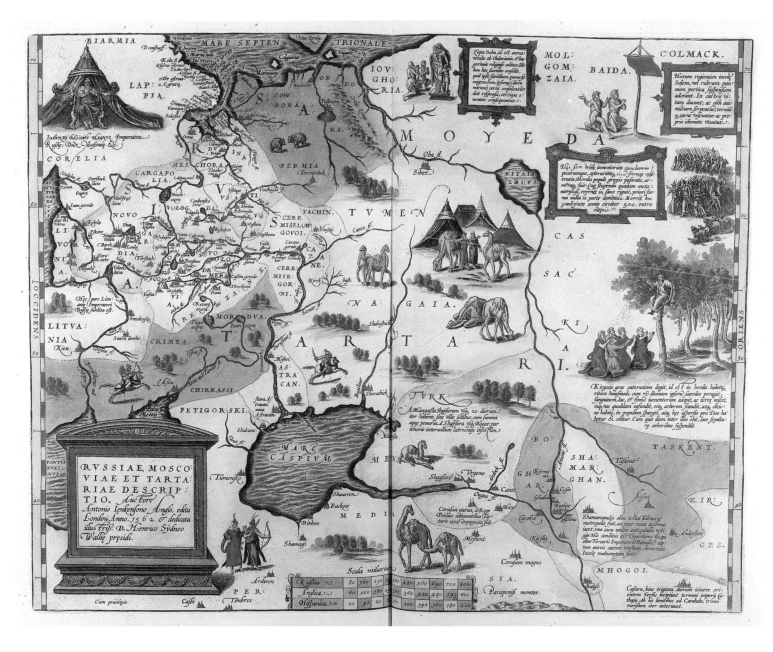

Kremlenagrad Castellum Urbis Moskvae ['The Kremlin Fortress of the City of Moscow']

Joan Blaeu (*c*.1599–1673)

Hand-coloured engraving

From *Geographiae Blavianae* ['Blaeu's Atlas'], vol. 2

Amsterdam, Labore & Sumptibus Ioannis Blaeu, 1662

Yale Center for British Art, Paul Mellon Collection, A/M Blaeu

Joan Blaeu expanded his father's printing business to include the printing of maps. Eventually the Blaeu press was the largest in seventeenth-century Europe. His maps of the world appeared in a series of volumes united under the title *Theatrum Orbis Terrarum* or *Atlas Maior*. By the 1660s this work consisted of some 600 maps, published in nine to twelve volumes, depending on the language in which it appeared.

C.P.

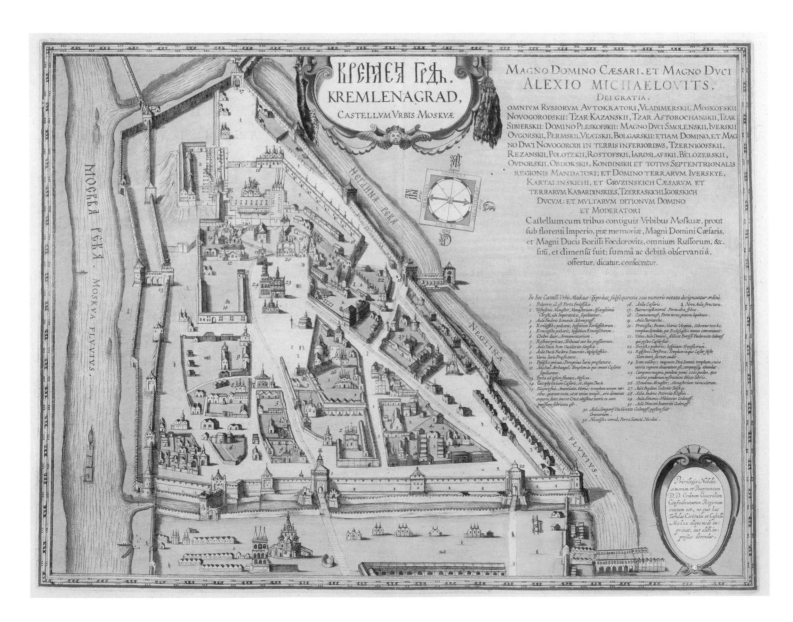

Tabula Russiae
['Map of Russia']

Joan Blaeu (*c.*1599–1673)

Hand-coloured engraving

From *Geographiae Blavianae* ['Blaeu's Atlas'], vol. 2

Amsterdam, Chez Jean Blaeu, 1667

Yale Center for British Art, Paul Mellon Collection,
Americana / Folio A / 1667

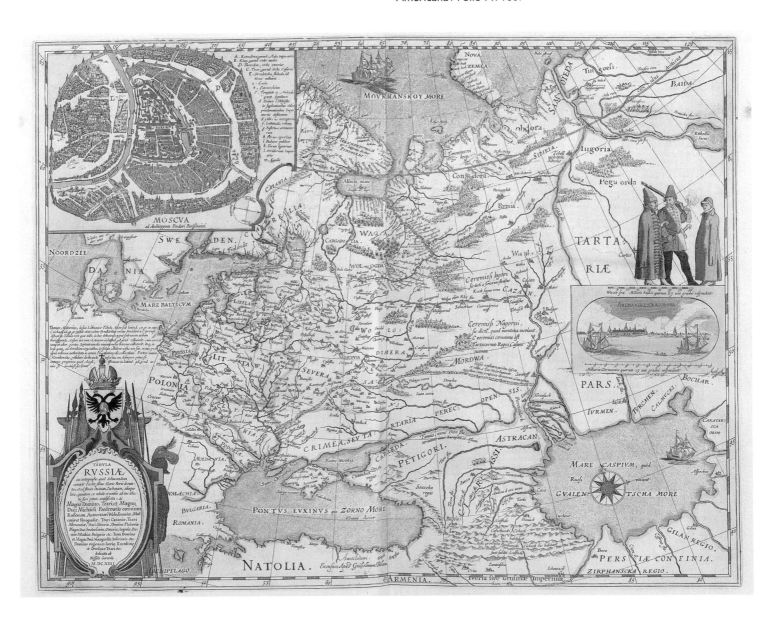

A Chart of the Sea Coasts of Russia Lapland Finmarke Nova Zemla and Greenland

John Seller (1632–97)

Engraving

From *The English Pilot: Describing the Sea Coasts, Capes, Head-lands, Soundings, Sands, Shoals, Rocks and Dangers; the Bayes, Roads, Harbors, Rivers and Posts in the Northern and Southern Navigation. Shewing the Courses and Distances from one Place to another; The Setting of Tydes and Currents; The Ebbing and Flowing of the Sea And many other necessary things belonging to the Practical Part of Navigation. Being furnished with New and Exact Draughts, Charts and Descriptions: Gathered from the latests and best Discoveries that have been made by divers Able and Expert Navigators of our English Nation*

London, J. Seller, 1671

Yale Center for British Art, Paul Mellon Collection, Maps 29, Folio A

John Seller began his career as a maker of compasses and other navigational instruments before dealing in maps and charts. He received a royal licence to produce maritime atlases and was appointed hydrographer to the King in 1671. Despite its claims to consist of 'new and exact draughts, charts and descriptions', *The English Pilot* in fact consisted partly of fifty-year-old Dutch printing plates, albeit somewhat updated.

C.P.

91

Audience des Ambassadeurs chez le Czar de Moscovie
Serment des Moscovites ['Ambassadors' audience with the Tsar of Muscovy' and 'The Muscovites' Sermon']

Engravings

From Pieter van der Aa (1659–1733), *La Galerie Agréable du Monde* ['The Pleasant Gallery of the World'], vol. 5

Leiden, Van der Aa, [1729]

Yale Center for British Art, Paul Mellon Collection, PM Bequest / M&A / Aa 1729

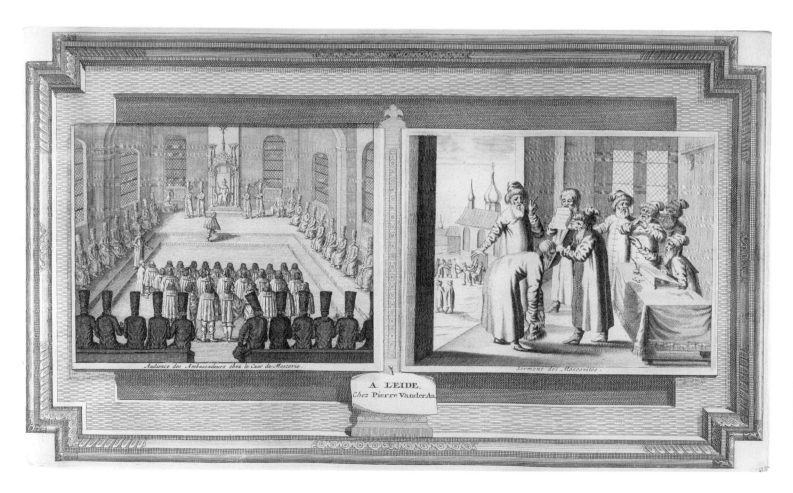

Audience des Ambassadeurs chez le Czar de Moscovie.

A LEIDE,
Chez Pierre Vander Aa.

Serment des Moscovites.

APPENDIX

List of English Silver of the Sixteenth and Seventeenth Centuries in the Armoury

Natalya Abramova

Font-shaped cup
London, 1557–8
Silver; chased, cast, gilded, engraved
Height 6⅛ in. (15.7 cm); bowl diameter 7⅛ in. (18 cm);
weight 31¼ oz (894.7 g)
Historic collection of the Armoury
Moscow Kremlin Museums inv. no. MZ–650

Ewer
London, 1571–2
Monogrammist TB
Silver; chased, cast, gilded, engraved
Height 7½ in. (19 cm); weight 18¼ oz (518 g)
Belonged to Patriarch Philaret; transferred from the
Patriarch's vestry in 1920
Moscow Kremlin Museums inv. no. MZ–703

Flagons
London, 1580–1
Monogrammist TF
Silver; chased, cast, gilded, engraved
MZ–656: Height 17¼ in. (44 cm); weight 99½ oz
(2,821.10 g)
MZ–657: Height 17¼ in. (44 cm); weight 104 oz
(2,972.5 g)
Historic collection of the Armoury
Moscow Kremlin Museums inv. nos. MZ–656, MZ–657

Standing cup
London, 1585–6
Maker's mark – three lilies
Silver, non-precious metal; chased, engraved cast,
gilded
Height 15¾ in. (40 cm); weight 36½ oz (1,030.5 g)
Historic collection of the Armoury
Moscow Kremlin Museums inv. no. MZ–614/1–2

Basin
London, 1594–5
Monogrammist VV
Silver; chased, cast, gilded, engraved
Diameter 16 in. (40.7 cm); weight 45½ oz (1,294.4 g)
Transferred from the Patriarch's vestry in 1920
Moscow Kremlin Museums inv. no. MZ–715

Ewer
London, 1594–5
Monogrammist IM
Silver; chased, cast, gilded
Height 13⅜ in. (34 cm); weight 59¼ oz (1,679 g)
Gift to Tsar Mikhail Romanov from Christian IV of
Denmark in 1644
Moscow Kremlin Museums inv. no. MZ–608

Ewer
London, 1594–5
Silver; chased, gilded, cast
Height 9⅞ in. (25 cm); weight 30½ oz (863 g)
Gift to Tsar Mikhail Romanov from Christian IV of
Denmark in 1644
Moscow Kremlin Museums inv. no. MZ–610

Salt
London, 1594–5
Monogrammist AS
Silver; chased, cast, gilded, engraved
Height 16⅛– 16⅜ in. (41–41.5 cm); weight 46½ oz
(1,325.2 g)
Historic collection of the Armoury
Moscow Kremlin Museums inv. no. MZ–651/1–2

Livery pot
London, 1594–5
Maker's mark – gryphon's head
Silver, glass; chased, cast, gilded, engraved
Height 15⅛ in. (38.5 cm); weight 93¾ oz (2,679.8 g)
Historic collection of the Armoury
Moscow Kremlin Museums inv. no. MZ–664

Basin
England, 1595
Monogrammist VV
Silver; chased, engraved, cast, gilded
Diameter 17⅜ in. (44 cm); weight 73¾ oz (2,093 g)
Gift to Tsar Mikhail Romanov from Christian IV of
Denmark in 1644
Moscow Kremlin Museums inv. no. MZ–606

Ewer
London, 1595–6
Silver; chased, cast, gilded
Height 17¼ in. (31 cm); weight 42 oz (1,190 g)
Gift to Tsar Mikhail Romanov from James I in 1619
Moscow Kremlin Museums inv. no. MZ–700

Gourd-shaped cup (standing cup)
London, 1589–90
Monogrammist K
Silver; cast, chased, gilded
Height 13¾–14½ in. (35–7 cm); weight 47¾ oz
(1,363.6 g)
Presented by the States General of Holland to Tsar
Alexey Mikhaylovich in 1647
Moscow Kremlin Museums inv. no. MZ–636

Leopards (decorative vessels)
London, 1600–1
Maker's mark – triangle with two crosses
Silver; chased, gilded, cast
MZ–693: Height 37 in. (94 cm); weight 1026¼ oz
(29,322.7 g),
MZ–694: Height 37 in. (94 cm); weight 1030¾ oz
(29,220 g)
Possibly derived from the English monarchy's Jewel
House and part of the 'Great Guilt Cubberd of Estate'
of 1626; brought by the merchant Fabian Smith for the
treasury of Tsar Mikhail Fyodorovich in 1629
Moscow Kremlin Museums inv. nos. MZ–693, MZ–694

Standing cup
London, 1601–2
Monogrammist IG
Silver; chased, gilded, cast
Height 7⅞ in. (20 cm); weight 9 oz (253.7 g)

Belonged to Patriarch Iosif; transferred from the Patriarch's vestry in 1920
Moscow Kremlin Museums inv. no. MZ–714

Standing cup
London, early seventeenth century
Maker Robert Blackwell
Silver; chased, gilded, cast
Height 13¾ in. (35 cm); weight 28 3.4 oz (814.2 g)
Presented by James I, via the embassy of John Merrick, to Tsar Mikhail Romanov in 1620
Moscow Kremlin Museums inv. no. MZ–637

Standing cup
London, 1604–5
Monogrammist IE
Silver; chased, cast, gilded
Height 19¾ in. (50 cm); weight 77 oz (2,182 g)
Historic collection of the Armoury
Moscow Kremlin Museums inv. no. MZ–625/1–2

Gourd-shaped cups (standing cups)
London, 1604–5
Silver; chased, cast, gilded, engraved
MZ–633: Height 16½ in. (42 cm); weight 47 oz (1,331 g)
MZ–634: Height 18½ in. (47 cm); weight 48¾ oz (1,394.1 g)
MZ–635: Height 16⅛ in. (41 cm); weight 46½ oz (1,315 g)
Historic collection of the Armoury
Moscow Kremlin Museums inv. nos. MZ–633/1–2, MZ–634/1–2, MZ–635/1–2

Water pots (ewers)
London, 1604–5
Monogrammist WI
Silver; chased, cast, gilded, engraved
MZ–642: Height 25⅛ in. (64 cm); weight 401¾ oz (11,476 g)
MZ–643: Height 24 in. (61 cm); weight 396 oz (11,311.9 g)
Derived from the English monarchy's Jewel House; formed part of the 'Great Guilt Cubberd of Estate' of 1626; brought by the merchant Fabian Smith for the treasury of Tsar Mikhail Fyodorovich in 1629
Moscow Kremlin Museums inv. nos. MZ–642, MZ–643

Livery pots
London, 1604–5
Monogrammist IH
Silver; chased, cast, gilded
MZ 644: Height 20 in. (51 cm); weight 132½ oz (3,756.6 g)
MZ 645: Height 20 in. (51 cm); weight 133¾ oz (3,823.1 g)
Presented by James I, via the embassy of John Merrick, to Patriarch Philaret in 1620 (?)
Moscow Kremlin Museums inv. nos. MZ–644, MZ–645

Livery pot
London, 1605–6
Monogrammist WI
Silver; chased, cast, gilded
Height 13 in. (33 cm); weight 54 oz (1,528.2 g)
Historic collection of the Armoury
Moscow Kremlin Museums inv. no. MZ–609

Standing cup
London, 1605–6
Silver, brass; chased, cast, gilded
Height 16½ in. (42 cm); weight 44¼ oz (1,255 g)
Presented by James I, via the embassy of John Merrick, to Tsar Mikhail Romanov in 1620 (?)
Moscow Kremlin Museums inv. no. MZ–624

Thistle cup (steeple cup)
London, 1605–6
Monogrammist AB
Silver; chased, cast, gilded
Height 20⅞ in. (53 cm); weight 52¼ oz (1,480.5 g)
Historic collection of the Armoury
Moscow Kremlin Museums inv. no. MZ–638/1–2

Steeple cup
London, 1605–7
Monogrammist LB
Silver; chased, cast, gilded
Height 21⅝ in. (55 cm); weight 47½ oz (1,356.8 g)
Presented by the Prior of the Monastery of the Nativity in Vladimir to Tsar Alexey Mikhaylovich in 1645
Moscow Kremlin Museums inv. no. MZ–629/1–2

Steeple cup
London, 1606–7
Monogrammist M
Silver; chased, cast, gilded
Height 22⅜ in. (57 cm); weight 55 oz (1,569 g)
Presented by the boyar Prince Fyodor Ivanovich Sheremetev to Tsar Alexey Mikhaylovich in 1645
Moscow Kremlin Museums inv. no. MZ–628/1–2

Large flagon
London, 1606–7
Monogrammist GC
Silver; chased, cast, gilded
Height 22⅞ in. (58 cm); weight 160 oz (4,568.5 g)
Presented by Charles I, via the embassy of Simon Digby, to Tsar Mikhail Fyodorovich in 1636
Moscow Kremlin Museums inv. no. MZ–658

Livery pot
London, 1606–7
Monogrammist TS
Silver; cast, chased, gilded
Height 15⅛ in. (38.5 cm); weight 69¼ oz (1,979.1 g)
Presented by James I, via the embassy of John Merrick, to Tsar Mikhail Fyodorovich in 1615 (?)
Moscow Kremlin Museums inv. no. MZ–701

Thistle cup (steeple cup)
London, 1608–9
Monogrammist CB
Silver; chased, cast, gilded
Height 17¾–18⅛ in. (45–6 cm); weight 37¾ oz (1,082.2 g)
Presented by Grigory Gavrilovich Pushkin to Tsar Alexey Mikhaylovich in 1645
Moscow Kremlin Museums inv. no. MZ–639/1–2

Cup
London, 1609–10
Maker John Wardlaw (?)
Silver; chased, cast, gilded
Height 12–12¼ in. (30.5–31 cm); weight 28¼ oz (806.1 g)
Belonged to boyar Prince Yury Yansheevich Suleshev; from the historic collection of the Armoury
Moscow Kremlin Museums inv. no. MZ–615

Livery pots
London, c. 1610
Monogrammist RP
Silver; chased, cast, gilded
MZ–662: Height 16½ in. (42 cm); weight 79½ oz (2,257 g)
MZ–663: Height 16½ in. (42 cm); weight 80 oz (2,262 g)
Historic collection of the Armoury
Moscow Kremlin Museums inv. nos. MZ–662, MZ–663

Livery pot
London, 1610–11
Monogrammist HS
Silver; chased, cast, gilded
Height 13⅜ in. (34 cm); weight 56¾ oz (1,618.2 g)
Transferred from the Patriarch's vestry in 1920
Moscow Kremlin Museums inv. no. MZ–702

Salts
London, 1611–12
Maker Robert Blackwell
Silver; chased, cast, gilded, engraved
MZ–652: Height 17½–17¾ in. (44.5–45 cm); weight 44¾ oz (1,280.5 g)
MZ–653: Height 12¼ in. (31 cm); weight 40½ oz (1,151 g)
Presented by James I, via the embassy of John Merrick, to Tsar Mikhail Fyodorovich in 1615 (?)
Moscow Kremlin Museums inv. nos. MZ–652, MZ–653

Livery pot
London, 1611–12
Monogrammist WR
Silver; chased, cast, gilded
Height 16⅛ in. (41 cm); weight 88½ oz (2,512.3 g)
Presented by Charles I, via the embassy of Simon Digby, to Tsar Mikhail Fyodorovich in 1636
Moscow Kremlin Museums inv. no. MZ–667

Livery pot
London, 1612–13
Monogrammist TC
Silver; chased, gilded, cast
Height 15⅜ in. (39 cm); weight 67 oz (1,901.3 g)
Gift to Tsar Mikhail Romanov from the merchant
Fabian Smith in 1615 (?)
Moscow Kremlin Museums inv. no. M7–607

Standing cup
London, 1612–13
Maker Robert Brooke
Silver; chased, cast, gilded
Height 35 in. (89 cm); weight 228¼ oz (6,469 g)
Historic collection of the Armoury
Moscow Kremlin Museums inv. no. MZ–616/1–2

Standing cup
London, 1612–13
Maker F. Terry
Silver; chased, cast, gilded
Height 17⅜ in. (44 cm); weight 47¼ oz (1,336.4 g)
Deposited in the Trinity Monastery of St Sergius, near
Moscow, after the death of Prince Vasily Yansheevich
Suleshev; a gift from the administration of the Trinity
Monastery to Tsar Alexey Mikhaylovich in 1645
Moscow Kremlin Museums inv. no. MZ–627

Standing cup
London, 1612–13
Monogrammist TC
Silver; chased, cast, gilded
Height 13 in. (33 cm); weight 25 oz (710 g)
Belonged to boyar Fyodor Ivanovich Sheremetev, then
Prince Yakov Cherkassky; presented to Tsar Alexey
Mikhaylovich (?)
Moscow Kremlin Museums inv. no. MZ–632

Standing cup
London, 1613–14
Maker Robert Brooke
Silver; chased, cast, gilded
Height 29½ in. (75 cm); weight 96 oz (2,724 g)
Presented by James I, via the embassy of John Merrick,
to Tsar Mikhail Romanov in 1620
Moscow Kremlin Museums inv. no. MZ–613/1–2

Standing cup
London, 1613–14
Monogrammist TC
Silver; chased, cast, gilded
Height 22½–23 in.(57–58.5 cm); weight 83¾ oz (2,395.9 g)
Historic collection of the Armoury
Moscow Kremlin Museums inv. no. MZ–618/1–2

Standing cup
London, 1613–14
Monogrammist TC
Silver; chased, cast, gilded
Height 20–20½ in. (51–2 cm); weight 71¼ oz (2,033.1 g)
Presented by James I, via the embassy of John Merrick,
to Tsar Mikhail Romanov in 1620
Moscow Kremlin Museums inv. no. MZ–619

Livery pot
London, 1613–14
Monogrammist WR
Silver; chased, cast, gilded
Height 16⅛ in. (41 cm); weight 85¾ oz (2,449.2 g)
Presented by Charles I, via the embassy of Simon
Digby, to Tsar Mikhail Fyodorovich in 1636; presented
by Tsar Alexey Mikhaylovich to Patriarch Iosif and
kept in the latter's treasury
Moscow Kremlin Museums inv. no. MZ–699

Standing cup
London, 1614–15
Makers John Middleton and Francis Brown
Silver; chased, cast, gilded
Height 17⅝ in. (44.6 cm); weight 42¼ oz (1,208.7 g)
Historic collection of the Armoury
Moscow Kremlin Museums inv. no. MZ–626

Standing cup
London, 1614–15
Makers John Middleton and Francis Brown
Silver; chased, cast, gilded
Height 15 in. (38 cm); weight 37 oz (1,048.4 g)
Historic collection of the Armoury
Moscow Kremlin Museums inv. no. MZ–630

Standing cup
London, 1614–15
Maker F. Terry
Silver; chased, cast, gilded
Height 13¾ in. (35 cm); weight 28½ oz (810 g)
Historic collection of the Armoury
Moscow Kremlin Museums inv. no. MZ–631

Water pots
London, 1615–16
Maker Robert Blackwell
Silver; cast, chased, gilded
MZ–640: Height 24⅜ in. (62 cm); weight 290 oz
(8,283 g)
MZ–641: Height 24⅜ in. (62 cm); weight 294¼ oz
(8,341.9 g)
Derived from the English monarchy's Jewel House;
formed part of the 'Great Guilt Cubberd of Estate'
of 1626; brought by Fabian Smith of the Muscovy
Company for the treasury of Tsar Mikhail Fyodorovich
in 1629
Moscow Kremlin Museums inv. nos. MZ–640, MZ–641

Beakers
London, 1615–16
Monogrammist IR
Silver; cast, chased, gilded, engraved
MZ–704: Height 4½ in. (11.5 cm); weight 9½ oz
(273.5 g)
MZ–705: Height 4¾ in. (12 cm); weight 10½ oz (295.7 g)
MZ–706: Height 4⅜ in. (11 cm); weight 9¼ oz (260 g)
MZ–707: Height 4½ in. (11.5 cm); weight 9 oz (259.5 g)
MZ–708: Height 4¾ in. (12 cm); weight 10¼ oz (286 g)
MZ–709: Height 4¾ in. (12 cm); weight 8¾ oz (247.8 g)
MZ–710: Height 4¾ in. (12 cm); weight 9¼ oz (267.8 g)

MZ–711: Height 4¾ in. (12 cm); weight 10¾ oz (308.7 g)
MZ–712: Height 4¾ in. (12 cm); weight 9¾ oz (276 g)
Belonged to boyar Prince Afanasy Vasilevich
Rostovsky; transferred from the Patriarch's vestry
in 1920
Moscow Kremlin Museums inv. nos. MZ–704 to
MZ–712

Standing cup
London, 1616–17
Monogrammist SF
Silver; chased, cast, gilded
Height 18⅛ in. (46 cm); weight 68 oz (1,925.6 g)
Presented by James I, via the embassy of John Merrick,
to Tsar Mikhail Romanov in 1620 (?)
Moscow Kremlin Museums inv. no. MZ–622

Standing cup (The Warwick Cup)
London, 1617–18
Maker F. Terry
Silver; chased, cast, gilded
Height 18¾ in. (47.8 cm); weight 63 oz (1,797.8 g)
Presented by James I, via the embassy of John Merrick,
to Tsar Mikhail Romanov in 1620
Moscow Kremlin Museums inv. no. MZ–623

Livery pots
London, 1617–18
Silver; chased, cast, gilded
MZ–665: Height 16½ in. (42 cm); weight 97¾ oz
(2,770 g)
MZ–666: Height 16½ in. (42 cm); weight 99¼ oz
(2,812.2 g)
Presented by Charles I, via the embassy of Simon
Digby, to Tsar Mikhail Fyodorovich in 1636
Moscow Kremlin Museums inv. nos. MZ–665, MZ–666

Standing cup
London, 1617–18
Monogrammist IP
Silver; chased, cast, gilded
Height 8¼ in. (21 cm); weight 9¼ oz (263 g)
Transferred from the Patriarch's vestry in 1920
Moscow Kremlin Museums inv. no. MZ–713

Standing cup
London, 1618–19
Maker Robert Brooke
Silver; chased, cast, gilded
Height 31⅛ in. (79 cm); weight 115 3.4 oz (3,281 g)
Presented by James I, via the embassy of John Merrick,
to Tsar Mikhail Romanov in 1620
Moscow Kremlin Museums inv. no. MZ–611/1–2

Standing Cup
London, 1619–20
Maker Robert Brooke
Silver; chased, gilded, cast
Height 17 in. (43 cm); weight 34½ oz (976.9 g)
Presented by Charles I, via the embassy of Simon
Digby, to Tsar Mikhail Fyodorovich in 1636
Moscow Kremlin Museums inv. no. MZ–612

Flagons
London, 1619–20
Monogrammist IS
Silver; chased, cast, gilded
MZ–654: Height 18⅞ in. (48 cm); weight 101¾ oz
(2,908.7 g)
MZ–655: Height 19¾ in. (50 cm); weight 97½ oz
(2,784.8 g)
Presented by James I, via the embassy of John Merrick,
to Tsar Mikhail Romanov in 1620
Moscow Kremlin Museums inv. nos. MZ–654, MZ–655

Candlestick
London, 1624–5
Maker's mark – trefoil
Silver; chased, cast, gilded
Height 9 in. (23 cm); weight 22½ oz (644.8 g)
Transferred from the Archangel Cathedral in the
Moscow Kremlin
Moscow Kremlin Museums inv. no. MZ–71

Standing cup
London, 1639–40
Maker F. Terry
Silver; chased, gilded, cast
Height 24⅜ in. (62 cm); weight 126½ oz (3,585 g)
Historic collection of the Armoury
Moscow Kremlin Museums inv. no. MZ–617/1–2

Platters
London, 1639–40
Monogrammist IM
Silver; chased
Diameter 7½ in. (19 cm); weight 8½ oz (240.5–244 g)
Historic collection of the Armoury
Moscow Kremlin Museums inv. nos. MZ–670, MZ–679

Platters
London, 1640–1
Monogrammist TI
Silver; chased
Diameter 7½ in. (19 cm); weight 9½– 9¾ oz
(265.5–274 g)
Historic collection of the Armoury
Moscow Kremlin Museums inv. nos. MZ–669, MZ–672,
MZ–688 to MZ–692

Platters
London, 1641–2
Monogrammist RS
Silver; chased
Diameter 7½ in. (19 cm); weight 7¾–8 oz
(222.4–228.8 g)
Historic collection of the Armoury
Moscow Kremlin Museums inv. nos. MZ–674, MZ–676,
MZ–680, MZ–681, MZ–683, MZ–684

Platters
London, 1643–4
Monogrammist CT
Silver; chased
Diameter 7½ in. (19 cm); weight 8¾ oz (247.9–248.7 g)
Historic collection of the Armoury
Moscow Kremlin Museums inv. nos. MZ–671, MZ–673,
MZ–675, MZ–677, MZ–678

Ewer
London, 1652–3
Monogrammist WB
Silver; chased, cast, gilded
Height 18¼ in. (46.2 cm); weight 97½ oz (2,766 g)
Transferred from the State Valuables Store in 1925;
formerly in the collection of the Princes Yusupov
Moscow Kremlin Museums inv. no. MZ–718

Standing cups
London, c.1663
Maker Francis Leake
Silver; chased, cast, gilded
MZ–620: Height 28¾ in. (73 cm); weight 140 oz
(3,964.7 g)
MZ–621: Height 28¾ in. (73 cm); weight 142½ oz
(4,073.50 g)
Presented by Charles II, via the embassy of Charles
Howard, Earl of Carlisle, to Tsar Alexey Mikhaylovich
in 1664
Moscow Kremlin Museums inv. nos. MZ–620/1–2,
MZ–621/1–2

Fruit dishes
London, 1663
Monogrammist TH
Silver; chased, gilded
Height 3⅜–3½ in. (8.5–9 cm); diameter 16¾ in.
(42.5 cm); weight 64–8 oz (1,828.5–1,930.8 g)
Presented by Charles II, via the embassy of Charles
Howard, Earl of Carlisle, to Tsar Alexey Mikhaylovich
in 1664
Moscow Kremlin Museums inv. nos. MZ–646 to
MZ–649

Livery pots
London, 1663
Maker Henry Greenway
Silver; chased, cast, gilded
MZ–660: Height 15¾ in. (40 cm); weight 169¼ oz
(4,835 g)
MZ–661: Height 15¾ in. (40 cm); weight 171½ oz
(4,864.1 g)
Presented by Charles II, via the embassy of Charles
Howard, Earl of Carlisle, to Tsar Alexey Mikhaylovich
in 1664
Moscow Kremlin Museums inv. nos. MZ–660, MZ–661

Perfuming pot and stand
London, c.1663
Monogrammist IN
Silver; chased, cast, gilded, openwork
Height 17¾ in. (45 cm); weight 202¼ oz (5,774.9 g)
Presented by Charles II, via the embassy of Charles
Howard, Earl of Carlisle, to Tsar Alexey Mikhaylovich
in 1664
Moscow Kremlin Museums inv. no. MZ–695/1–4

Candlesticks
London, c.1663
Silver; chased, cast, gilded
MZ–697: Height 18⅞ in. (48 cm); diameter 14⅛ in.
(36 cm); weight 143¼ oz (4,062.3 g)
MZ–698: Height 18⅞ in. (48 cm); diameter 14⅛ in.
(36 cm); weight 142 oz (4,027 g)
Presented by Charles II, via the embassy of Charles
Howard, Earl of Carlisle, to Tsar Alexey Mikhaylovich
in 1664
Moscow Kremlin Museums inv. nos. MZ–697/1–2,
MZ–698/1–2

Flagon
London, c.1663
Maker Robert Smythier
Silver; cast, chased, gilded
Height 15 in. (38 cm); weight 150¾ oz (4,308.7 g)
Presented by Charles II, via the embassy of Charles
Howard, Earl of Carlisle, to Tsar Alexey Mikhaylovich
in 1664
Moscow Kremlin Museums inv. no. MZ–659

Bibliography

I. Works cited: Abbreviations

Manuscript sources

Ambassadorial Affairs 1644
'V'ezd v Moskvu datskogo korolevicha Val'demara s poslami Olafom Pazbergom i Sten Billem …' ['The Entry in Moscow of the Danish Crown Prince Waldemar with Ambassadors Olaf Pazberg and Sten Bill …']. Russian State Archive of Ancient Acts, Moscow, fund 53, *opis'* 1, part 2, 1644, no. 1.

Ambassadorial Book 1614-17
'Priezd v Rossiyu posla Ivana Merika s pozdravleniyami o vstuplenii na prestol gosudara tsarya Mikhaila Fyodorovicha i s predlozheniem 1) o primirenii rossiyskogo dvora so shvedskim po pros'be o sem shvedskogo korolya, 2) o podtverzhdenii zhalovannoy gramoty angliyskim kuptsam besposhlinno torgovat', 3) o dozvolenii angliyskim kuptsam s tovarami ezdit' Volgoyu v Indiyu …' ['The Arrival in Russia of Ambassador John Merrick with congratulations on the Accession of Sovereign Tsar Mikhail Fyodorovich to the throne and with the suggestion 1) of the reconciliation of the Russian court with that of Sweden at the request to that effect of the Swedish king, 2) of confirmation of the charter granted to the English merchants to trade without payment of duties, 3) of permitting English merchants to travel with their goods along the River Volga to India …']. Russian State Archive of Ancient Acts, Moscow, fund 35, *opis'* 1, part 1, *delo* 4.

Ambassadorial Book 1620-1
'Priezd v Rossiyu knyazya Ivana Merika s pozdravleniyami ob uchinyonnom mezhdu Russkim i Pol'skim gosudarstvami peremirii i o vozvrashchenii iz plena patriarkha Filareta, s predlozheniem ob uchinenii soyuza protiv obshchikh nepriyateley i o dozvolenii po-prezhnemu angliyskim kuptsam khodit' Volgoy v Persiyu v rassuzhdenii ponesyonnykh imi v torgovle ubytkov. Tut zhe i otpusk ego …' ['The Arrival in Russia of Prince [sic] John Merrick with congratulations on the peace concluded between the Russian and Polish states and on the return from captivity of Patriarch Philaret, with the suggestion of conclusion of a peace against common enemies and permitting English merchants as before to travel the River Volga to Persia, with regard to the losses they have made in trade. Also his departure …']. Russian State Archive of Ancient Acts, Moscow, fund 35, *opis'* 1, *delo* 7.

Ambassadorial Book 1635-6
'Priezd v Moskvu angliyskogo dvoryanina Semyona Digbi dlya bytiya emu v Rossii agentom i otzyv preemniku ego Tomasu Rikhardu Benchu' ['The Arrival in Moscow of the English Nobleman Simon Digby to stay as agent in Russia and recall his predecessor Thomas Richard Bench']. Russian State Archive of Ancient Acts, Moscow, fund 35, *opis'* 1, 1635, no. 123.

Ambassadorial Book 1641
'Priezd v Rossiyu i otpusk polnomochnykh datskikh poslov korolevich Val'demara i Grigoriya Krabe s predlozheniem obnovleniya i podtverzhdeniya drevnego mezhdu oboimi gosudarstvami mirea i vechnoy druzhby …' ['The Arrival in Russia and Departure of Plenipotentiary Danish Ambassadors Crown Prince Waldemar and Grigory Krab with the proposal for renewing and reaffirming the peace and eternal friendship that is long-standing between the two states …']. Russian State Archive of Ancient Acts, Moscow, fund 53, *opis'* 1, part 1, *delo* 6.

Ambassadorial Book 1647-8
'Priezdy v Rossiyu Gollandskikh Shtatov i otpuski … posla Al'berta Burkha (kotoryy ne byl na posol'stve, v Narve gorode umer) i syna ego Konrada Burkha, kotoryy pravit' posol'stvo khodataystvoval, o zavodchikakh tul'skikh …' ['Arrivals in Russia from the Dutch States and Departures … of the ambassador Albert Burch (who did not arrive with the embassy but died in the town of Narva) and his son Conrad Burch, who petitioned to lead the embassy, on Tula factory-owners …']. Russian State Archive of Ancient Acts, Moscow, fund 50, *opis'* 1, part 1, *delo* 4.

Ambassadorial Book 1662-3
'Otpravlenie v Angliyu k korolyu Karlu II velikikh poslov stol'nika Petra Prozorovskogo da dvoryanina Ivana Zhelyabuzhskogo da dlya perevody polkovnika Andreya Forota s pozdravleniyami korolyu i prinyatii im do dolgovremennom izgnanii trona' ['The Despatch to England to King Charles II of Two Great Ambassadors *stol'nik* Pyotr Prozorovsky and Noble Ivan Zhelyabuzhsky and as Translator Colonel Andrey Forot with Congratulations to the King and on his Reception after the Long Exile from the Throne']. Russian State Archive of Ancient Acts, Moscow, fund 35, *opis'* 1, *delo* 8.

Ambassadorial Book 1663-4
'Priezd v Moskvu angliyskogo velikogo i polnomochnogo posla Charlusa Govorta s synom i s zhenoyu, i s sekretaryom Andreem Morvelem s predlozheniem o podtverzhdenii mezhdu oboimi gosudarstvami druzhby i lyubvi i o dozvolenii besposhlinnoy torgovli …' ['The Arrival in Moscow of the Senior and Plenipotentiary Ambassador Charles Howard with his son and wife, and with his secretary Andrew Marvell, with the suggestion that the friendship and love between the two states be confirmed, and that duty-free trade be permitted …']. Russian State Archive of Ancient Acts, Moscow, fund 35, *opis'* 1, *delo* 11.

Ambassadorial Book 1667
'Priezd v Moskvu pol'skikh poslov Stanislav Benevskiy, Kiprian Brostovskiy, Sekretarya Shmelinga s gramotoyu korolevskoyu o podtverzhdenii Andrusovskogo peremiriya' ['The Arrival in Moscow of Polish Ambassadors Stanislaw Benewski, Cyprian Brostowski, Secretary Smeling, with a royal letter confirming the Peace of Andrusovo']. Russian State Archive of Ancient Acts, Moscow, fund 79, *opis'* 1, part 1, *delo* 115.

Ambassadorial Book 1676
'Priezd v Moskvu i otpusk chrezvychaynogo poslannika Ivan Gebdona s pozdravleniem gosudaryu tsaryu Fyodora Alekseevicha o vstuplenii na rossiyskiy prestol …' ['The Arrival in Moscow and Departure of Envoy Extraordinary John Hebdon with Congratulations to the Sovereign Tsar Fyodor Alexeevich on his Accession to the Russian Throne …']. Russian State Archive of Ancient Acts, Moscow, fund 35, *opis'* 1, *delo* 18.

Ambassadorial Book 1686
'Bytnost' v Moskve i ot'ezd polnomochnykh pol'skikh poslov Kristopa Grimultovskogo, voevody poznan'skogo, s tovarishchi …' ['The Stay in Moscow and Departure of Plenipotentiary Polish Ambassadors Cristof Grimultowski, Commander of Poznan, with Comrades …']. Russian State Archive of Ancient Acts, Moscow, fund 79, *opis'* 1, part 1, *delo* 224.

Annunciation Cathedral Inventory 1701
'Opis' Blagoveshchenskogo sobora 1701 g.' ['Inventory of the Annunciation Cathedral 1701']. Russian State Archive of Ancient Acts, Moscow, fund 196, *opis'* 1, *delo* 1564.

Annunciation Cathedral Inventory 1745
'Opis' tserkovnogo imushchestva Blagoveshchenskogo sobora za 1745 g, Kn. 1' ['Inventory of the Church Property of the Annunciation Cathedral for 1745, Book 1]. Department of Manuscripts, Printed and Graphic Reserves of the Moscow Kremlin Museums, fund 3, *delo* 85.

Annunciation Cathedral Inventory 1771-2
'Opis' tserkovnogo imushchestva Blagoveshchenskogo sobora za 1771-2 g.' ['Inventory of the Church Property of the Annunciation Cathedral for 1771-2]. Department of Manuscripts, Printed and Graphic Reserves of the Moscow Kremlin Museums, fund 3, *delo* 90.

Armoury and Royal Treasury Inventory Book 1686-7
'Perepisnaya kniga Oruzheynoy i vsyakoy tsarskoy kazne i krasok chto v Oruzheynoy palate, v Bol'shoy kazne, i v prochikh palatakh …1687 g.' ['Inventory Book of Arms and Armour and all kinds of royal treasures and paints that are in the Armoury, in the Great Treasury and in other such rooms …1687']. Russian State Archive of Ancient Acts, Moscow, fund 396, *opis'* 2, book 936.

Armoury Inventory 1808
'Opis' Veshcham Masterskoy i Oruzheynoy palaty po Vysochayshemu poveleniyu sostavlennoy v 1808 g.'

['Inventory of Objects in the Workshop and Armoury compiled in 1808 by Highest Command']. Central State Historical Archive, St Petersburg, fund 468, *opis*' 1, part 2, *delo* 400.

Armoury Inventory 1835
'Opis' Veshcham Moskovskoy Oruzheynoy Palaty, Chast' pyataya, 1835 g.' ['Inventory of the Objects in the Moscow Armoury, part five, 1835']. Department of Manuscripts, Printed and Graphic Reserves of the Moscow Kremlin Museums, fund 1, *opis*' 1, *delo* 6.

Armoury Inventory 1914–30
'Opis' Oruzheynoy palaty 1914–30 ['Inventory of the Armoury 1914–30]. Department of Manuscripts, Printed and Graphic Reserves of the Moscow Kremlin Museums, fund 20, *delo* 16.

Armoury Inventory 1922–4
'Opis' Oruzheynoy palaty 1922–4 gg.' ['Inventory of the Armoury for 1922–4]. Department of Manuscripts, Printed and Graphic Reserves of the Moscow Kremlin Museums, fund 20, *delo* 13.

Book of Deposits 1539–1776
'Kniga vkladnaya ot Velikikh Gosudarey patriarkhov i arkhiereev boyar kuptsov i prochikh lyudey' ['Book of Deposits from Great Monarchs, Patriarchs and Members of the Higher Clergy, Boyars, Merchants and Such People']. Moscow Kremlin Museums inv. no. Ruk–1238.

Book of Receipts 1613
'Kniga prikhodnaya rukhlyadi i uzoroch'yu 1613 g.' [Book of Receipts of Goods and Decorative Items 1613]. Russian State Archive of Ancient Acts, Moscow, fund 396, *opis*' 2, part 1, *delo* 21.

Book of Receipts 1613–14
'Prikhodnaya kniga denezhnoy kazne Kazyonnogo prikaza za 1613–14 gg' ['Book of Receipts of the Monetary Treasury of the Treasury Office for 1613–14']. Russian State Archive of Ancient Acts, Moscow, fund 396, *opis*' 2, part 1, *delo* 139.

Book of Receipts 1620–1
'Prikhodnaya kniga myagkoy rukhlyadi, tovaram i veshcham: postupivshim iz raznykh prikazov, a takzhe podnesyonnym inostrannymi poslami, vymenyannym na soboli i prochee, 7129 (1620–1) g.' ['Book of Receipts of Soft Items, Goods and Objects received from Various Offices, and also presented by Foreign Ambassadors, exchanged for sables and such like, 7129 (1620–1)']. Russian State Archive of Ancient Acts, Moscow, *opis*' 2, part 1, *delo* 154.

Book of Receipts 1636–7
'Prikhodnaya kniga myagkoy rukhlyadi, tovaram i veshcham prinyatym iz prikazov, podnesyonnym ot krymskikh i litovskikh poslov i prochee. Za 1636–7 g.' ['Book of Receipts of Soft Items, Goods and Objects received from Offices, presented by Crimean and Lithuanian ambassadors and such like. For 1636–7']. Russian State Archive of Ancient Acts, Moscow, fund 396, *opis*' 2, part 1, *delo* 142.

Book of Receipts 1645–6
'Prikhodnaya kniga tovaram i veshcham, podnesyonnym tsaryu Alekseyu Mikhaylovichu dukhovenstvom, boyarami, posadskimi lyud'mi i proch., po sluchayu venchaniya Gosudarya na tsarstva s 29-go sentyabrya po 15-e marta 7154 (1645–6) g.' ['Book of Receipts of Goods and Objects presented to Tsar Alexey Mikhaylovich by the clergy, boyars, tradespeople and others, on the occasion of the Sovereign's Coronation, between 29 September and 15 March 7154 (1645–6)']. Russian State Archive of Ancient Acts, Moscow, fund 396, *opis*' 2, part 1, *delo* 153.

Book of Receipts 1647–8
'Prikhodnaya kniga myagkoy rukhlyadi, tovaram i veshcham prinyatym … za 1647–8 g.' ['Book of Receipts of Soft Items, Goods and Objects received … for 1647–8']. Russian State Archive of Ancient Acts, Moscow, fund 396, *opis*' 2, part 1, *delo* 164.

Book of Receipts and Allocations 1625
'Kniga prikhodnaya-raskhodnaya rukhlyadi i uzoroch'yu 1625 g.' ['Book of Receipts and Allocations of Goods and Decorative Items 1625']. Russian State Archive of Ancient Acts, Moscow, fund 396, *opis*' 2, book 145.

Church Inventory Nineteenth Century
'Glavnaya tserkovno–riznichnaya opis' kon-ets XIX v.' ['Main Church Vestry Inventory of the late Nineteenth Century']. Moscow Kremlin Museums inv. no. Ruk–1438.

Gifts Presented to the Tsar 1664
'O podnesyonnykh tsaryu podarkakh ot Angliyskogo posla i peredache ikh v Oruzheynyy prikaz, 1664 g.' ['On the Gifts Presented to the Tsar by the English Ambassador and their transfer to the Armoury Office, 1664']. Russian State Archive of Ancient Acts, Moscow, fund 396, *opis*' 1, *delo* 8909.

Solovetsky Collection 1928, part 1
'Opis' Solovetskogo sobraniya' ['Inventory of the Solovetsky Collection', part 1]. Department of Manuscripts, Printed and Graphic Reserves of the Moscow Kremlin Museums, fund 20, *opis*' 1928, *delo* 68.

Solovetsky Collection 1928, part 3
Opis' Solovetskogo sobraniya' ['Inventory of the Solovetsky Collection', part 3]. Department of Manuscripts, Printed and Graphic Reserves of the Moscow Kremlin Museums, fund 20, *opis*' 1928, *delo* 70.

Solovetsky Inventory 1824
'Opis' stavropigial'nogo pervoklassnogo Solovetskogo monastyrya riznym veshcham, Uchinyonnaya 1824-go goda' ['Inventory of the First Class Solovetsky Monastery of Vestry Items, Compiled in 1824']. Moscow Kremlin Museums inv. no. Ruk–1427.

Treasury Inventory 1634
'Opis' tsarskoy kazny na Kazennom dvore 1634 g.' ['Inventory of the Tsar's Treasury in the Treasury Office 1634']. Russian State Archive of Ancient Acts, Moscow, fund 396, *opis*' 2, part 1, *delo* 3.

Treasury Inventory 1640
'Opis' tsarskoy kazny na Kazennom dvore, sostavlennaya Samoylom Kirkinym i d'yakom Timofeem Golosovym v 1640 g.' ['Inventory of the Tsar's Treasury in the Treasury Office, Compiled by Samoyl Kirkin and *d'yak* Timofey Golosov in 1640']. Russian State Archive of Ancient Acts, Moscow, fund 396, *opis*' 2, part 1, *delo* 4.

Treasury Inventory 1663–6
'Opis' tsarskoy kazny na Kazennom dvore 1663–6 gg.' ['Inventory of the Tsar's Treasury in the Treasury Office 1663–6']. Russian State Archive of Ancient Acts, Moscow, fund 396, *opis*' 2, part 1, *delo* 8.

Treasury Inventory 1676
'Opis' tsarskoy kazny na Kazennom dvore 1676 g.' ['Inventory of the Tsar's Treasury in the Treasury Office 1676']. Russian State Archive of Ancient Acts, Moscow, fund 396, *opis*' 2, part 1, *delo* 9.

Treasury Inventory 1690
'Opis' tsarskoy kazny na Kazennom dvore 1690 g.' ['Inventory of the Tsar's Treasury in the Treasury Office 1690']. Russian State Archive of Ancient Acts, Moscow, fund 396, *opis*' 2, part 1, *delo* 13.

Treasury Inventory 1721
'Opis' tsarskoy kazny Kazennogo prikaza 1721 g., sostavlennaya po predydushchey opisi (No. 17)' ['Inventory of the Tsar's Treasury of the Treasury Office 1721, Compiled according to the previous inventory (No. 17)']. Russian State Archive of Ancient Acts, Moscow, fund 396, *opis*' 2, part 1, *delo* 18.

Published sources

Alexeev 1946
M. P. Alexeev. 'Angliya i anglichane v pamyatnikakh moskovskoy pis'mennosti' ['England and the English in Moscow, Written Material']. *Uchenye Zapiski LGU: Seriya istoricheskikh nauk* ['Scientific Notes of Leningrad State University: Historical Sciences Series'] 15 (1946), pp. 47–109.

Alexeev 1982
M. P. Alexeev. *Russko-angliyskie literaturnye svyazi (XVIII vek – pervaya polovina XIX veka)* ['Russo-English Literary Connections (Eighteenth Century–First half of the Nineteenth Century)']. Moscow, 1982.

Ambassadors' Travels 1954
Puteshestviya russkikh poslov XVI–XVII vv.: Stateynye spiski ['The Travels of Russian Ambassadors in the Sixteenth–Seventeenth Centuries: Ambassadors' Reports']. Moscow and Leningrad, 1954.

Annunciation Cathedral 1990
I. Y. Kachalova, N. A. Mayasova and L. A. Shchennikova. *Blagoveshchenskiy sobor Moskovskogo Kremlya: K 500–letiyu unikal'nogo pamyatnika russkoy kul'tury* ['The Annunciation Cathedral of the Moscow Kremlin: On the 500th Anniversary of a Unique Russian Cultural Monument']. Moscow, 1990.

Annunciation Cathedral Inventory 17th century
'Perepisnaya kniga Moskovskogo Blagoveshchenskogo sobora XVII veka po spiskam arkhiva Oruzheynoy palaty i Donskogo monastyrya' ['Inventory Book of the Moscow Annunciation Cathedral in the Seventeenth Century from Lists in the Armoury Archive and the Monastery of the Don']. In *Sbornik obshchestva drevnerusskogo iskusstva pri Moskovskom Publichnom muzee na 1873 g.* ['Anthology of the Society of Old Russian Art of the Moscow Public Museum for 1873']. Moscow, 1873.

Antiquities 1849–53
Drevnosti Rossiyskogo gosudarstva, izdannye po vysochayshemu poveleniyu ['Antiquities of the Russian State, published by highest command']. Moscow, 1849–53.

Applied Art of France 1995
Prikladnoe iskusstvo Frantsii XVII–XX vekov ot barokko do suprematizma: Katalog ['Applied Art of France, Seventeenth–Twentieth Centuries from Baroque to Suprematism: Catalogue']. Moscow Kremlin Museums exh. cat. Moscow, 1995.

Arel and Bogatyryov 1997
M. S. Arel and S. N. Bogatyryov. 'Anglichane v Moskve vremyon Borisa Godunova (po dokumentam posol'stva T. Smita 1604–5 godov)' ['The English in Moscow During the Age of Boris Godunov (From Documents Relating to Thomas Smith's Embassy 1604–5)']. *Arkheograficheskiy ezhegodnik za 1997* ['Archaeographical Annual for 1997']. Moscow, 1997.

Armoury 1954
Gosudarstvennaya Oruzheynaya palata Moskovskogo Kremlya ['State Armoury of the Moscow Kremlin']. Moscow, 1954.

Armoury 1958
Gosudarstvennaya Oruzheynaya palata Moskovskogo Kremlya ['State Armoury of the Moscow Kremlin']. Moscow, 1958.

Armoury Inventory 1884–93
Opis' Moskovskoy Oruzheynoy palaty ['Inventory of the Moscow Armoury']. 9 parts, 7 books. Moscow, 1884–93

Artistic Treasures 1902
Khudozhestvennye sokrovishcha Rossii ['Artistic Treasures of Russia']. Nos. 9, 10. St Petersburg, 1902.

Bantysh-Kamensky 1894
N. N. Bantysh-Kamensky. *Obzor vneshnikh snosheniy Rossii (po 1800 god)* ['Overview of Russia's International Relations (to 1800)']. Moscow, 1894.

Bartenev 1912–16
S. P. Bartenev. *Moskovskiy Kreml' v starinu i teper'* ['The Moscow Kremlin in Days of Old and Today']. 2 vols. Moscow, 1912–16.

Bencard and Markova 1988
M. Bencard and G. Markova. *Christian IV's Royal Plate.* Copenhagen, 1988.

Bimbenet-Privat 2002
M. Bimbenet-Privat. *Les Orfèvres et l'orfèvrerie de Paris au XVIIe siècle.* 2 vols. Paris, 2002.

Bimbenet-Privat and de Fontaines 1995
M. Bimbenet-Privat and G. de Fontaines. *La Datation de l'orfèvrerie parisienne sous l'Ancien Régime.* Paris, 1995.

Blackmore 1965
H. L. Blackmore. *Guns and Rifles of the World.* London, 1965.

Blackmore 1968
H. L. Blackmore. *Royal Sporting Guns at Windsor.* London, 1968.

Blackmore 1986
H. L. Blackmore. *A Dictionary of London Gunmakers 1350–1850.* Oxford, 1986.

Blackmore 1990
D. Blackmore. *Arms and Armour of the English Civil Wars.* London, 1990.

Blackmore 1999
H. L. Blackmore. *Gunmakers of London, Supplement 1350–1850.* New York, 1999.

Bushkovitch 2001
P. Bushkovitch. *Peter the Great: The Struggle for Power 1671–1725.* Cambridge, 2001.

Calendar of State Papers, Domestic
Calendar of State Papers, Domestic series, of the reign of Charles I, 1625–6 … preserved in … Her Majesty's Public Record Office. Edited by J. Bruce. 23 vols. London, 1858–97.

Calendar of State Papers, Venetian
Calendar of the State Papers and Manuscripts Relating to English Affairs in the Archives and Collections of Venice and in Other Libraries in Northern Italy. 80 vols. London, 1900–25.

Carlisle 1669
Guy de Miège. *A Relation of the Three Embassies from his Sacred Majestie Charles II to the Great Duke of Muscovie . . . Performed by the Right Honorable the Earle of Carlisle in the Years 1663 & 1664.* London, 1669.

Collins 1671
S. Collins. *The Present State of Russia, in a Letter to a Friend in London.* London, 1671.

Collins 1955
A. J. Collins. *The Jewels and Plate of Queen Elizabeth.* London, 1955.

Court and Times of James I 1973
Court and Times of James I. Edited by T. Birch. 2 vols. London, 1848; repr. New York, 1973.

Crown Jewels 1998
The Crown Jewels. Edited by C. Blair. 2 vols. London, 1998.

Crummey 1987
R. Crummey. *The Formation of Muscovy 1304–1613.* London and New York, 1987.

Czars 2002
Czars: 400 Years of Imperial Grandeur. Edited by A. K. Levykin. Memphis, 2002.

Dosifey 1836
Archimandrite Dosifey. *Geograficheskoe, istoricheskoe i statisticheskoe opisanie stavropigial'nogo pervoklassnogo Solovetskogo monastyrya* ['Geographical, Historical and Statistical Description of the First Class Solovetsky Monastery']. 3 vols. Moscow, 1836.

Drejholt 1996
N. Drejholt. *Firearms of the Royal Armouries.* Stockholm, 1996.

Dutch Guns 1996
Dutch Guns in Russia. Edited with an Introduction by E. A. Yablonskaya. Amsterdam, 1996.

Dyomkin 1994
A. V. Dyomkin. *Zapadnoevropeyskoe kupechestvo v Rossii v XVII v.* ['The Western European Merchant Class in Russia in the Seventeenth Century']. 2 issues. Moscow, 1994.

Eaves 1976
I. Eaves. 'Further Notes of the Pistol in early Seventeenth-Century England'. *Journal of the Arms and Armour Society* 8, no. 5 (1976), pp. 269–329.

Elizabeth 2003
Elizabeth. Edited by S. Doran. National Maritime Museum exh. cat. London, 2003.

England and the North 1994
England and the North: The Russian Embassy of 1613–14. Edited by M. Jansson and N. Rogozhin. Translated by P. Bushkovitch. American Philosophical Society Memoirs. Philadelphia, 1994.

English Silver 1991
English Silver Treasures from the Kremlin: A Loan Exhibition. Sotheby's exh. cat. London, 1991.

Filimonov 1893
G. D. Filimonov. *Polnyy khronologicheskiy ukazatel' vsekh marok na serebre Moskovskoy Oruzheynoy palaty* ['Full Chronological Index of all Marks on Silver in the Moscow Armoury]. Moscow, 1892.

Forbes 1999
J. S. Forbes. *Hallmark: A History of the London Assay Office.* Foreword by P. Glanville. London, 1999.

Gamel 1865–9
I. K. Gamel. *Anglichane v Rossii v XVI i XVII stoletiyakh* ['The English in Russia in the Sixteenth and Seventeenth Centuries']. Essays I and II. St Petersburg, 1865–9.

Gifts to the Tsars 2001
Gifts to the Tsars 1500–1700: Treasures from the Kremlin. Edited by B. Shifman and G. Walton. New York, 2001.

Glanville 1987
P. Glanville. *Silver in England.* London, 1987.

Glanville 1990
P. Glanville. *Silver in Tudor and Early Stuart England.* London, 1990.

Goldberg 1954
T. G. Goldberg. 'Iz posol'skikh darov XVI–XVII vekov: Angliyskoe serebro' ['From Ambassadorial Gifts of the Sixteenth to Seventeeth Centuries: English Silver']. In Armoury 1954.

Gordon 2002
Patrick Gordon. *Dnevnik 1659–67 gg.* ['Diary 1659–67'].Translated by D. G. Fedosov. Moscow, 2002.

Great Britain, USSR 1967
Great Britain, USSR: An Historical Exhibition. Victoria and Albert Museum exh. cat. London, 1967.

Hackenbroch 1969
Y. Hackenbroch. *English and Other Silver in the Irwin Untermyer Collection.* New York, 1969.

Hakluyt 1598
R. Hakluyt. *The Principal Navigations, Voyages, Traffiques and Discoveries of the English Nation.* London, 1589; revised and enlarged 1598.

Hayward 1960
J. F. Hayward. 'English Firearms of the Sixteenth Century'. *Journal of the Arms and Armour Society* 3, no. 5 (1960).

Hayward 1976
J. F. Hayward. *Virtuoso Goldsmiths and the Triumph of Mannerism, 1540–1620.* London, 1976.

Hernmarck 1977
C. Hernmarck. *The Art of the European Silversmith, 1430–1830.* 2 vols. London and New York, 1977.

History of Russia 1997
Istoriya Rossii i doma Romanovykh v memuarakh sovremennikov, XVII–XX: Utverzhdenie dinastii ['The History of Russia and the House of Romanov in Contemporary Memoirs, Seventeenth–Twentieth Centuries: Establishment of the Dynasty]. Moscow, 1997.

Hoff 1978
A. Hoff. *Dutch Firearms.* Ed. W. A. Stryker. London, 1978.

Hollstein 1949–2001
F. W. Hollstein. *Dutch and Flemish Etchings, Engravings, and Woodcuts 1450–1700.* 58 vols. Amsterdam, 1949–2001.

Italy and the Court of Moscow 2004
Italiya i moskovskiy Dvor ['Italy and the Court of Moscow']. Moscow Kremlin Museums exh. cat. Moscow, 2004.

Jackson 1921
C. Jackson. *English Goldsmiths and their Marks.* London, 1921.

Jackson 1989
C. Jackson. *English Goldsmiths and their Marks.* London 1921; repr. London, 1989.

Jones 1909
A. E. Jones. *The Old English Plate of the Emperor of Russia.* London, 1909.

Kleyn 1925
V. K. Kleyn. 'Inozemnye tkani, bytovavshie v Rossii do XVIII veka i ikh terminologiya' ['Foreign Textiles in Russia Before the Eighteenth Century and their Terminology']. In *Sbornik Oruzheynoy palaty* ['Armoury Anthology']. Moscow, 1925.

Kologrivov 1911
S. N. Kologrivov. *Materialy dlya istorii snosheniy Rossii s inostrannymi derzhavami v XVII v.* ['Material on the History of Russia's Relations with Foreign Powers in the Seventeenth Century']. St Petersburg, 1911.

Konovalov 1953
S. Konovalov. 'Anglo-Russian Relations, 1620–4'. *Oxford Slavonic Papers* 4 (1953), pp. 71–131.

Loomie 1987
A. J. Loomie. *Ceremonies of Charles I: The Notebooks of John Finet 1628–41.* New York, 1987.

Makarius 1996
Metropolitan Makarius. *Istoriya russkoy Tserkvi* ['History of the Russian Church']. Moscow, 1996.

Markova 1976
G. A. Markova. 'O vliyanii risunkov i gravyur Al'brekhta Dyurera na formy i dekor nemetskogo khudozhestvennogo serebra' ['On the Influence of Drawings and Prints by Albrecht Dürer on the Form and Decoration of German Artistic Silver']. *Materialy i issledovaniya: Gosudarstvennye muzei Moskovskogo Kremlya* ['Material and Research: State Museums of the Moscow Kremlin'] 2 (1976).

Markova 1980
G. A. Markova. 'Nyurnbergskoe serebro v Oruzheynoy palate Moskovskogo Kremlya' ['Nuremberg Silver in the Armoury of the Moscow Kremlin']. In *Muzey: Khudozhestvennye sobraniya SSSR* ['Museum: Art Collections in the USSR']. Moscow, 1980.

Markova 1988
G. A. Markova. 'Diplomaticheskie privozy Anglii: Posol'skie dary Gollandii i Danii' ['Diplomatic Imports from England: Ambassadorial Gifts from Holland and Denmark']. In *Gosudarstvennaya Oruzheynaya palata* ['The State Armoury']. Moscow, 1988.

Markova 1990
G. A. Markova. *Gollandskoe serebro v sobranii Gosudarstvennoy Oruzheynoy palaty: Katalog* [Dutch Silver in the Collection of the State Armoury: Catalogue]. Moscow, 1990.

Markova 1996
G. A. Markova. 'Pamyatniki evropeyskogo zolotogo i serebryanogo dela' ['Monuments of European Gold and Silver Work']. In *Sokrovishcha Oruzheynoy palaty: Posol'skie dary* ['The Treasures of the Armoury: Diplomatic Gifts']. Moscow, 1996.

Martynova 2002
M.V. Martynova. *Moskovskaya emal' XV–XVII vekov* ['Moscow Enamels Fifteenth–Seventeenth Centuries']. Moscow, 2002.

Meierberg 1997
'Puteshestvie v Moskoviyu barona Avgustina Avgustina Meyerberga, chlena Imperatorskogo pridvornogo soveta, i Goratsiya Vil'gel'ma Kal'vuchchi, kavalera i chlena Pravitel'stvennogo soveta Nizhney Avstrii, poslov avgusteyshego rimskogo imperatora Leopol'da k tsaryu i velikomu knyazyu Alekseyu Mikhaylovichu v 1661 godu, opisannoe samim baronom Meyerbergom' ['The Journey to Moscow of Baron Augustin Augustin Meierberg, member of the Imperial Court Council, and Horatio Wilhelm Calvucci, Knight and Member of the Governing Council of Lower Austria, Ambassadors of the Most August Roman Emperor Leopold to the Tsar and Grand Duke Alexey Mikhaylovich in 1661, Described by Baron Meierberg Himself']. In History of Russia 1997.

Millar 1926
E. G. Millar. *English Illuminated Manuscripts from the Tenth to the Thirteenth Century.* Paris, 1926.

Milton 1682
J. Milton. *A brief History of Moscovia and of other less-known Countries lying eastward of Russia as far as Cathay. Gathered from the Writings of several Eye-witnesses.* London, 1682.

Musée de l'Armée 1997
'Musée de l'Armée Acquires Important Snaphaunce'. *Arms Collecting* 35, no. 3 (1997).

Nenarokomova and Sizov 1978
N. Nenarokomova and E. Sizov. *Khudozhestvennye sokrovishcha Gosudarstvennykh muzeev Moskovskogo Kremlya* ['Artistic Treasures of the State Museums of the Moscow Kremlin']. Moscow, 1978.

Nichols 1966
J. Nichols. *The Progresses, Processions, and Magnificent Festivities of King James the First, His Royal Consort, Family, and Court.* 4 vols. London, 1828; repr. New York, [1966].

Oman 1961
C. Oman. *The English Silver in the Kremlin.* London, 1961.

293

Oman 1970
C. Oman. *Caroline Silver 1625–88*. London, 1970.

Oman 1978a
C. Oman. *English Engraved Silver, 1150–1900*. London, 1970.

Oman 1978b
C. Oman. 'Niçaise Roussel and the Mostyn Flagons'. *Leeds Arts Calendar* 83 (1978).

Pakhomova 1989
V. A. Pakhomova. *Grafika Gansa Gol'beyna Mladshego* ['The Graphic Works of Hans Holbein the Younger']. Leningrad, 1989.

Penzer 1958
N. M. Penzer. 'Tudor Font-shaped Cups'. *Apollo*, February & March 1958, pp. 44–9, 82–6.

Penzer 1960a
N. M. Penzer. 'The Steeple Cup, Part II'. *Apollo*, April 1960, pp. 103–9.

Penzer 1960b
N. M. Penzer. 'The Steeple Cup, Part V'. *Apollo*, December 1960, pp. 173–8.

Philaret Inventory 1876
'Opis' keleynoy kazny patriarkha Filareta Nikiticha 1630 goda' ['Inventoy of the Cell Inventory of Patriarch Philaret Nikitich for 1630'], *Russkaya istoricheskaya biblioteka* ['Russian Historical Library'], vol. 3. St Petersburg, 1876.

Popov 1910
N. Popov. *Opis' Patriarshey riznitsy 1720 g.* ['Inventory of the Patriarchal Vestry for 1720']. Moscow, 1910.

Postnikova-Loseva 1954
M. M. Postnikova-Loseva. 'Zolotye i serebryanyye izdeliya Masterov Oruzheynoy palaty XVI–XVII vekov' ['Gold and Silver Works by Masters of the Armoury Sixteenth–Seventeenth Centuries']. In Armoury 1954.

Prakhov 1907
A. Prakhov. *Al'bom istoricheskoy vystavki predmetov iskusstva v 1904 g. v Peterburge* ['Album of a Historical Exhibition of Artistic Objects in 1904']. St Petersburg, 1907.

Purchas 1626
S. Purchas. *Purchas his Pilgrimage, or Relations of the World and the Religious Observed in all Ages and places Discovered, from the Creation unto this Present*. London, 1626.

Rashkovan 1988
N.V. Rashkovan. 'Iskusstvo frantsuzskikh masterov XVII–XVIII vekov' ['Art of French Masters of the Seventeenth and Eighteenth Centuries']. In *Gosudarstvennaya Oruzheynaya palata* ['The State Armoury']. Moscow, 1988.

Rogozhin 2002
N. M. Rogozhin. *U del gosudarevykh byt' ukazano* ['In the Service of the Sovereign']. Moscow, 2002.

Rogozhin 2003
N. M. Rogozhin. *Posol'skiy prikaz kolybel' rossiyskoy diplomatii* ['The Ambassadorial Office, Cradle of Russian Diplomacy']. Moscow, 2003.

Rude and Barbarous Kingdom 1968
Rude and Barbarous Kingdom: Russia in the Accounts of Sixteenth-Century English Voyagers. Edited by L. E. Berry and R. O. Crummey. Madison, 1968.

Russia–Britain 2003
Rossiya–Britaniya: K 450-letiyu ustanovleniya diplomaticheskikh otnosheniy ['Russia–Britain: To Commemorate the 450th Anniversary of Diplomatic Relations']. Moscow Kremlin Museums exh. cat. Moscow, 2003.

Russian Enamel 1974
Russkie emali XI–XIX vekov iz sobraniy Gosudarstvennykh muzeev Moskovskogo Kremlya, Gosudarstvennogo Istoricheskogo muzeya, Gosudarstvennogo Ermitazha ['Russian Eleventh–Nineteenth-century Enamels from the Collections of the State Museum of the Moscow Kremlin, State History Museum, State Hermitage']. Edited by L.V. Pisarskaya, N. G. Platonova and B. L. Ulyanova. Moscow, 1974.

Russian Gold 1984
Russkoe zoloto XIV–nachala XX vv. iz fondov Gosudarstvennykh Muzeev Kremlya ['Russian Gold of the Fourteenth to early Twentieth Centuries in the Collections of the State Kremlin Museums']. Edited by S. Y. Kovarskaya, I. D. Kostina and E.V. Shakurova. Moscow, 1984

Savva 1896
Savva, Bishop of Tver. *Ukazatel' dlya obozreniya Moskovskoy Patriarshey (nyne Sinodal'noy) riznitsy i biblioteki* ['Index for an Overview of the Moscow Patriarchal (now Synodal) Vestry and Library']. Moscow, 1896.

Seizième siècle en Europe 1965–6
Le XVIe siècle en Europe. Exh. cat. Paris, 1965–6.

Smirnova 1964
E. I. Smirnova, 'Zapadnoe serebro XIII–XIX vekov' ['Western Silver of the Thirteenth to Nineteenth Centuries']. In *Oruzheynaya palata* [The Armoury]. Moscow, 1964.

Smirnova and Shumilov 1961
E. I. Smirnova and V. N. Shumilov. 'Kollektsiya angliyskogo serebra v Oruzheynoy palate Kremlya' ['The Collection of English Silver in the Armoury of the Kremlin']. *Voprosy arkhivovedeniya* ['Archive Matters'] 1 (1961).

Smith 1605
Sir Thomas Smithes *Voiage and Entertainment in Rushia*. London, 1605.

Smith 2003
E. Smith. 'Richard Blackwell and Son', *Silver Society Journal* 15 (2003), pp. 19–45.

Sobolev and Ermolov 1954
N. I. Sobolev and B. A. Ermolov. 'Ognestrel'noe privoznoe oruzhie XVI–XVII vekov' ['Imported Firearms of the Sixteenth–Seventeenth Centuries']. In Armoury 1954.

Sokolov 1992
A. Sokolov. *Navstrechu drug drugu: Rossiya i Angliya v XVI–XVIII vv.* ['Meeting Each Other Half Way: Russia and England in the Sixteenth–Eighteenth Centuries]. Yaroslavl, 1992.

Solovetsky Monastery 1899
Istoriya pervoklassnogo stavropigial'nogo Solovetskogo monastyrya ['The History of the First Class Solovetsky Monastery']. St Petersburg, 1899.

Solovetsky Monastery 2001
Sokhranyonnye svyatyni Solovetskogo monastyrya ['The Surviving Sacred Sites and Objects of the Solovetsky Monastery']. Moscow, 2001.

Sovereign's Armoury 2002
Gosudareva Oruzheynaya palata ['The Sovereign's Armoury']. St Petersburg, 2002.

Taylor 1984
G. Taylor. 'Some London Platemakers' Marks, 1558–1624', *Proceedings of the Silver Society* 3, no. 4, 1984, pp. 97–9.

Temps d'exubérance 2002
Un temps d'exubérance: Les arts décoratifs sous Louis XIII et Anne d'Autriche. Grand Palais exh. cat. Paris, 2002.

Tolstoy 1875
Y.V. Tolstoy. *Pervye sorok let snosheniy mezhdu Rossiey i Angliey 1553–93: Gramoty* ['The First Forty Years of Relations between England and Russia 1553–93: Letters']. Documents collected, copied and edited by G. Tolstoy. St Petersburg, 1875.

Treasures 1979
Treasures from the Kremlin. Metropolitan Museum of Art exh. cat. New York, 1979.

Treasures 1995
Treasures of the Czars from the State Museums of the Moscow Kremlin. London, 1995.

Treasures 1998
Treasures of the Moscow Kremlin: Arsenal of the Russian Tsars. Royal Armouries exh. cat. London, 1998.

Trésors 1979–80
Trésors des Musées du Kremlin. Grand Palais exh. cat. Paris, 1979–80

Troytsky 1861
V. I. Troytsky. *Serebryanye bratiny Patriarshey riznitsy* ['Silver Bratinas from the Patriarch's Vestry']. Moscow, 1861.

Ulfeldt 2002
J. Ulfeldt. *Puteshestvie v Rossiyu* ['Journey to Russia']. Russian translation of *Hodoeporicon Ruthenicum*, 1608. Moscow, 2002.

URSS 1974
L'URSS et la France: Les grands moments d'une tradition. Grand Palais exh. cat. Paris, 1974.

Van der Doort 1960
Abraham van der Doort's Catalogue of the Collection of Charles I. Edited with an introduction by O. Millar. Walpole Society 37. Oxford, 1960.

Veltman 1843
A. Veltman. *Dostopamyatnosti Moskovskogo Kremlya* ['Sights of the Moscow Kremlin']. Moscow, 1843.

Veltman 1844
A. Veltman. *Moskovskaya Oruzheynaya palata* ['The Moscow Armoury']. Moscow, 1844.

Versailles 1993–4
Versailles et les tables royales en Europe XVII–XIXe siècles. Versailles exh. cat. Paris, 1993–4.

Viktorov 1875
A. Viktorov. 'Starinnye opisi Patriarshey riznitsy: Kritika i bibliografiya' ['Old Inventories of the Patriarch's Vestry: Criticism and Bibliography']. In *Vestnik Obshchestvu Drevnerusskogo Iskusstva pri Moskovskom publichnom muzee* ['Herald of the Society of Ancient Russian Art at the Moscow Public Museum']. Moscow, 1875, pp. 6–10.

Viktorov 1877–83
A. Viktorov. *Opisanie zapisnykh knig i bumag starinnykh dvortsovykh prikazov v 1584–1725 gg.* ['Description of the Notebooks and Papers of the Old Palace Offices for 1584–1725']. 2 issues. Moscow, 1877–83.

Vishnevskaya 2002
I. I. Vishnevskaya. *Prikladnoe iskusstvo Italii iz muzeyz-zapovednika 'Moskovskiy Kreml': Ital'yanskie tkani XVI–XVII vekov v Rossii* ['Italian Applied Art from the Moscow Kremlin Museum Reserve: Sixteenth–Seventeenth-Century Italian Textiles in Russia']. Moscow, 2002.

Warncke 1979
C.-P. Warncke. *Die ornamentale Groteske in Deutschland, 1500–1650* ['The Ornamental Grotesque in Germany, 1500–1650']. Berlin, 1979.

Wilson 1927
H. Wilson. *The Plague in Shakespeare's London.* Oxford, 1927.

Yablonskaya 1990
E. A. Yablonskaya. 'Zapadnoevropeyskoe vooruzhenie XV–XVII vekov' ['Western European Arms and Armour of the Fifteenth–Seventeenth Centuries.]. In *Gosudarstvennaya Oruzheynaya palata* ['The State Armoury']. Moscow, 1990.

Yablonskaya 1999
E. A. Yablonskaya. 'English Seventeenth-Century Firearms in the Kremlin Armoury Chamber'. *Royal Armouries Yearbook* 4 (1999).

Zabelin 1902
I. Zabelin. *Istoriia goroda Moskvy* ['History of the City of Moscow']. Moscow, 1902; repr. Moscow, 1995.

II. Anglo-Russian Relations: Subject Bibliography

This bibliography offers a starting point to guide the reader towards selected original texts by English visitors to Russia and others in the sixteenth and seventeenth centuries, and towards some general background literature relating to the period.

British Ambassadors in the Sixteenth and Seventeenth Centuries

Primary sources

Baldwin, T. *The Privileges of an Ambassador.* London, 1654.

Hotman, J. *The Ambassador.* Translated from French. London, 1603.

Thynne, F. T. *The Perfect Ambassador Treating of the Antiquity, Privileges, and Behaviour of Men belonging to that Function.* London, 1651.

Secondary sources

Bell, G. M. *A Handlist of British Diplomatic Representatives 1509–1688.* Royal Historical Society Guides and Handbooks 16. London, 1990.

Jansson, M. 'English Ambassadorial Gift Exchange in the Seventeenth and Eighteenth Centuries'. *Journal of Early Modern History* 9, nos. 3–4 (2005), pp. 348–70.

Mattingly, G. *Renaissance Diplomacy.* Boston, 1955.

Trade and Diplomatic Relations Between England and Russia

Primary sources

Milton, J. *A brief History of Moscovia and of other less-known Countries lying eastward of Russia as far as Cathay. Gathered from the Writings of several Eye-witnesses.* London, 1682.

Secondary sources

Alexeev, M. P. *Russko-angliyskie literaturnye svyazi (XVIII vek – pervaya polovina XIX veka)* ['Russo-English Literary Connections (Eighteenth Century–First half of the Nineteenth Century)']. Moscow, 1982.

Anderson, M. S. *Britain's Discovery of Russia, 1553–1815.* London, 1958.

Bogoushevsky, N. S. 'The English in Muscovy during the Sixteenth Century'. *Transactions of the Royal Historical Society* 7 (1878), pp. 58–129.

England and the North: The Russian Embassy of 1613–14. Edited by M. Jansson and N. Rogozhin. Translated by P. Bushkovitch. American Philosophical Society Memoirs. Philadelphia, 1994.

Gamel, I. K. 'Nachalo torgovykh i politicheskikh snosheniy mezhdu Angliey i Rossiey' ['The Commencement of Trading and Political Relations Between England and Russia']. *Zhurnal Ministerstva Narodnogo Prosveshcheniya* ['Journal of the Ministry of Public Education'] 2–3 (1856).

_____. *Anglichane v Rossii v XVI i XVII stoletiyakh* ['The English in Russia in the Sixteenth and Seventeenth Centuries']. Essays I and II. St Petersburg, 1865–9.

Hamel, J. [I. K. Gamel]. *Early Voyages to Northern Russia*. London, 1875.

Konovalov, S. 'Anglo-Russian Relations, 1620–4'. *Oxford Slavonic Papers* 4 (1953), pp. 71–131.

Lubimenko, I. I. 'Les marchands anglais en Russie au XVIe siècle'. *Revue historique* 109 (1912), p. 1.

_____. *Istoriya torgovykh snosheniy Rossii s Angliey* ['The History of Trading Relations Between Russia and England']. Yurev, 1912.

_____. 'Torgovye snosheniya Rossii s Angliey pri pervykh Romanovykh' ['Trading Relations Between Russia and England Under the First Romanovs']. *Zhurnal Ministerstva Narodnogo Prosveshcheniya* ['Journal of the Ministry of Public Education'], November 1916.

_____. 'Moskovskiy rynok kak arena bor'by Gollandii s Angliey' ['The Moscow Market as an Arena for the Battle Between Holland and England']. In *Russkoe proshloe* ['The Russian Past']. Vol 5. Moscow, 1923.

_____. *Les relations commerciales et politiques de l'Angleterre avec la Russie avant Pierre le Grand*. Bibliothèque de l'École des Hautes Études: Sciences philologiques et historiques 261. Paris, 1933.

_____. 'Torgovye snosheniya Rossii s Angliey i Gollandiey s 1553 po 1649 g.' ['Russia's Trading Relations with England and Holland from 1553–1649']. *Izvestiya AN SSSR: Otdelenie obshchestvennykh nauk* ['News of the USSR Academy of Sciences: Department of Social Sciences'], seventh series 10 (1933).

Lure, Y. S. 'Angliyskaya politika na Rusi kontsa XVI veka' ['English Politics in Rus at the End of the Sixteenth Century']. *Uchonye zapiski Leningradskogo gosudarstvennogo pedagogicheskogo instituta im. A. I. Gertsena* ['Scientific Notes of the Leningrad Herzen State Pedagogical Institute'] 61 (1947).

_____. 'Russko-angliyskie otnosheniya i mezhdunarodnaya politika vtoroy poloviny XVI v.' ['Russo-English Relations and International Politics in the Second Half of the Sixteenth Century']. In *Mezhdunarodnye svyazi Rossii do XVII v.* ['Russia's International Connections Before the Seventeenth Century']. Moscow, 1961.

Martens, F. F. 'Rossiya i Angliya v prodolzhenie XVI–XVII vekov' ['Russia and England in the Course of the Sixteenth–Seventeenth Centuries']. In *Russkaya mysl* ['Russian Thought']. Books 1–2. Moscow, 1891.

Nikashidze, N. T. *Russko-angliyskie otnosheniya vo vtoroy polovine XVI v.* ['Russo-English Relations in the Second Half of the Sixteenth Century']. Tbilisi, 1956.

Sokolov, A. *Navstrechu drug drugu: Rossiya i Angliya v XVI–XVIII vv.* ['Meeting Each Other Half Way: Russia and England in the Sixteenth–Eighteenth Centuries']. Yaroslavl, 1992.

Stuart, A. F. 'Early Russian Embassies to Britain'. *Twentieth Century Russia* 2 (1917), pp. 281–7.

Tolstoy, Y. V. 'Pervye snosheniya Anglii s Rossiey' ['England's First Relations with Russia']. *Russkiy vestnik* ['Russian Herald'] 6 (1873).

_____. 'Angliya i eyo vidy na Rossiyu v XVI veke' ['England and Her Intentions for Russia in the Sixteenth Century']. *Vestnik Evropy* ['Herald of Europe'] 12 (1875).

Vinogradoff, I. 'Russian Missions to London, 1569–1687: Seven Accounts by the Masters of the Ceremonies'. *Oxford Slavonic Papers*, new series 14 (1981), pp. 36–72.

Wretts-Smith, M. 'The English in Russia during the Second Half of the Sixteenth Century'. *Transactions of the Royal Historical Society*, fourth series 3 (1920), pp. 72–102.

Yakobson, S. 'Early Anglo-Russian relations, 1553–1613'. *Slavonic and East European Review* 13 (1934–5), pp. 597–610.

History of the Muscovy Company

Primary sources

'A copie of the first Privileges graunted by the Emperour of Russia to the English Marchants in the yeere 1555'. In Hakluyt 1598, pp. 265–7.

'The Charter of the Marchants of Russia, graunted upon the discoverie of the saide Countrey, by King Philip and Queene Marie'. In Hakluyt 1598, pp 267–72.

'A letter of the Company of the Marchants adventurers to Russia unto George Killingworth, Richard Gray, and Henry Lane their Agents there, to be delivered in Colmogro or els where: sent in the Iohn Evangelist [1577]'. In Hakluyt 1598, pp. 297–302.

'The Priviledges graunted by the Emperour of Russia to the English merchants of that company: obtained the 22. of September, Anno 1567, by M. Anthony Ienkinson'. In Hakluyt 1598, pp. 372–4.

'A copie of the priviledges granted by the right high and mightie Prince, the Emperour of Russia, &c. unto the right worshipfull fellowship of English merchants, for the discoverie of new trades: and hither sent by Thomas Randolfe esquire, her Maiesties Ambassadour to the sayd Emperour, and by Andrew Savin his Ambassadour in the yere of our Lord God 1569'. In Hakluyt 1598, pp. 379–82.

'A most gracious letter given to the English Merchants Sir Iohn Hart and his company, by Theodoro Ivanowich, the King, Lord, and great duke of all Russia, the onely upholder thereof 1596'. In Hakluyt 1598, pp. 505–7.

Secondary sources

Arel, M. S. *The Muscovy Company in the First Half of the Seventeenth Century: Trade and Position in the Russian State. A Reassessment*. PhD thesis, Yale University, 1995.

Baron, S. H. 'The Muscovy Company, the Muscovite Merchants and the Problem of Reciprocity in Russian Foreign Trade'. *Forschungen zur osteuropäischen Geschichte* ['Studies in East European History'] 27 (1980).

Bushkovitch, P. *The Merchants of Moscow 1580–1650*. Cambridge, 1980.

Cherkashina, N. P. *Istoriya Moskovskoy torgovoy kompanii v XVI–XVII vv.* ['The History of the Muscovy Trading Company in the Sixteenth and Seventeenth Centuries']. M.Phil. dissertation, Moscow, 1952

Dyomkin, A. V. *Zapadnoevropeyskoe kupechestvo v Rossii v XVII v.* ['The Western European Merchant Class in Russia in the Seventeenth Century']. 2 issues. Moscow, 1994.

Gerson, A. J. 'The Origin and Early History of the Muscovy Company'. In *Studies in the History of English Commerce in the Tudor Period*. New York, 1912.

Lubimenko, I. I. 'Angliyskaya torgovaya kompaniya v Rossii v XVI veke' ['The English Trading Company in Russia in the Sixteenth Century']. *Istoricheskoe obozrenie* ['Historical Review'] 16, books 3–4 (1911).

Page, W. S. *The Russia Company from 1553–1660*. London, 1912.

Willan, T. S. *The Muscovy Merchants of 1555*. Manchester, 1953.

_____. *The Early History of the Russia Company 1553–1605*. Manchester, 1956.

Moscow and the Kremlin

Aristotele Fioravanti a Mosca 1475–1975. Special issue of *Arte Lombarda*, new series 44–5 (1976).

Bartenev, S. P. *Moskovskiy Kreml' v starinu i teper'* ['The Moscow Kremlin in Days of Old and Today']. 2 vols. Moscow, 1912–16.

Batalov, A. L. *Moskovskoe kamennoe zodchestvo kontsa XVI veka* ['Stone Architecture in Moscow in the late Sixteenth Century']. Moscow, 1996.

Cracraft, J. *The Petrine Revolution in Russian Architecture*. Chicago, 1988.

Drevnerusskoe iskusstvo: Russkoe iskusstvo pozdnego srednevekov'ya, XVI vek ['Ancient Russian Art: Russian Art of the Late Mediaeval Period, Sixteenth Century']. Edited by A. L. Batalov. St Petersburg, 2003.

Zabelin, I. *Istoriya goroda Moskvy* ['History of the City of Moscow']. Moscow, 1902; repr. 1995.

——————. *Domashniy byt russkikh tsarey i tsarits v XVI i XVII stoletiiakh* ['The Home Life of Russian Tsars and Tsarinas in the Sixteenth and Seventeenth Centuries]. 3 vols. in 4 parts. 3rd–4th edn. Moscow, 1915–18; repr. 2000–3.

Russian sources of Information on England

Alexeev, M. P. 'Angliya i anglichane v pamyatnikakh moskovskoy pis'mennosti' ['England and the English in Moscow Written Material']. *Uchenye Zapiski LGU: Seriya istoricheskikh nauk* ['Scientific Notes of Leningrad State University: Historical Sciences Series'] 15 (1946), pp. 47–109.

Alpatov, M. A. *Russkaya istoricheskaya mysl' i Zapadnaya Evropa XII–XVII* ['Russian Historical Thought and Western Europe in the Twelfth–Seventeenth Centuries']. Moscow, 1973.

Kazakova, N. A. *Zapadnaya Evropa v russkoy pis'mennosti XV–XVI vekov* ['Western Europe and Russian Written Sources in the Fifteenth–Sixteenth Centuries']. Leningrad, 1980.

Tudor Correspondence with Russian Tsars

Evans, N. E. 'Queen Elizabeth I and Tsar Boris: Five Letters, 1597–1603'. *Oxford Slavonic Papers* 12 (1965), pp. 49–68.

Lubimenko, I. I. 'The Correspondence of Queen Elizabeth with Russian Tzars'. *American Historical Review* 19, no. 3 (1914), p. 526.

——————. 'Les relations diplomatiques de l'Angleterre avec la Russie au XVIe siècle'. *Revue historique* 121 (1916), pp. 33–4.

Tolstoy, Y. V. *Pervye sorok let snosheniy mezhdu Rossiey i Angliey 1553–93: Gramoty* ['The First Forty Years of Relations Between Russia and England 1553–93: Letters']. Documents collected, copied and edited by G. Tolstoy. St Petersburg, 1875. [Bilingual publication with introductory essay in English and Russian and original texts and the contemporary translations that were provided of them]

Stuart Correspondence with Russian Tsars

Konovalov, S. 'Seven Russian Royal Letters (1613–23)'. *Oxford Slavonic Papers* 7 (1957), pp. 118–34.

——————. 'Twenty Russian Royal Letters (1626–34)'. *Oxford Slavonic Papers* 8 (1958), pp. 117–56.

Lubimenko, I. I. 'Perepiska i diplomaticheskie snosheniya Romanovykh s pervymi Styuartami' ['Correspondence and Diplomatic Relations Between the Romanovs and the First Stuarts']. *Zhurnal Ministerstva narodnogo Prosveshcheniya* ['Journal of the Ministry of Public Education'], July 1915, pp. 62–7.

The English in Russia

Dyomkin, A. V. *Zapadnoevropeyskoe kupechestvo v Rossii XVII v.* ['Western European Merchant Classes in Russia in the Seventeenth Century']. Issues 1–2. Moscow, 1994.

Gotye, Y. V. and S. V. Bakhrushin. 'Kul'turnye i politicheskie svyazi Rossii i Anglii v XVI–XVII vv.' ['Cultural and Political Links Between Russia and England in the Sixteenth–Seventeenth Centuries']. *Istoricheskiy zhurnal* ['Historical Journal'] 12 (1941).

Hakluyt, R. *The Principal Navigations, Voyages, Traffiques and Discoveries of the English Nation*. London, 1589; revised and enlarged 1598.

Lubimenko, I. I. 'Anglichane v dopetrovskoy Rusi' ['The English in Pre-Petrine Rus']. In *Russkaya mysl'* ['Russian Thought'], March 1918.

——————. 'Trud inozemtsev v Moskovskom gosudarstve' ['The Labours of Foreigners in the Muscovite State']. In *Arkhiv istorii truda v Rossii* ['Archive of the History of Labour in Russia']. Books 6–7. Petrograd, 1923.

Orlenko, S. P. *Vykhodtsy iz Zapadnoy Evropy v Rossii XVII veka: Proavovoy status i real'noe polozhenie* ['Western Europeans in Seventeenth-Century Russia: Legal Status and Real Situation']. Moscow, 2004.

Phipps, G. M. *Britons in Seventeenth-Century Russia: A Study of the Origins of Modernization*. PhD thesis, University of Pennsylvania, 1973.

——————. 'Britons in Russia: 1613–82'. *Scietas: A Review of Social History* 7 (1977), pp. 19–45.

——————. 'Britons in Seventeenth-Century Russia: An Archival Search'. In *The Study of Russian History from British Archival Sources*. Edited by J. M. Hartley. New York, 1986, pp. 27–50.

Platonov, S. F. *Moskva i Zapad v XVI–XVII vekakh* ['Moscow and the West in the Sixteenth–Seventeenth Centuries']. Moscow, 1999.

Zapadnoevropeyskie spetsialisty v Rossii XV–XVII vekov ['Western European Specialists in Russia in the Fifteenth to Seventeenth Centuries']. Moscow, 2002.

English Travellers

Primary sources

Hakluyt, R. *The Principal Navigations, Voyages, Traffiques and Discoveries of the English Nation*. London, 1589; revised and enlarged 1598.

Secondary sources

Rude and Barbarous Kingdom: Russia in the Accounts of Sixteenth-Century English Voyagers. Edited by L. E. Berry and R. O. Crummey. Madison, 1968.

Jerome Bowes

Primary sources

'A copie of the Commission given to Sir Ierome Bowes, authorizing him her Maiesties Ambassadour unto the Emperour of Russia, Anno 1583'. In Hakluyt 1598, pp. 456–7.

'A Letter sent from her Highnesse to the sayd great Duke of Russia, by sir Hierome Boywes aforesaid, her Maiesties Ambassadour'. In Hakluyt 1598, pp. 457–8.

'A briefe discourse of the voyage of Sir Ierome Boyes knight, her Maiesties ambassadour to Ivan Vasilivich, the Emperour of Muscovia, in the yeere 1583'. In Hakluyt 1598, pp. 458–64.

Letters exchanged by Elizabeth I, Lord Burghley and Russian Tsars reflecting Russian displeasure at the behaviour of some of British ambassadors. In Hakluyt 1598, pp. 498–505.

'Extracts out of Sir Ierome Horseys Observations in Seventeene yeeres travels and experience in Russia, and other countries adioyning'. In Purchas 1626, pp. 982–5.

Secondary sources

Croskey, R. A. 'A Further Note on Sir Jerome Bowes'. *Oxford Slavonic Papers*, new series 10 (1977), pp. 39–45.

_____ 'Hakluyt's Account of Sir Jerome Bowes's Embassy to Ivan IV'. *Slavonic and East European Review* 61, no. 4 (1983), pp. 546–64.

Tolstoy, Y. V. 'Poslednee posol'stvo Elizavety k tsaryu Ivanu Vasil'yevichu: Ser Eremey Baus' ['Elizabeth's Last Embassy to Tsar Ivan Vasilievich: Sir Jerome Bowes']. *Russkiy vestnik* ['Russian Herald'] 36 (1861), pp. 5–29.

Samuel Collins

Collins, S. *The Present State of Russia, in a Letter to a Friend in London*. London, 1671.

Giles Fletcher

Primary sources

'The Ambassage of M. Giles Fletcher, Doctor of the Civil Law, sent from her Maiestie to Theodor the Emperor of Russia, Anno 1588'. In Hakluyt 1598, pp. 473–92.

Fletcher, G. *Of the Russe Commonwealth*. London, 1591.

Secondary sources

Baron, S. H. 'Ivan the Terrible, Giles Fletcher and the Muscovite Merchants: A Reconsideration'. *Slavonic and East European Review* 56 (1978), pp. 563–85.

_____. 'Fletcher's Mission and the Anthony Marsh Affair'. *Forschungen zur osteuropäischen Geschichte* ['Studies in East European History'] 46 (1992), pp. 107–30.

Seredonin, S. M. *Sochinenie Dzhil'sa Fletchera 'Of the Russe Commonwealth' kak istorichyeskiy istochnik* ['Giles Fletcher's "Of the Russe Commonwealth" as a Historical Source']. St Petersburg, 1891.

Tolstoy, Y. V. 'Fletcher i ego kniga o russkom gosudarstve pri tsare Fyodore Ivanoviche' ['Fletcher and his Book on the Russian State under Tsar Fyodor Ivanovich']. *Biblioteka dlya chteniya: Zhurnal Slovesnosti, nauk i politiki* ['Library for Readers: Journal of Philology, Science and Politics'] 158, no. 1 (1860).

Volodikhin, D. M. 'Istochniki traktata Dzh. Fletchera "O gosudarstve russkom" ' ['Sources for G. Fletcher's Treatise "Of the Russe Commonwealth" ']. In *Rossiya i Zapad: Dialog kul'tur* ['Russia and the West: A Dialogue of Cultures']. Moscow, 1994, pp. 31–5.

John Hebdon

Gurlyand, I. Y. *Ivan Gebdon, kommissarius i resident* ['John Hebdon, Commissary and Resident']. Yaroslavl, 1903.

Jerome Horsey

Primary sources

'Travels of Sir Jerome Horsey, 1572–89', British Library, Harl. MS 1813.

'The most solemne, and magnificent coronation of Pheodor Ivanowich, Emperour of Russia &c. the tenth of Iune, in the yeere 1584 – seene and observed by Master Ierom Horsey gentleman, and servant to her Maiesty, a man of great travel, and long experience in those parts: wherwith is also joined the course of his journey over land from Mosco to Emden'. In Hakluyt 1598, pp. 466–73.

'Extracts out of Sir Ierome Horseys Observations in Seventeene yeeres travels and experience in Russia, and other countries adioyning'. In Purchas 1626, pp. 973–92.

Secondary sources

Croskey, R. 'The Composition of Sir Jerome Horsey's "Travels"'. *Jahrbucher für Geschichte Osteuropas* ['Yearbook of East European History'] 26, no. 3 (1978), pp. 362–75.

Lure, Y. S. 'Pis'ma Dzheroma Gorseya' ['The Letters of Jerome Horsey']. *Uchonye Zapiski LGU: Seriya istoricheskikh nauk* ['Scientific Notes of Leningrad State University: Historical Sciences Series'] 8 (1941), pp. 189–201.

Moir, T. L. *The Addled Parliament of 1614*. Oxford, 1958.

Perrie, M. 'Jerome Horsey's Account of the Events of May 1591'. *Oxford Slavonic Papers*, new series 13 (1980), pp. 28–49.

Sevastyanova, A. A. *Sochineniia Dzheroma Gorseya kak istochnik po istorii Rossii XVI – nach. XVII v.* ['The Writings of Jerome Horsey as a Source in the History of Russia of the Sixteenth and early Seventeenth Centuries']. M.Phil. dissertation, Moscow, 1974

_____. 'Zapiski Dzheroma Gorseia o Rossii v kontse XVI–nachale XVII vekov: Raznovremennye sloi istochnika i ikh khronologiia' ['The Notes of Jerome Horsey on Russia in the late Sixteenth–early Seventeenth Centuries: The Source's Different Layers of Time and their Chronology']. In *Voprosy istoriografii i istochnikovedeniia otechestvennoi istorii: sbornik trudov* ['Questions in Historiography and Sources of the History of the Fatherland: Anthology of Papers']. Edited by V. B. Kobrin. Moscow, 1974, pp. 63–124.

_____. 'Dzherom Gorsey i ego sochineniya o Rossii' ['Jerome Horsey and his Writings on Russia']. In Dzherom Gorsey. *Zapiski o Rossii XVI–nachala XVII v.* ['Jerome Horsey. Notes on Russia of the Sixteenth–early Seventeenth Centuries']. Moscow, 1990.

Tolstoy, Y. V. 'Skazaniya anglichanina Gorseya o Rossii v iskhode XVI stoletiya' ['Tales of Russia by the Englishman Horsey at the End of the Sixteenth Century']. *Otechestvennye zapiski* ['Notes of the Fatherland'] 107 (1859).

Charles Howard, 1st Earl of Carlisle

Miège, G. de. *A Relation of the Three Embassies from his Sacred Majestie Charles II to the Great Duke of Muscovie ... Performed by the Right Honorable the Earle of Carlisle in the Years 1663 & 1664*. London 1669.

Anthony Jenkinson

Primary sources

'The first voyage made by Master Anthonie Ienkinson, from the Citite of London toward the land of Russia, begun the twelfth of may, in the yeere 1557'. In Hakluyt 1598, pp. 310–14.

'The voyage, wherein Osep Napaea the Moscovite Ambassadour returned home into his countrey, with his entertainment at his arrival at Colmogro: and a large description of the maners of the Countrey'. In Hakluyt 1598, pp. 314–23.

'The voyage of Master Anthony Ienkinson, made from the city of mosco in Russia, to the citie of Boghar in Bactria, in the yeere 1558: written by himselfe to the Merchants of London of the Moscovie companie'. In Hakluyt 1598, pp. 324–35.

'The Queenes Maiesties Letters to the Emperour of Russia, requesting licence, and safe conduct for M. Anthony Ienkinson to passe thorow his kingdom of Russia, into Persia, to the Great Sophie, 1561'. In Hakluyt 1598, pp. 339–40.

'A remembrance given by us the Governours, Consuls, and Assistants of the company of Merchants trading to Russia, the eight day of May 1561, to our trustie friend Anthonie Ienkinson, at his departure towards Russia, and so to Persia, in this our eight journey'. In Hakluyt 1598, pp. 341–3.

'A compendious and briefe declaration of the iourney of M. Anth. Ienkinson, from the famous citie of London into the land of Persia, passing in this same iourney thorow Russia, Moscovia ... sent and imployed therein by the right worshipfull Societie of the Merchants Adventurers, for discoverie of Lands, Islands, etc. Being begun the fourteenth day of May, Anno 1561 ...' In Hakluyt 1598, pp. 343–52.

'The Priviledges graunted by the Emperour of Russia to the English merchants of that company: obtained the 22. of September, Anno 1567, by M. Anthony Ienkinson'. In Hakluyt 1598, pp. 372–4.

'A note of the proceeding of M. Anthonie Ienkinson, Ambassadour from the Queenes most excellent Maiestie, to the Emperour of Russia, from the time of his arrival there, being the 26. of Iuly 1571, until his departure from thence the 23 of Iuly 1572'. In Hakluyt 1598, pp. 402–11.

Early Voyages and Travels to Russia and Persia by Anthony Jenkinson and Other Englishmen, with Some Account of the First Intercourse of the English with Russia and Central Asia by Way of the Caspian Sea. Hakluyt Society, First Series. London, 1886.

Secondary sources

Huttenbach, H. R. 'The Search for and Discovery of New Archival Materials for Ambassador Jenkinson's Mission in 1571–2: Four Letters by Queen Elizabeth to Tsar Ivan IV. *Canadian-American Slavonic Studies* 6, no. 3 (1972), pp. 416–25.

_____. 'Anthony Jenkinson's 1566 and 1507 Missions to Muscovy Reconstructed from Unpublished Sources'. *Canadian-American Slavic Studies* 9, no. 2 (1975), pp. 179–203.

Morton, M. B. G. *The Jenkinson Story.* Glasgow, 1962.

John Merrick

Phipps, G. M. *Sir John Merrick: English Merchant-Diplomat in Seventeenth-Century Russia.* Newtonville, MA, 1983.

Thomas Randolph

'The Ambassage of the right worshipfull Master Thomas Randolfe, Esquire, to the Emperour of Russia, in the yeere 1568, briefly written by himselfe'. In Hakluyt 1598, pp. 376–8.

'A copie of the priviledges granted by the right high and mightie Prince, the Emperour of Russia, &c. unto the right worshipfull fellowship of English merchants, for the discoverie of new trades: and hither sent by Thomas Randolfe esquire, her Maiesties Ambassadour to the sayd Emperour, and by Andrew Savin his Ambassadour in the yere of our Lord God 1569'. In Hakluyt 1598, pp. 379–82.

'Certaine letters in verse, written by master George Turbervile out of Moscovia, when went as Secretarie thither with Master Tho. Randolph, her Maiesties Ambassadour to the Emperour 1568, to certeine friends of his in London, describing the maners of the Countrey and people…'. In Hakluyt 1598, pp. 384–9.

Thomas Smith

Primary sources

Sir Thomas Smithes Voiage and Entertainment in Russia. London, 1605.

Secondary sources

Arel, M. S. and S. N. Bogatyryov. 'Anglichane v Moskve vremyon Borisa Godunova (po dokumentam posol'stva T. Smita 1604–5 godov)' ['The English in Moscow During the Age of Boris Godunov (From Documents Relating to Thomas Smith's Embassy 1604–5)']. *Arkheograficheskiy ezhegodnik za 1997* ['Archaeographical Annual for 1997']. Moscow, 1997.

Bogatyryov, S. N. '"Ot Volgi do potoka Amazonki": Zhizn i puteshestvie sera Tomasa Smita' ['"From the Volga to the Flowing of the Amazon": The Life and Journey of Sir Thomas Smith']. *Zerkalo istorii* ['Mirror of History'] 2 (1995), pp. 52–66.

Russian Travellers

Primary sources

The original reports of Russian embassies to England in the sixteenth and seventeenth centuries have been published in:

Puteshestviya russkikh poslov XVI–XVII vv: Stateynye spiski ['The Travels of Russian Ambassadors, Sixteenth–Seventeenth Centuries: Reports']. Moscow and Leningrad, 1954.

Sbornik Russkogo Istoricheskogo Obshchestva ['Anthology of the Russian Historical Society']. Vol. 38. St Petersburg, 1883.

English contemporary accounts may be found in the diaries of John Evelyn and Samuel Pepys as well as:

'A discourse of the honourable receiving into England of the first Ambassador from the Emperor of Russia, in the yeere of Christ 1556, and in the third yeere of the raigne of Queene Marie, serving for the third voyage to Moscovie. Registered by Master Iohn Incent Protonotarie'. In Hakluyt 1598, pp. 285–90.

Finetti Philoxenis, some choice Observations of Sr John Finett, Knight and Master of the Ceremonies to the two last kings touching the Reception and Precedence, the Treatment and Audience, the Puntillios and Contests of Forren Ambassadors in England. London, 1656.

Holinshed, R. *Chronicles of England, Scotland and Ireland.* London, 1587.

Secondary sources

Court and Times of James I. Edited by T. Birch. 2 vols. London, 1848; repr. New York, 1973.

England and the North: The Russian Embassy of 1613–14. Edited by M. Jansson and N. Rogozhin. Translated by P. Bushkovitch. American Philosophical Society Memoirs. Philadelphia, 1994.

Loomie, A. J. *Ceremonies of Charles I: The Notebooks of John Finet 1628–41.* New York, 1987.

Nichols, J. *The Progresses, Processions, and Magnificent Festivities of King James the First, His Royal Consort, Family, and Court.* 4 vols. London, 1828; repr. New York, [1966].

Osip Nepeya

Primary sources

Holinshed, R. *Chronicles of England, Scotland and Ireland.* London, 1587.

Secondary sources

Robertson, J. 'Documents Relating to the First Russian Embassy to England in 1556'. *Archaeological Journal* 13 (1876), pp. 77–80.

Baron, S. H. 'Osip Nepea and the Opening of Anglo-Russian Commercial Relations'. *Oxford Slavonic Papers*, new series 11 (1978), pp. 42–63.

Gerasim Dokhuturov

Roginsky, Z. I. *Poezdka gontsa Gerasima Semyonovich Dokhutorova v Angliyu v 1645–6* ['The Journey of Messenger Gerasim Semyonovich Dokhutorov to England in 1645–6']. Yaroslavl, 1959.

_____. *London 1645–6 godov: Novye istochniki o poezdki gontsa G. S. Dokhutorova v Angliyu* ['London in 1645–6: New Sources Regarding the Journey by Messenger G. S. Dokhutorov to England']. Yaroslavl, 1960.

Index

Illustrations are indicated by italic page numbers.

Photo Credits

Beinecke Rare Book and Manuscript Library, Yale University, 2, 4, 6, 7, 8, 10, 14, 38, 54, 70
By Permission British Library Cotton MS Tiberius D.x, f.411, 44
By Permission British Library 8005.a.41, 60
© Copyright The Trustees of the British Museum, 25, 61
By permission of the Syndics of Cambridge University Library, 17
The Governing Body of Christ Church, Oxford, 39
© The Worshipful Company of Goldsmiths, 31
Guildhall Library, Corporation of London, 24
Reproduced by kind permission the Hon. Simon Howard, photo by Peter Smith Photography, 34
Hungarian National Museum, Budapest, 59
© Museum of London, 23
© The National Gallery, London, 27
National Portrait Gallery, London, 62
Rare Books Division, The New York Public Library, Astor, Lenox and Tilden Foundations, 3, 69
Slavic and Baltic Division, The New York Public Library, Astor, Lenox and Tilden Foundations, 1, 42, 66, 71, 72
With permission of the Princeton University Library, 68
The Royal Collection © 2005, Her Majesty Queen Elizabeth II, 26
The State Hermitage Museum, St. Petersburg, 67
State History Museum, Moscow, 45, 46, 47, 48, 51
©V&A Images / Victoria and Albert Museum, 21
Copyright: Dean and Chapter of Westminster, 28
Willis Museum, Basingstoke, 13
Richard Caspole, Yale Center for British Art, 5, 9, 11, 64, 65